Toni Morrison

Bloomsbury Studies in Contemporary North American Fiction

Series Editor: Sarah Graham, Lecturer in American Literature,
University of Leicester, UK

This series offers up-to-date guides to the recent work of major
contemporary North American authors. Written by leading
scholars in the field, each book presents a range of original
interpretations of three key texts published since 1990, showing
how the same novel may be interpreted in a number of different
ways. These informative, accessible volumes will appeal to
advanced undergraduate and postgraduate students, facilitating
discussion and supporting close analysis of the most important
contemporary American and Canadian fiction.

TITLES IN THE SERIES INCLUDE:

Bret Easton Ellis: American Psycho, Glamorama, Lunar Park
Edited by Naomi Mandel

*Cormac McCarthy: All the Pretty Horses, No Country for
Old Men, The Road*
Edited by Sara Spurgeon

Don Dellio: Mao II, Underworld, Falling Man
Edited by Stacey Olster

*Louise Erdrich: Tracks, The Last Report on the Miracles at Little
No Horse, The Plague of Doves*
Edited by Deborah L. Madsen

*Margaret Atwood: The Robber Bride, The Blind Assassin,
Oryx and Crake*
Edited by J. Brooks Bouson

*Philip Roth: American Pastoral, The Human Stain, The Plot
Against America*
Edited by Debra Shostak

Toni Morrison

Paradise, Love, A Mercy

Edited by
Lucille P. Fultz

B L O O M S B U R Y
LONDON • NEW DELHI • NEW YORK • SYDNEY

Bloomsbury Academic
An imprint of Bloomsbury Publishing Plc

50 Bedford Square	175 Fifth Avenue
London	New York
WC1B 3DP	NY 10010
UK	USA

www.bloomsbury.com

First published 2013

British Library Cataloguing-in-Publication Data
A catalogue record for this book is available from the British Library.

ISBN: HB: 978-1-4411-3013-6
PB: 978-1-4411-1968-1

Library of Congress Cataloging-in-Publication Data
Toni Morrison : Paradise, Love, A mercy / edited by Lucille P. Fultz.
p. cm. — (Continuum studies in contemporary North American fiction)
Includes bibliographical references and index.
ISBN 978-1-4411-3013-6 (hardcover)—ISBN 978-1-4411-1968-1 (pbk.)—
ISBN 978-1-4411-2539-2 (PDF)—ISBN 978-1-4411-6791-0 (epub)
1. Morrison, Toni—Criticism and interpretation. 2. African Americans in literature.
I. Fultz, Lucille P., 1937—

PS3563.O8749Z914 2012
813'.54—dc23

2012011976

Typeset by Newgen Imaging Systems Pvt Ltd, Chennai, India
Printed and bound in India

I am accused of tending to the past
as if I made it,
as if I sculpted it
with my own hands. I did not.
this past was waiting for me
when I came,
a monstrous unnamed baby,
and I with my mother's itch
took it to breast
and named it
History.
she is more human now,
learning language everyday,
remembering faces, names and dates.
when she is strong enough to travel
on her own, beware, she will.

Lucille Clifton[1]

1 Lucille Clifton, "i am accused of tending to the past . . ." from *Quilting: Poems 1987–1990*. Copyright 1991 by Lucille Clifton. Reprinted with the permission of The Permissions Company, Inc. on behalf of BOA Editions Ltd., www.boaeditions.org.

CONTENTS

SERIES EDITOR'S INTRODUCTION

Each study in this series presents ten original essays by recognized subject specialists on the recent fiction of a significant author working in the United States or Canada. The aim of the series is to consider important novels published since 1990 either by established writers or by emerging talents. By setting 1990 as its general boundary, the series indicates its commitment to engaging with genuinely contemporary work, with the result that the series is often able to present the first detailed critical assessment of certain texts.

In respect of authors who have already been recognized as essential to the canon of North American fiction, the series provides experts in their work with the opportunity to consider their latest novels in the dual context of the contemporary era and as part of a long career. For authors who have emerged more recently, the series offers critics the chance to assess the work that has brought authors to prominence, exploring novels that have garnered acclaim both because of their individual merits and because they are exemplary in their creative engagement with a complex period.

Including both American and Canadian authors in the term "North American" is in no sense reductive: studies of Canadian writers in this series do not treat them as effectively American, and assessment of all the chosen authors in terms of their national and regional identity, as well as their race and ethnicity, gender and sexuality, religion and political affiliation is essential in developing an understanding of each author's particular contribution to the representation of contemporary North American society.

The studies in this series make outstanding new contributions to the analysis of current fiction by presenting critical essays chosen for their originality, insight and skill. Each volume begins with a substantial introduction to the author by the study's editor, which establishes the context for the chapters that will follow through a discussion of essential elements such as the writer's career, characteristic narrative strategies, themes and preoccupations, making clear the author's importance and the significance of the novels chosen for discussion. The studies are all comprised of three parts, each one presenting three original essays on three key recent works by the author, and every part is introduced by the volume's editor, explaining how the chapters to follow engage with the fiction and respond to existing interpretations. Each individual chapter takes a critical approach that may develop existing perceptions or challenge them, but always expands the ways in which the author's work may be read by offering a fresh approach.

It is a principle of the series that all the studies are written in a style that will be engaging and clear however complex the subject, with the aim of fostering further debate about the work of writers who all exemplify what is most exciting and valuable in contemporary North American fiction.

Sarah Graham

ACKNOWLEDGMENTS

My heartfelt thanks to Sarah Graham, the series editor of Bloomsbury's Studies in Contemporary North American Fiction, who lured me from the bliss of unencumbered retirement to edit this volume, for her confidence in my ability (my dotage not withstanding) to see the project to fruition, and for her advice, guidance, and editorial assistance throughout the preparation of the manuscript. Special thanks to the Morrison cohorts who agreed to participate in the project before realizing they would have to contend with my constant inquiries through a barrage of emails. This volume is a result of their endurance, and they deserve extra credit for hanging in. I am also indebted to the School of Humanities and the staff of Fondren Library at Rice University. Other Morrison scholars served as peer reviewers but prefer to remain anonymous; however, their contributions are reflected in the final version of this volume.

Audrey Crawford deserves enormous thanks for her editorial and technical support. With her knowledge and skills, she patiently and unswervingly guided me through the intricacies of word processing and the mystical and saving power of my computer.

The following group deserves special thanks for in/tangible support and for contributions too numerous to list: my SAGE Sisters Patricia Bell-Scott, Miriam Decosta-Willis, and Janet Sims-Wood, inspiring examples of diligence and perseverance; Sarah Bentley, Saundra Boyd, Marcia Carter, Monica Cobb, Vincent Cobb, Thomas Diggs, Ikuseghan Eno, Dara Flinn, Amanda Focke, Karen Fultz, Shirley Grob, Mildred Jackson, Felecia Jordan, Ife Mawusi, K Krueger McDonald, Lauren Meyers, Tom Murray, Lee Pecht, Malissia Pilgrim, Petra Pilgrim, Jacsun Shah, Iris Sizemore, DeAndrea Smither, Karen Stumpf, Justine Tally, Mary Tobin, Melissa Torrey, and Sandra Torrey.

Finally, and most importantly, I wish to express my deepest gratitude to Toni Morrison, whose literary works comprise the donnée for this volume.

1

Introduction: The Grace and Gravity of Toni Morrison

Lucille P. Fultz

Toni Morrison in the international context

We are a group of 100 "spectators"—here to *see* Toni Morrison receive the 2010 Médaille Vermeil Grand Prix Humanitaire de France/Honor Medal of the City of Paris. Twenty-five of us are members of the Toni Morrison Society, in Paris for the Society's biennial meeting. One hundred pairs of eyes (more if you include the professional cameras and camera phones) are directed toward Morrison, while she gazes intently and unblinkingly at the speaker, Christophe Girard, Deputy Mayor of Paris in charge of culture. She is regal in bright autumn colors redolent of the trees skirting the River Seine and elegantly appropriate to the occasion. Not so many years prior, the audience would have been instructed not to take photos, and had someone inadvertently done so, she might have been the object of Morrison's discomfiting glance or her long unsettling pause.

The room—reminiscent of Medieval pageantry—is in the l'Hôtel de Ville (site of the administrative offices for the city and Mayor). It is a sunny, chilly November day in Paris. As the center of all the fuss,

Morrison seems at ease, truly at home in this royal setting, while most in the audience seem eager and restive as they press against one another for a better view or a closer shot. It is as though she has been primed for this moment since she received the Nobel Prize in 1993. We are her guests—better stated, her devotees—invited by the Mayor of Paris to witness yet another recognition of Morrison's extraordinary achievements as a writer.

The previous evening Morrison was inducted into la Legion d'Honneur/the French Legion of Honor. Referring to Morrison as "the greatest American novelist of her time," Frederic Mitterrand, France's minister of culture, spoke of her "modest" background and her "exceptional destiny," as he reminded her, "we [the French] admire you and we love you." Accepting the Legion of Honor Medal, Morrison averred that the award was an affirmation that she was both "welcomed" and "prized" by the French: "I've always felt welcomed in France and especially in Paris" (Barchfield). Indeed, she has been at home in Paris, where, in November 2006, she guest-curated a multigenres program—"Étranger chez soi"/"The Foreigner's Home"—at the Louvre Museum. In conjunction with "The Foreigner's Home," the Toni Morrison Society sponsored the "Symposium: International Perspectives on Toni Morrison." To further link Morrison to France, and especially Paris, a few days later, the Toni Morrison Society placed a "Bench by the Road" on Rue Delgrès in Paris, to commemorate Louis Delgrès—"insurgent revolutionary, and freedom fighter." In response to Morrison's lament that there were no public monuments honoring the lives of enslaved Africans, the Society established a "bench project," the placement of metal benches at sites important to African American history and culture. (The Toni Morrison Society's website provides details about the bench projects.)

In addition to her French connections, Morrison has garnered accolades elsewhere around the world. Most recently, in collaboration with the singer/songwriter Rokia Traoré, she has written the text for the musical "Desdemona," which celebrated its 2011 World Premier on three continents—Europe (Vienna), North America (New York), and Africa (Bamako). In 1994, she merited, in Vitoria-Gasteiz, Spain, graffiti on the in/famous wall and, in Italy, the Rhegium Julii Prize. That her novels are studied across the globe is perhaps among her highest honors. A recent survey in Taiwan, for example, noted that Morrison "ranks as the most-studied African

American writer" in that country. The survey recorded 134 entries for Morrison and 24 for Alice Walker, her closest competitor (Wenching Ho 515).

On the evening of the day she received the Médaille Vermeil, Morrison invited two other scholars and me to her Paris hotel for an informal evening of wine and conversation. During the course of the evening, I asked her three questions: How do you *feel* about all the recognition and honors you've received this week and over the years? What do you *think* about such honors? And what do you see as *your responsibility* in relation to such honors? To the first question, she offered a warm and almost tearful reply, "At first I felt it was for my people and I was pleased." Her response to the second question came with no hint of arrogance or prepossession, "I think—in fact, I know—I deserve all the recognition because I work hard to produce what I know is my best work. I don't put my work out there until I'm satisfied that it's a polished piece of writing."

Before she could answer the third question, she went to answer her telephone. When she returned, she asked, "What was your third question?" Then, she responded, "What is my responsibility? My responsibility is to my art and to no one else. My responsibility is to present what I know is my best work regardless of what anyone else thinks." Morrison has repeated this conviction several times in interviews and public appearances. It is the same advice she offers to others, whether it is about writing or other projects. In a conversation with *Roll Out*, she insisted, "You must know when you're at your best. . . . And, and no matter what, you must be unblinking, be really unblinking and really, really true" ("Toni Morrison: More Than Words Can Say" 17). Then speaking about her numerous awards and her attendant responsibilities:

> I don't know how to say this without sounding churlish. I love prizes and accolades and so on. But my responsibilities are to do the best work I can do and to be the best human being I can be. Now the Nobel [P]rize doesn't help that. It doesn't make it easier to write the book that I had to write. None of it helps that. What it does do, I think, which is one of my assumed responsibilities, is make it thinkable, possible, doable, for others—other African Americans and other women. (Verdelle 169)

Chloe Ardelia Wofford/Chloe Anthony Wofford/Toni Morrison

Frederic Mitterrand referred to Morrison's "exceptional destiny" as "what's most beautiful about America"—that a child of working-class African American parents could and would achieve the pinnacle of literary success. Who is this woman the world knows as Toni Morrison? Who is this woman who has introduced African American life to readers around the globe? A brief review of the discussions about her names offers a glimpse of the conjecture that surrounds her. If one mills around groups at a Toni Morrison Society conference one may overhear her son refer to her as "my mother" or her niece address her as "Aunt Chloe." Before she was any of these, of course, she was Chloe Ardelia Wofford, daughter of Ramah (Willis) and George Wofford of Lorain, Ohio, where she was born on February 18, 1931.

She became Chloe Anthony at 12 when she converted to Catholicism and chose St Anthony as her patron saint. Anthony was shortened to Toni, and this became the name by which she was known in college. When asked about how she became famous as "Toni Morrison," she explains that she was "upset. They (her publishers) had the wrong name. Toni Morrison. My name is Chloe Wofford. Toni's a nickname." Toni Morrison became her official nom de plume when her publisher at Holt "misnamed" her. The mix-up occurred because she sent the manuscript as Toni Morrison since the editor "knew [her] that way" (Dreifus 101)—an interesting twist for a writer who devotes much of her craft to misnamed characters.

John Duvall has enlarged the mystique surrounding the name "Toni Morrison" by inventing his own narrative to explain it. Frustrated by his inability to locate sufficient auto/biographical information about Morrison, he searches for Morrison's "self-making" in her fiction (Duvall 3). In one of numerous speculations, he suggests that Morrison dropped the name "Chloe" in favor of "Toni" "to distance herself" from a name that "often signals a particularly hated form of racial oppression and servility in the South," and that her readings in college revealed "unflattering Chloes in American literature besides the one in [Ralph] Ellison's novel" (Duvall 37–8). He might also have considered the not-so-remote possibility that Morrison, like many young girls of her generation, dropped or added a name out of vanity or pure fantasy. Granting Duvall his argument for a moment, one must then ask the question: Why would Toni Morrison, who has never run from her early life of poverty and who has always included the names of her family members in her books, disavow her given name? She has been quite adamant about her relationship to her family, "all my family call me Chloe. It was Chloe, by the way, who went to Stockholm . . . to get the Nobel Prize" (Dreifus 101). In the final analysis, Duvall is forced to admit that he is engaging in high speculation as he searches for the woman behind the name.

The grace and gravity of Morrison's fiction

One thing is certain: when Chloe Ardelia/Chloe Anthony Wofford submitted *The Bluest Eye* to her editor, she signed her name "Toni Morrison." And due to that un/fortunate error, she will forever be known to the world as Toni Morrison. Her astonishing accomplishments as a writer have made her an important point of reference on the international literary scene. Since receiving the Nobel Prize in Literature, Morrison has been a familiar and frequent presence on the world's stages. Of her achievement as a writer the Swedish Academy noted that her "novels [are] characterized by visionary force and poetic import [through which she] gives life to an essential aspect of American reality." Of her craft, the Academy observed, "She delves into the language itself, a language she wants to liberate from the fetters of race. And she addresses us with the luster of poetry."

Sentient artistry

Paul Gray has remarked that the force of Morrison's art resides in "a mélange of high literary rhetoric and plain talk. She can turn pecan shelling into poetry: "the tick of nut meat tossed in the bowl" ("Paradise Found" 66). Morrison deftly captures the sensual, reminding readers that characters are not merely speaking and moving but that their entire bodies are engaged in activities that involve a larger environment. Consider this image created by boiling water that greets Junior Viviane when she first enters Christine Cosey's kitchen, "A bouquet of steam wandered away from water lifting to a boil on the stove" (*Love* 21). Similar examples abound across Morrison's oeuvre. Consider two examples from *Paradise* when the church lights are turned off in preparation for the Christmas pageant: "Quiet coughing domesticates the dark" (208); and a description of African Americans confronting unearned suffering, "people who made Job's patience look like restlessness. Elegance when all around was shabby" (160). What reader can forget 11-year-old Pecola Breedlove's father "snatch[ing] his genitals out of the dry harbor of her vagina" (*The Bluest Eye* 163)? Two final images should underscore what I am calling Morrison's sentient artistry. First, this is L's description of Cosey's decaying hotel: "*The wood siding of the hotel looks silver-plated, its peeling paint like the streaks on an unpolished tea service*" (*Love* 7). The language and imagery are appropriate to L, who worked many years in the hotel's kitchen. Finally, this description of Sethe preparing biscuits:

> Quickly, lightly she touched the stove. Then she trailed her fingers through the flour, parting, separating small hills and ridges of it, looking for mites. Finding none, she poured soda and salt into the crease of her folded hand and tossed both into the flour. Then she reached into a can and scooped half a handful of lard. Deftly she squeezed the flour through it, then with her left hand sprinkling water, she formed the dough. . . . Now she rolled the dough out with a wooden pin. (*Beloved* 18–19)

Sensual and sensuous language pervades Morrison's fiction. For Morrison it is as much about secondary gestures as it is about primary ones. What occurs while the major events are unfolding tells us as much about characters—sometimes more—as do their spoken words. Moreover, such gestures locate events in space and time. Francine Prose suggests that when used effectively, gestures "are like windows opening to let us see a person's soul . . . the precise relations between that person and the self, between the self and the world" (213).

Daunting narratives

Not everyone who reads Morrison's fiction is impressed. Many readers approach her novels with predetermined expectations and are sometimes disappointed when they are faced with a daunting narrative requiring intensive labor on their part. Some readers, for example, expecting a linear narrative become frustrated and set the novels aside, while others hang in for a while then surrender because the texts require so much input from the reader. Such readers have to be reminded that Morrison writes for readers who are willing to work with her. Stated another way, she expects readers to meet her on her terms—not theirs. Carol Shields has observed that Morrison defies expectations, "consistently, book after book, she remakes the novel as we know it" ("Heaven on Earth" 33).

While many praise Morrison's literary art, others are eager to point to what they perceive as "flaws." Brooke Allen has this to say about the language of *Jazz*: "her aim was obviously to produce a prose poem, an evocation and lilt of the jazz music that filled the air of Harlem in the 1920s. She succeeded magnificently, but as fiction "*Jazz* fails to move" (Allen 7). Allen is, however, kinder than Charles Johnson, who has stated that *Jazz* has "no characters, there's no story, there's no plot, and even the poetry which Morrison is good at is not there. I'm not sure why she released that book at all." And, to *Beloved*'s selection as the best American novel of the past 25 years, Charles Johnson responded, "It's an interesting middle-brow book. I don't think it's an intellectual achievement, because I'm not sure where the intellectual probing is going on" (Little 107).

The African American cultural critic, Stanley Crouch, one of Morrison's most virulent critics, has argued that *Beloved* "is designed to placate sentimental feminist ideology, and to make sure that the vision of black woman as the most scorned and rebuked of the victims doesn't weaken." Crouch, like Johnson, admits that Morrison "has real talent, an ability to organize her novel in a musical structure, deftly using images as motifs," but he seems most annoyed that Morrison "perpetually interrupts her narrative with maudlin ideological commercials" (Crouch 205). What some critics see as the power of Morrison's writing, Crouch sees as a lack of "control." He insists that Morrison "can't resist the temptation of the trite or the sentimental" (Crouch 209).

It is conceivable that Crouch, like other reviewers of *Beloved*, may have read the novel too quickly and failed to grasp not just Morrison's narrative strategies but the full import of the kind of stories she adumbrates in that novel. Countering Crouch's comparison of Sethe Suggs to her historical model, Morrison has noted that "Margaret Garner didn't do what Medea did and kill her children because of some guy. It [infanticide] was for me this classic example of a person determined to be responsible" (Gilroy 177). Finally, Geoffrey Bent has called *Paradise* Morrison's "weakest book" because of its "didactic purity that underlies every paradise." He contends that flaws in this novel "can only send ripples of reappraisal back over the rest of her oeuvre" ("Less Than Divine" 145).

I have elected to include such negative critiques of Morrison's writing in order to provide a range of opinions about her work. But I have also elected to mobilize these critiques in order to show that there is a consistency about her art—even her critics speak of the poetic power of her prose. She writes with the sensibility of a poet and the deeply probing mind of a novelist who creates narrative environments for readers to find their own truths about African Americans.

The issue of language

Because so much has been written about the "luster of poetry" in Morrison's fiction, it may be helpful at this point to review some of what Morrison herself has to say about her use of black speech and what she hopes to achieve with it. She has stated that her desire is "to polish and show, and make it [black idiom] a literary vehicle" (Als 73). In her *Nobel Lecture*, Morrison focuses her remarks around the issue of language and the efforts, at times, to stifle or censor it or, in her words, "the tendency of its users to forgo its nuanced, complex mid-wifery properties, replacing them with menace and subjugation" (15–16). Referring to the Tower of Babel in her *Nobel Lecture*, she observes, "Perhaps the achievement of Paradise was premature, a little hasty if no one could take the time to understand other languages, other views, other narratives" (19). But she also acknowledges in her *Nobel Lecture* the writer's limitations in the deployment of language: "Language can never 'pin down' slavery, genocide, war. Nor should it yearn for the arrogance to be able to do so. Its force, its felicity, is in its reach toward the ineffable" (21); after all, she proffers, language is "an act with consequences" (*Nobel Lecture* 13).

About the music in her writing, Morrison tells the cultural critic Paul Gilroy:

> The power of the word is not music, but in terms of aesthetics, the music is the mirror that gives me the necessary clarity. . . . I don't have the resources of a musician, but I thought that if it was truly black literature, it would not be black because I was . . . . It would be something intrinsic, indigenous, something in the way it was put together—the sentences, the structure, texture and tone—so that anyone who read it would realize. . . . Sometimes I hear blues, sometimes spirituals or jazz and I've appropriated it. I've tried to reconstruct the texture of it in my writing—certain kinds of repetition—its profound simplicity. (Gilroy 181–2)

What Morrison hears is what also resonates with her readers and what they often refer to when they speak of the poetic and musical powers of her language. For example, when I wrote to Morrison about her limited edition, *Five Poems*, she replied that the pieces in that volume "are lyrics, not poems," which is to say, they are meant to be sung, not read or interpreted as poetry. Nevertheless, the fact that these lyrics are published under the sign of poetry speaks to the overwhelming identifying quality in Morrison's writing—its lyrical and poetic dimensions.

Grace in language

To dissect Morrison's language is to be privy to a majestic mind at work. The late critic John Leonard, in a conversation with Bill Moyers lamenting the absence of freshness and the paucity of seriousness in contemporary writing, averred, "I have to read a Toni Morrison novel to find gravity and grace" ("Bill Moyers Interviews").

Sula and the folk idiom

Morrison's use of language is unquestionably powerful and arresting, but that language, de rigueur, must be more than mere adornment: it must be functional in detail and specificity. As Francine Prose has observed, "the elements of good writing depend on the writer's skill in choosing one word instead of another. And what grabs and keeps our interest has everything to do with those choices" (Prose 16). While Morrison is applauded for her artistic use of folk idioms, that language has a primary function: to serve the narrative by contributing to readers' understanding of characters and their environment. To that end, the language should be appropriate to the speaker and situation; it should be relevant to the narrative; and it should advance the novel's larger purposes. This involves what Charles Baxter terms "staging," or "putting characters in specific strategic positions in the scene so that some unvoiced nuance is revealed." This process may entail the distance between characters and "what their particular gestures and facial expressions might be at moments of dramatic emphasis, exactly how their words are said, and what props appear inside and outside" (Baxter 13). To illustrate Morrison's "staging" in her fiction, I would like to focus on two mise-en-scènes—the first, from *Sula*; the second, from *Love*. Both at once capture Morrison's rhetorical virtuosity and reveal her employment of language and gesture to mediate time and exposition.

Below are four brief passages from *Sula* that I will parse as examples of Morrison's ability to distill information through language and gesture.

1   The second strange thing was Hannah's coming into her mother's room with an empty bowl and a peck of Kentucky Wonders and saying, "Mamma, did you ever love us?" She sang the words like a small child saying a piece at Easter, then knelt to spread a newspaper on the floor and set the basket on it; the bowl she tucked in the space between her legs. (67)

2   Hannah pinched the tips off the Kentucky Wonders and snapped their long pods. What with the sweet sound of the cracking and snapping and her swift-fingered movements, she seemed to be playing a complicated instrument. Eva

watched her a moment and then said, "You gone can them?" (68)

3   Hannah went off to the Kitchen. . . . She turned the spigot on, letting water break up the tight knots of Kentucky Wonders and float them to the top of the bowl. She swirled them about with her fingers, poured the water off and repeated the process. Each time the green tubes rose to the surface she felt elated and collected whole handfuls at a time to drop in the twos and threes back into the water. (72)

4   Hannah put the Kentucky Wonders over the fire, and struck by a sudden sleepiness, she went off to lie down. . . . She dreamed of a wedding in a red bridal gown until Sula came in and woke her. (73)

The beans, a recurring motif in this scene, which runs for six and a quarter pages, are mentioned more than a dozen times between the snapping and the cooking. They serve several functions: they at once reveal Hannah's actions during and after her conversation with her mother, provide a window on the present and the past, and anticipate the immediate future. The period is 1923, several years before the Great Depression; Hannah is in her mid-thirties, yet she approaches her mother as a child-woman. The conversation between Hannah and Eva, the essential gesture, is about the past and the present, while the beans reveal the current economic situation in the Peace household. A closer scrutiny of the conversation that ensues from Hannah's question about Eva's maternal love prompts Eva to give a history of the family's fortune. However, before answering Hannah, Eva wants to be certain that she heard the question, "Give me that again. Flat out to fit my head" (67). Satisfied that she understands Hannah's question, Eva asks Hannah if she plans to can the beans, to which Hannah replies, "A peck ain't enough to can. [Uncle Paul] say he got two bushels for me" (68).

The peck (8 quarts) and two bushels of beans become a part of the scheme of Eva's story of the family and the larger narrative. While Hannah snaps beans, Eva narrates the family's history of poverty beginning in 1895 when her husband abandoned the family in the dead of winter and under the worst possible circumstances. Eva recalls for Hannah just how dire their situation was then. To feed the four of them she had "$1.65, five eggs, three beets" (32).

Besides their poor economic conditions, the three children were ill:
Hannah had mouth sores; Pearl, intestinal worms (69); and Plum,
locked bowels that Eva loosened with "[t]he last food staple in the
house" (70). Moreover, Eva explains to Hannah, "Wasn't nobody
playin' in 1895." And she warns Hannah not to take their current
good fortune for granted: "Just 'cause you got it good now you
think it was always that good?" (68). "I stayed alive for you," she
reminds Hannah (69). For Eva, love is figuring out how to feed a
family of four and keeping her children alive.

The next sentence returns to the present and the beans: "Hannah
had enough beans now. With some tomatoes and hot bread, she
thought, that would be enough for everybody. . . . She pick[s] up the
basket and [stands] with it and the bowl of beans over her mother"
(69–70) then asks Eva why she murdered Plum if she loved him.
Eva explains that she "just thought of a way he could die like a
man" (72) rather than from the illicit drugs that had taken over his
rational mind and behavior. After Eva's revelation, Hannah goes
to the kitchen to wash and cook the beans, then to her nap and
the portentous dream. The tempos unfold in the phenomenon of
time and events: present, past, and future are collapsed into a single
moment of narration. The immediate future, of course, will bring
Hannah's death by fire and Eva's near-death leap to save her.

To return briefly to the first passage cited above and the "second
strange thing," it is worth noting that such ordering of events is a
recurring Morrison gesture at complicating the narrative—positing
an expectation and teasing the reader with the order of events that
may take a while to sort out. Ultimately, we learn that there are
five "strange things"—the fifth is Hannah's death. This ordering of
events explains why the chapter begins with Hannah's question and
ends with her death rather than with "the wind, which had been the
first," strange event: "The very night before the day Hannah had
asked Eva if she had ever loved them, the wind tore over the hills
rattling roofs and loosening doors" (73). The wind is obviously an
omen of Hannah's death and a concrete and metaphorical answer
to her question, "an evil wonderin'," according to Eva (67). Rather
than begin with the omen, which would clearly prompt readers'
expectations of some terrible outcome, Morrison elects to begin
with what appears to be an ordinary day and an unanticipated
question in the midst of a quotidian activity—the preparation of a
meal that turns out to be the family's last supper together.

Finally, a brief word about the language in this scene—Eva's and the narrator's. Eva's language is folksy, direct, and colorful. And by folksy, I do not mean the kind of language Zora Neale Hurston attempts to capture through the sharp and jarring distinction between her narrator's prestige discourse and the exaggerated vernacular speech of her black characters. Morrison terms Hurston's gesture at representing African American folk speech "slumming" (Als 73). By contrast, Morrison captures the poetry in Eva's and Hannah's gestures, and she moves quite nimbly between their direct, colorful idiom and the more sophisticated language of the narrator. What follows is a breakdown of the dialogue to facilitate scrutiny of its linguistic features.

Eva:	"Give me that again. Flat out to fit my head."
Hannah:	"I mean, did you? You know. When we was little."
Narrator:	Eva's hand moved snail-like down her thigh toward her stump, but stopped short of it to realign a pleat.
Eva:	"No, I don't reckon I did. Not the way you thinkin'."
Hannah:	"Oh, well. I was just wonderin'."
Narrator:	Hannah appeared to be through with the subject. . . . Eva was not through.
Eva:	"An evil wonderin' if I ever heard one."
Hannah:	"I didn't mean nothing by it, Mamma."
Eva:	"What you mean you didn't *mean* nothing by it? How you gone not mean something by it?"
Narrator:	"Hannah pinched the tips off the Kentucky Wonders . . ." (67–8)

Several linguistic features are noteworthy: neither Eva nor Hannah drops the final *g* on every word. Consider, for example, *wonderin'* and *something*. Their grammatical constructions do not require transliteration: "When we was little"; "Thought you was gone can some." The force and directness of their language communicate the homespun practicality of their lives: "Flat out to fit my head"; "A peck ain't enough to can." The complexity and dramatic import of this vernacular speech may be summarized in a single sentence that contains the elements previously mentioned. Here is Eva, still answering Hannah's question, "I'm talkin' 'bout 18 and 95 when I set in that house five days with you and Pearl and Plum and three beets, you snake-eyed ungrateful hussy" (69).

Speaking about her use of language, Morrison stated, "I was just determined to take the language that for me was so powerfully metaphoric, economical, lunatic, and intelligent at the same time—just these short sentences or these developments of ideas that was the language of my family and neighbors and so on—and not make it exotic or comic or slumming" (Als 73). She continues, "I wanted it to come from inside the culture, and speak to people inside the culture . . . to reveal and raise questions" (Als 73–4). This direct, to-the-point speech is referenced in *Love* when Sandler Gibbons comments on the language of his grandson's generation, a language that says little and probably means less. "Nineties [1990s] children didn't want to hear 'sayings' or be managed by lessons too dusty to read, let alone understood. They got better advice from their hammering music. Straight no chaser. Black no sugar. Direct as a bullet" (151). This shift from the spoken word to music suggests both the generational shift and economic progress for African Americans.

Morrison trusts the metaphorical content and folk rhythms to convey texture and meaning. And that, I would argue, is part of the grace of her texts: her ability to move seamlessly between these two levels of discourse. And in doing so, she avoids the awkward shift between the poetry of the folk and lyricism of the author/narrator. Two examples may serve to underscore my point. In *Love*, for example, Christine's unsettled life is described in identical ways, but in two different discourses. In one instance someone refers to her "mismanaged life" (83)—the folk idiom; in another, it is compared to "an engine adjusting to whatever gear the driver chose" (100)—the narrator's description. Now consider the blending of the two voices, "all felt the tick of entitlement, of longing turned to belonging in the vicinity of the fabulous, successful resort controlled by one of their own" (42). Again, a close reading yields Morrison's facility in melding the folksy and lyrical—both metaphorically powerful in their import.

Love and the discourse of nostalgia

To further explore Morrison's poetic language, by way of summary, I would now like to turn to a mise-en-scène in *Love*. Like the scene involving Eva and Hannah, this scene is at once remarkable for its blend of folk idiom and lyricism and in its commentary on the present and the past. The scene involves a single character—Sandler—who, in his domestic, psychological, social situation, reveals Morrison's adroitness in exposing the interior man through his relationship with his external environment. The moon is the controlling image that frames the essential moment—contrasting the past and present and complicating the notion of progress. While Eva measures her move from poverty to progress in pecks and bushels of beans, Sandler measures his progress by the shape and light of the moon. And while Eva has no desire to return to her life of struggle and poverty, Sandler questions whether his new Oceanside house is an improvement over the small cabin he grew up in. As in the scene of Hannah and the beans, Morrison elides several discourses in a single moment while advancing the larger themes of *Love*: change and progress.

> As he did on almost every day, as now, on every cold night, longing for the crackle of fire in a stingy pot-belly stove, the smell of clean driftwood burning. He couldn't forget the picture the moon turned those Up Beach cabins into. Here, in this government-improved and -approved housing with too much man-made light, the moon did nothing of the kind. . . . Only in fine neighborhoods and the country were people entrusted to shadow. So even when the moon was full and blazing, for Sandler it was like a bounty hunter's far-off torch, not the blanket of beaten gold it once spread over him and the ramshackle house of his childhood, exposing the trick of the world, which is not to make us think it is ours. He wanted his own moon again releasing a wide gold finger to travel the waves and point directly at him. (*Love* 39)

This brief passage, part of a single paragraph totaling about 250 words, reveals several things. It shows Morrison's adroit shift between Sandler's folk idiom ("stingy potbelly stove" and "his ramshackle house") and the narrator's lyrical voice ("bounty hunter's far-off torch," "blanket of beaten gold," and "wide gold finger"). We are, in fact, privy to two visions—Sandler's and the unidentified narrator's feelings about the changes and losses brought to the community. The elision of these voices is so skillful that it is hardly noticeable until the pace of reading slows. The passage also exposes the interior life of a character who is first revealed as a sensuous man attracted to a young woman who approaches him for directions; he "scanned her legs and reckoned her knees and thighs were stinging from the cold her tiny skirt exposed" (15). The "bounty hunter's moon," an allusion to *"Police-heads—dirty things with big hats who shoot up out of the ocean to harm loose women and eat disobedient children"* (5), is the diametric opposite of the moon that allowed Sandler to roam freely at night in his old neighborhood.

As Morrison shapes this narrative, it is simultaneously *now* and *then*. We also hear Sandler's interior voice and the narrator's exterior voice reinforcing the novel's themes of present/past, gain/ loss, segregation/integration. This passage also reveals something about Sandler: he is both reflective and nostalgic. Recognizing the need for improvements in their material lives, he admits to himself, and later on to his wife, that there is an irrevocable loss that modern houses in a crowded town cannot compensate for— something important to the human spirit—the loss of direct access to nature. Measuring his present community, with "too much man-made light," against moonlight in his old community, he chooses the latter.[1] The passage further exposes the trade-off between material progress and spiritual well-being and urges a reconsideration of conditions that determine progress.

The gravity

Love and *Paradise*: Gender and the civil rights movement

In the preface to *Freedom's Daughters*, Lynne Olson cites Stokely Carmichael's admission that "the ones who came out first for the movement were women. If you follow the mass meeting, not the stuff on TV, you'd find women out there giving all the direction. As a matter of fact, we used to say, 'Once you got the women, the men got to come'" (15). The preponderance of women within the civil rights movement notwithstanding, most women were relegated to minor roles, and even when they were responsible for major decisions and operations within the movement, the men were the ones publicly touted for the progress and success of the movement. Several theories have been advanced to explain this gender stratification. One theory holds that women were kept in the background so that black men could emerge as macho leaders to counter their years of subservience to white men. It was, however, the takeover of the movement by the Black Panthers, more than any other cause that elevated black machismo to its nationalistic fervor at the expense of black women. Peter J. Ling and Sharon Monteith have observed that "[t]he dominant image of black manhood had become interwoven with a political discourse of death and defiance, but it also disregarded the ways in which black power organizations expressed masculine power in ways that marginalized women in the movement" (7). Elaine Brown describes a moment at a black power meeting in Oakland, California, that provides some insight into gender divisions within the movement. After purchasing meal tickets at a Black Panther meeting, Brown and her female friend joined a line of black males. The two women were advised of the protocol by a young woman, "Sisters, . . . you will have to wait until our Brothers are served. . . . our Brothers are warriors. Our warriors must be fed first, Sisters." When the women refused to step out of line, they were confronted by a Brother, "Sisters, he explained, did not challenge Brothers. Sisters, he said, stood behind their black men, supported their men, and respected them" (Brown 109). Brown also notes that "A woman in the Black Power movement was considered, at best, irrelevant. . . . If a woman assumed a role of leadership she was said to be eroding black manhood, to be hindering the progress of the black race" (357). Stokely Carmichael, responding to women's complaints about their role in the movement, asked, "What is the position of women in SNCC?" Jesting, he answered the question himself, "The position of women in SNCC is prone" (quoted in Olson 336). Carmichael's remark came to define an aspect of the late civil rights movement.

In *Love*, Morrison starkly portrays the treatment of women in the civil rights movement. Christine Cosey, after years of promiscuousness and a failed marriage, meets Fruit, a civil rights activist, "eight years younger than she was" (165) and remains with him for nine years. Christine and Fruit strikingly resemble Elaine Brown and Huey Newton of the Black Panther party. Brown recounts the conflicts in the movement related to dress and hair; they were criticized for "not being "black," and for "wearing European-style clothing." They were expected to "sport 'naturals'" and relinquish their "slave names" and stop "associating with Whitey" (Brown 142). In *Love*, Christine apologizes for her "light skin, gray eyes, and hair, threatening a lethal silkiness"—features antithetical to the movement's dedication to all things African-like—and tries to compensate in other ways. She "became a dedicated helpmate . . . changed her clothing to "motherland," learned the obligatory "slogans" and "hid her inauthentic hair in exquisite gelés" and did whatever else was necessary to *look* like someone dedicated to the movement. Surrendering to the black power movement meant learning a new vocabulary. She learns new epithets for members of her family: "bourgeois traitor"; "handkerchief—head"; "a field hand wannabe" (163). She accedes to "female surrender" to black masculinity. So when she discovers she is pregnant for the seventh time, she has an abortion. Tellingly, "no one stopped her or suggested she do otherwise: Revolutions needed men—not fathers" (164). Moreover, she accepts Fruit's infidelity because "[t]hat was the beauty, the honesty of their relationship" (165).

According to Elaine Brown, Huey Newton discouraged monogamous relationships (Brown 259). Following the Panther line, Fruit's infidelity is expected and accepted because "having men meant sharing them" (165). Yet, Christine is not entirely acquiescent; she questions Fruit when a "Comrade" rapes a young woman in the movement. The victim, not the rapist, is at fault because, according to the rapist, "the girl was all over him braless sitting sloppy" (166). While the other women sympathize with the victim, for Christine their response is troubling, "What did *she* [the victim] do? Why didn't *she* . . .?" Christine "shut up about it and the good work of civil disobedience and personal obedience went on." Morrison's scathing attack on this aspect of the movement is summarized in a brief phrase, "the good work of disobedience was merging with disguised acquiescence" and Christine was considered "too old," "irrelevant" (167).

However, Morrison's critique of the serious work of the movement, the major contributions of everyday people, is summed up in *Paradise*. Rev. Richard Misner, the former civil rights worker and new minister at Calvary, calls attention to the important and essential contributions of everyday folk who "formed the spine on which the televised ones stood." Misner is convinced that by

1975 "all sorts of people will claim pivotal, controlling, defining positions in the rights movement" and that "few would be justified," but "most would be frauds." And what seems to trouble Misner and what is at the heart of his comments is the scant attention to those most deserving of recognition for their valor: "What could not be gainsaid, but would remain invisible in the newspapers and the books he bought for his students, were the ordinary folk. . . . the grandmother who kept all the babies so the mothers could march; the backwoods women with fresh towels in one hand and a shotgun in the other . . . their small stories part of no grand record or even its footnotes" (212). History has indeed confirmed Misner's conviction: It is the public faces of Martin Luther King, Jr and Rosa Parks that overshadow those faces of everyday folk who fought in the trenches and risked their lives and property in the struggle for civil rights.

Finally, readers are reminded that the "disruptive presence" of Africans in America pervades all of Morrison's fiction. Taken together, her novels provide a template for the study of American life from the early years of the emergent nation to the present. They offer readers some paths toward understanding the role of race, gender, class, social, political, economic status, as well as definitions of self and community. They posit a spectrum of human life that encompasses and transcends the African American experience. Combined, they expose the frailties and virtues, the selfishness and generosity, and ultimately what is profoundly human in all people.

PART I

Paradise

Morrison has stated that she "always wanted to write the kind of books that could invite, as well as sustain, subsequent readings" (Hoofard 7). *Paradise*, a dense landscape with a plethora of characters and multiple voices, indeed, invites and demands subsequent and sustained readings as evidenced by the chapters in this volume. The authors in this section extrapolate from Morrison's patriarchal community visions of female resistance and transcendence.

In *Paradise*, Toni Morrison asks: What happens when the oppressed become the oppressor? She interrogates African American identity under conditions of freedom and black leadership by exposing the blind adherence to unexamined Western values of patriarchy and oppression of women. The novel, on the one hand, celebrates the rapid economic advancement of African Americans after Emancipation and, on the other hand, questions whether blacks have forgotten the lessons of slavery and have become corrupted by wealth and power. Prejudices based upon color (Who is black?), class (Whose forebears were among the first to build the original black settlement?), gender (Who decides women's destinies?), and politics (Who has power?) permit Morrison to hold a mirror up to African Americans in which to view themselves and ask whether they have slavishly emulated those who once held them in thrall. The novel further examines the failure of black leaders to search for the best modalities to establish social, economic, and political institutions in an all-black town.

Employing Lacanian concepts to explore the hierarchal order in *Paradise*, Shirley A. Stave initiates the discussion with a focus on the role of gender and place. She delineates the parameters of gender formation and domination by respectively locating the sites of oppression and resistance in the town of Ruby and the Convent. She examines the master narrative that frames and controls the Morgan brothers' vision of the town ruled by the law of the Founding Fathers and continued through the flawed vision of the New Fathers. She points to the appearance of Ruby as an ideal community and the hidden reality of a patriarchy that subjugates women and threatens those who would question male authority or consider altering the status quo. Stave contrasts the contradictions in the tightly controlled segregated community of Ruby—which Morrison calls "outrageously racist" (Hoofard 4)—and its putative independence with the community of women at the Convent, where freedom and individuality are not only respected but encouraged. Stave further notes that the motley group of Convent Women, in contrast to the "model" women of Ruby, search for wholeness, which they achieve through a shared spiritual experience. But that feminine space is disrupted by the Ruby men no longer able to control their insular society. Stave argues that in trying to divert attention from their internal problems and crumbling social order, these men use the Convent Women as scapegoats to mask their failures.

If Stave establishes the grounds on which patriarchy and female subjection are based, Gurleen Grewal lays out the foundation on which women are able to escape domination and find tangible and effective ways to heal. She takes Stave's argument to the next stage by explaining the women's access to healing from their discrete traumatic experiences prior to settling at the Convent. Reading *Paradise* through the lens of Dominick LaCapra's notion of trauma and healing, Grewal examines how these women work out and through their traumatic past. For Grewal, Ruby is not just a closed community but a violent one where men carry forward the intergenerational pain of rejection and repeat it through their own form of "disallowing." Contrastingly, the Covent becomes both a refuge and a place of healing for damaged women from around the country as well as for a few women in Ruby.

Analyzing *Paradise* from a historical and an ecocritical perspective, Aoi Mori builds on Stave's and Grewal's explications of resistance, trauma, and healing by exploring Morrison's revision of the passive feminine power of the Virgin Mary through ancient and transgressive figures such Isis and Mary Magdalene and their modern counterparts—Lone DuPres and Consolata Sosa. These women combine what is considered traditional, occult, and natural in expressing Morrison's argument for a union of body, mind, and spirit in a quest for wholeness. Mori stresses that Morrison's transgressive women offer strategies for moving through and beyond oppression and violence toward a state of healing and transcendence.

2

Separate Spheres?: The Appropriation of Female Space in *Paradise*

Shirley A. Stave

The ideology of "separate spheres" is commonly regarded as the social mechanism regulating the obligations of men and women and segregating them from each other in their daily lives. In Western culture specifically, women have been charged with maintaining the home and overseeing the domestic realm, while men have been entrusted with public life in all its aspects. Feminists over time have decried women's restriction to the home and consequent exclusion from opportunities for paid labor even as they have recognized the enabling possibilities inherent in women sharing life experiences and cultivating talents typically regarded as unavailable to men. Fundamental to the concept of "separate spheres" is the notion that the home represents the uncontested site of woman's authority. While she may have no voice in the economic or political status of her family, the household, and specifically the kitchen, is the woman's domain.

Toni Morrison's novel *Paradise* explores the implications for women's lives when not even the home functions as a space over which a woman exercises authority. In *Paradise*, the town of Ruby with its sinister sense of "perfection," recalls the small town in Ira Levin's horror novel, *The Stepford Wives* (1972). Perfectly laid out, with "enormous lawns cut to dazzle . . . and pastel-colored houses," Ruby gives the impression that "no one lived there" (45). The lives of the women and of the young people in the town are so rigidly constrained by the New Fathers that one might maintain that life is being squeezed out of them. Created as an intentional community by a small group of young men returning home from World War II, to replace an intentional community established by a wandering group of ex-slaves during Reconstruction, Ruby "becomes an imaginative location, a space created by longing and nostalgia for an original place, complete with an affective investment by idealized notions of wholeness" (Yoon 70).

Morrison's choosing to label the men of Ruby as Old Fathers or New Fathers highlights the privilege that fathers—patriarchs— have wielded in culture. French psychoanalyst-philosopher Jacques Lacan coined the phrase the Law of the Father to signify the social order that humans enter once they learn language. Lacanian philosophy perceives gender hierarchy as coterminous with the development of language, at which point a child leaves what Lacan calls the Imaginary Order, in which the child, perceiving him/ herself in a mirror, mistakenly believes he/she possesses agency and wholeness. The acquisition of language lands one in the Symbolic Order and ruptures the fantasy of a unified self. Lacan believes both men and women are constituted as subjects once they accept the limitations imposed on them by the Symbolic Order, but that the process of how this occurs differs for men and women. This chapter will use concepts from Lacanian philosophy to analyze the gendered identities of the characters in the novel and to explore Morrison's use of alternative geographic spaces as enabling or thwarting healthy human subjectivity.

Ruby as the death of the mother

While Haven, especially in its early years, was a community characterized by charity and compassion, by the time the Morgan twins, Deacon and Steward Morgan, were teenagers, they were clearly eager to escape the dwindling village. They resist interrogating the reasons behind Haven's demise, which suggests that the "original place" driving their nostalgia is something more profound than simply revitalizing their community. They seem to seek originary wholeness, the body of the mother lost to them as the result of birth. Not surprisingly, the settlement founded by these men is named Ruby in honor of the young mother who died shortly after the town's inception. Her death is reflected in the static nature of the town itself, which is constrained by the overarching narrative of the original Disallowing. The founding story of the wandering group of ex-slaves who were turned away from an all-black town they had hoped to join, presumably because of their blue-black skin, freezes time and forecloses any possibility of advancement.

Thus, the founding of Ruby commemorates the death of a mother in a narrative created and controlled by the men of the town. One explanation for the emergence of male dominance can be found in Lacan, who has suggested that "civilization" is predicated on the death of the mother, which precipitates men into the Symbolic Order, the realm of language and law, and specifically, the Law of the Father (Stave 219). Debra Bergoffen offers a summary of this trajectory:

> Lacan introduces us to the following formula/condition of the symbolic: woman must disappear into the image of the mother; the image of the mother must efface itself into the Name of the Father. According to this formula, Freud is correct. Civilization is grounded in an act of violence. But he is also wrong. The primal crime is not the murder of the father but the destruction, first of woman and then of the mother. (287)

While the name of the town commemorates one dead woman, it is noteworthy that any reference to women is missing from the story remembered by Steward and Deacon (Kella 215). In the narrative they venerate, the decisions were made primarily by Zechariah, the Morgan patriarch. The women circulate a counter-narrative with subversive details. While the men "forbade the women to eat the food" or take the money or the blankets given to them by the town that rebuffed them, "Soane said her grandmother, Celeste Blackhorse, sneaked back and got the food, . . . to distribute to the children" (195). The paradigm that defines Ruby was inherent in their forebears' decision that "their" women work in the fields rather than in the kitchens of their masters' homes in order to minimize the possibility of rape. The women themselves have no part in the decision affecting their life situation. Prior to the founding of Haven, then, the men were already engaged in the project of policing the sexuality of their female companions and barring their participation in decisions affecting the entire group.

Public versus private spheres in Ruby

The town of Haven grew up around a communal brick cook-oven available for all families to use. While such a facility is practical in a frontier town, where homes heated by woodstoves and housefires always presented a risk of fire, by the time Ruby was settled the communal oven no longer served any realistic function. Understanding this, the women resent the time and labor the men devote to disassembling the oven, packing the bricks in straw, and rebuilding what has become a shrine. For the men of Ruby, the oven has a more symbolic meaning. It represents a refusal to tolerate private space. Noelle Morrisette has pointed out that the existence of the oven "creates the imperative of making the private public" (146). The loss of privacy is annoying to the women. Laura Sloan Patterson describes how Soane Morgan's resentment of the bother over the oven is heightened by the fact that the men do not even put a door on the communal outhouse until the oven is lovingly reassembled. Soane objects to being "exposed to [her] neighbors in even [her] most private acts because of the men's insistence on rituals and appearances of communitarianism" (Patterson 166).

Even courtship allows for no private sphere. When Anna Flood makes dinner for Rev. Misner, "they made sure the parsonage blazed with light, and he drove or walked her home by seven-thirty for all Ruby to see" (214). If, then, no distinction can be drawn between what is public and what is private, and given that the town has "no recognizable business district" (45), one might argue that an economy of one exists in Ruby—that the entire town, named for a dead woman, functions as the body of Woman, over which the men assume authority. Kella argues that "[b]y the strange logic of racialized and sexualized violence, both the black women and white men function as others to the townsmen" (214). In this case, we are back to another economy of one: only men can be said to "live" in Ruby. Kella claims that the men "symbolically en/gendered Ruby's public space as female, and thus as requiring vigilant male control" (216). However, if, as we have seen, no public space exists in Ruby, then all space requires male control and the home—even the kitchen—provides no site of either sanctuary or even enabling possibility for the women.

Dogmatic patriarchy

Morrison's narrative highlights the lengths to which the New Fathers go to regulate the vestiges of the domestic in Ruby. Steward Morgan scrutinizes his wife Dovey's meals, questioning whether "the clove [should] be down in the tissue, not just sitting on top of the ham" and whether one should use "Vidalia onions or Spanish" in preparing chicken-fried steak (81). When the women begin to cultivate flower gardens to fill up empty time, the husbands grumble about the "disappointingly small harvest of radishes, or the too short rows of collards, beets" (89). To conform to the moral dogma of the New Fathers, who claim that "there wasn't a slack or sloven woman anywhere in town" (8), the women of Ruby "did not powder their faces and they wore no harlot's perfume" (143).

Rev. Richard Misner himself, for all his compassion and decency, falls prey to the mind-set that drives the New Fathers. When K. D. strikes Arnette in public (which, in Ruby, could also be in the home since there is no distinction between public and private), Misner calls the men of the families together to discuss what is to be done. Since Arnette and her mother are absent from the meeting, this scene makes clear the "dogmatic patriarchal structure of the town, in which women are denied a voice and, indeed, remain possessions of men that must be negotiated by men" (Michael 649).

The men completely objectify the women around them. When Arnette is effectively sold in exchange for college tuition, Steward questions whether Arnette will agree to the plan, and Arnold Fleetwood brays, "I'm her father. I'll arrange her mind" (61). K. D. recalls the aftermath of his slapping Arnette as "screaming tits closing in on [him and his friends]" (55). His statement identifies a woman's capacity for speech as part of her body. Since "tits" cannot "scream," K. D.'s comment conveys his attitude that women cannot possibly communicate anything meaningful.

Although submission to male dominance supposedly provides "safety," the emptiness of women's lives is apparent, and the women resist in limited ways. Even K. D., hardly the most sensitive of observers, considers that Soane "worked thread like a prisoner: daily, methodically, for free, producing more lace than could ever be practical" (53). Anna Flood complains to Richard Misner that the women's lives revolve around "choir competitions and Bible class and ribbons for fat vegetables and baby showers" (118). The fact that the women of Ruby drive to Demby to shop rather than buy the shoddy items available to them in Fleetwood's hardware store (Patterson 152) is indicative of their dissatisfaction with what the men have deemed adequate for them.

The Convent as private sphere

Ironically, while the Convent was never actually a convent, during the time it was a school for Native American girls administrated by Roman Catholic nuns, it, too, had no public-private divide. The schoolgirls most obviously did not regard it as a home, since their primary objective appears to have been to escape, and it is hard to imagine even well-meaning nuns providing their wards with the kind of privacy one associates with sanctuary. As a girl, Consolata Sosa, a.k.a. Connie, slept in the kitchen, obviously not a private space. In addition, the rituals of a nun's life, where prayer, labor, and meals are shared, meant that only in sleep would a sister be solitary. However, once only Connie and Mary Magna occupy the Convent, and later, when wandering women find their way there, the situation changes. The novel highlights how each woman has affixed her name to the door of her room, disclosing how each one has claimed a private space. Although what the town calls the Convent is a far cry from a conventional home, it provides asylum for the desolate women who have fled oppression to take up residence there. In saying that these women *live* at the Convent, we understand the site is their home, and, its disorder and serendipitous nature notwithstanding, its challenge to the New Fathers of Ruby permeates the text.

The kitchen is the center of the community at the Convent. Despite their squabbles, the Convent Women are almost always represented in the kitchen, and they are frequently cooking or eating food. In contrast, although food in Ruby is mentioned, including people's memories of meals, there is no scene in the novel that describes a family in Ruby actually sitting down to a meal.

Significantly, when the men enter the Convent to commit their massacre, they focus overwhelmingly on domestic details. They are attuned to "the yeast-and-butter smell of rising dough," which they immediately associate with "female malice," and they experience disgust at the fact that the women have not begun their fall canning. Their attention is drawn to "an old hen" with "puffed and bloody hind parts," which they understand as associated with the abundance of the eggs she lays. They notice the garments the women wear—"dirty non-fit dresses and nothing you could honestly call shoes" (7). They choose to ignore the loaves of freshly baked bread and the piles of freshly chopped vegetables ready to go into the pot of boiling stock. Evidence of such industry would challenge their conviction that the Convent Women "call into question the values of almost every woman" (8) in Ruby, and might force them to confront the lack of nurturance in their own homes. Even though the men have already shot the white girl and know that the others may be running for cover, one of the men takes the time to swig milk from a pitcher as he surveys the kitchen. In spite of their aggression, it appears that the men need the maternal comfort represented by the milk, and by extension, the Convent.

The town of Ruby, after all, has depended on the Convent, even during the years when the outcast women were at each others' throats. Nicole Schroder points out how the Convent functions as the polar opposite of the town. The Convent offers food and shelter to all who arrive there (Schroder 179), whereas Ruby rejects strangers. The townspeople have routinely bought food from the Convent, and many women—and even men—have sought sanctuary there when their empty lives in Ruby became more than they could manage. Even the garden at the Convent embodies openness and a celebration of diversity. In contrast to the manicured ones in Ruby, "the Convent is surrounded by vegetation that is the embodiment of an open attitude, a garden that shows traces of wilderness instead of the neat cultivation of civilization," one with a mélange of "flowers, plants, herbs, and weeds" (Schroder 190), with chickens foraging among the plants.

Controlling the Symbolic Order

In an intriguing Lacanian analysis of the novel, Chia Tsai maintains that the Convent "both constitutes and destabilizes Ruby's socio-symbolic network [and] epitomizes the Lacanian feminine structure not because it is a space inhabited by women but because it points to a domain that is beyond the grasp of phallic function" (189). In the opening scene in *Paradise*, the narrator's statement "[t]hey have never been *this deep in* the Convent" (3, emphasis added) suggests that the men perceive their attack on the Convent as a kind of rape. However, it is also intriguing that Morrison describes the building itself as "[s]haped like a live cartridge" (71). Although the original owner of the house was male, the building has subsequently been inhabited solely by women—first by a group of nuns, effectively ignored if not disowned by the Catholic Church, and then by the women who arrive there simply because they have nowhere else to go. Essentially, all these women, whether by choice or not, have been freed from conventional notions of femininity and male control. As such, they possess the Phallus in a way that no one—male or female—can do within the bounds of the Symbolic Order.

In Lacan's articulation of the development of subjectivity, a child, encountering his/her image in a mirror, projects a fantasy ideal of the self as whole and possessing of agency, a stage Lacan refers to as the Imaginary. Upon learning language and grammar, the child learns of his/her subordination to the Father and to the Law—at which point both girls *and* boys are effectively "castrated," recognizing their limitations and understanding that ultimate power (i.e. the Phallus) always exists somewhere else. This "castration" is a necessary stage in the process of maturation, in that it reins in the kind of arrogance and self-obsession that is detrimental to community. It goes without saying, however, that many, many adults never successfully arrive at the stage of accepting their own diminished status. Understandably, women are more inclined than men to feel bounded by law, having been inculcated by language to accept their own subordination. However, a man achieves healthy subjectivity when he comes to realize that power and authority are always to some degree illusory, that they will always be contested and challenged by someone else. The New Fathers of Ruby, specifically Deek and Steward Morgan, have resisted this process of maturation. They do not recognize personal limitations and continue to consider themselves the "ultimate power." Because the men are twins, each functions as an ongoing mirror for the other, permitting both men to remain in the Imaginary stage. According to Lacan, when a child perceives him/

herself in a mirror, the child mistakenly assumes that the image represented in the mirror is his/her true self. Since what the child sees in the mirror is a complete person, the child begins to believe that he/she is unified and whole. The obvious rupture between the "I" that perceives the "other" in the mirror is not questioned until the child learns language and must negotiate among labels such as "son," "brother," "student," and understand that the being represented by those various labels is multiple. The being that functions as "son" is in some ways different from the one who functions as "friend." The Morgan twins never grow beyond their misrecognition. Their shared blackness shields them from the alienation of black oppression (Tsai 169) and masks their status in the Symbolic Order as "subjects equally subjected to the law" (Bergoffen 287). Deek and Steward perceive themselves as *the* law, above and outside any previous law, even that established by the Old Fathers.

Control of language is a fundamental part of the control Deek and Steward wield. A major motivation for the massacre at the Convent is the tension created by the mostly obliterated words on the Oven. When the young people suggest an alternative to the phrase that tradition claims was Zechariah's original words (though the event precedes the memory of any of the living members of Ruby), Steward asserts his authority in ultimate terms: "If you, any one of you, ignore, change, take away, or add to the words in the mouth of that Oven, I will blow your head off just like you was a hood-eye snake" (87).

In Lacan's paradigm of subjectivity, the Morgan twins would feel diminished by the immensity of what the Old Fathers achieved—outlasting slavery, becoming successful during the period immediately following Emancipation, surviving the horrors of Reconstruction, maintaining their integrity after the Disallowing, and founding the town of Haven. And, indeed, as young men, they did experience a sense of their subordination—they enlisted in the military during World War II to escape a life "where all was owed, nothing owned" (12). However, upon their return from the war, finding the town of Haven a shabby remnant of its earlier self, the New Fathers chose to replicate the achievement of the Old Fathers, claiming complete power—over the women and the children, as well as over men they considered inferior to themselves. Whereas in Haven, "families shared everything, mak[ing] sure no one was short" (109), in Ruby, the Morgan twins, through their practice of high-interest loans and foreclosing on mortgages, are slowly taking possession of the entire town. The delusion that they actually possess the Phallus has consequences. The subsequent actions of the Morgan twins demonstrate that the failure to integrate into the Symbolic Order is "indiscriminate aggressivity" (Bergoffen 281).

If, in Lacanian theory, the Symbolic Order is tied to language and law, it can be ruptured by a moment of what Lacan calls *jouissance*, a bliss that has been described as "sexual, spiritual, physical, conceptual at one and the same time" (Hawthorn 186). *Jouissance* is tied to the *semiotique*, sound that is not language (cries, screams, murmurs) or not structured grammatically (poetry)—sound that specifically destabilizes the Symbolic Order. Sound of this nature can be seen as akin to real prayer—to the ecstasy of the mystic, essentially to an encounter with the spiritual. *Paradise* presents many such language ruptures. On the originary journey to found Haven, Big Papa knelt to pray, but "after a few seconds of total silence, he began to hum the sweetest saddest sounds Rector [his son] had ever heard" (96). That he has entered a spiritual realm inaccessible to many is evident from the appearance of the "walking man," who is visible to no one except Big Papa and "sometimes a child" (98), but who leads the group to the place where their community will settle.

In the town of Ruby, Dovey Morgan temporarily escapes the rigidity of the town's codes of femininity through a mysterious visitor who speaks without moving his lips. In response, Dovey "talked nonsense"—another example of the *semiotique*. Dovey understands that "once she asked him his name, he would never come again" (92). Naming would tie him to the Symbolic Order. Her fear that he might destabilize her life leads her to resist him the first time he comes to her house at night. As a result, she loses him completely, never again experiencing the jouissance that he enabled. Morrison's play with the multiple meanings of "jouissance" becomes apparent in the dream Dovey has long after her final encounter with the mysterious visitor in her garden. Having dreamed that she was washing the mysterious man's hair, she awakens "pleased to see that her hands were wet from the suds" (287). As repressed as she is, Dovey does not understand that she has been masturbating and that the "pleasure" she feels is multivalent, both sexual and emotional.

Outside of Ruby, the Convent and its inhabitants challenge the Morgan brothers' fantasy of total power, since both the structure and the women remain out of their control. The women transgress not only the New Fathers' fiction of acceptable femininity, but general societal expectations of acceptable human behavior. Connie retreats to the Convent basement where she exists in a mostly inebriated half-sleep, Seneca cuts into her veins, and Mavis buys toys and treats for children who died years before.

Connie is offered the possibility of transformation through a spiritual encounter with her male self, her animus, who shares her language and appearance because he is an aspect of her own self. Connie's god-self speaks in the cadences of the pidgin English she spoke as a child, sounds so seductive that "Consolata was beginning to slide toward [it] like honey oozing from a comb" (252). Unlike Dovey, who shrinks from the possibility of escaping the Law of the Fathers, Connie transforms herself into Consolata Sosa, "a new and revised Reverend Mother" (265). She foregoes her alcoholic stupor to take charge of the women in the Convent, initiating a regimen of physical and mental discipline that will ultimately enable the fractured women to heal. Not surprisingly, the ritual she creates forgoes language in the sense it is usually understood. "Loud dreaming," in which "monologue is no different from a shriek," and in which "it was never important to know who said the dream or whether it had meaning" (264) replaces speech and breaks down the barriers of individual subjectivity. At the same time, it removes the women more completely from the Symbolic Order and the Law of the Father, so that in the novel's astounding conclusion, the women are no longer subject to either the men of Ruby or their violence.

Excess and the feminine

While *Paradise* invites an interrogation of the symbolic/semiotique split, it also points toward an understandable friction between the Symbolic Order, which is obviously inextricable from the human community, and the natural world, which exists in a relationship with the human but also maintains an independence from it. While the citizens of Ruby live off the land for the most part and are intimate with the natural world—evident in their ability to predict the ferocious blizzard that kills the family less schooled in reading nature—they nevertheless must contend with blazing summers

and violent storms. The rigidity and restraint that constitute the
Symbolic Order is inconsequential to nature's diversity and excess.
The devotion the women in Ruby have for their flower gardens—so
vibrant and luxuriant that "new butterflies journeyed miles to brood
in Ruby" (90)—contrasts sharply with the men grumbling about the
insufficiency of vegetables. The men's dissatisfaction reflects their
fear of a beauty and an abundance they cannot control. Lindsay M.
Christopher points out that for the men of Ruby the "landscapes
surrounding them were something to look at, to *domesticate*" (92,
emphasis added). Soane's relentless lace-making, in its beauty and
excess, creates for her a space free of male restraint. In contrast, her
husband is reassured by "orderly cupboards minus surfeit" (111),
and he measures beauty by conformance to rules: Soane is "as
beautiful as it was possible for a good woman to be" (112).

The 19 pastel Negro ladies of Deek's youth are memorable
for their delicacy and their defined margins. They pose no threat
because they possess neither strength nor excess and are identified
with domestication and cultivation rather than extravagance or self-
indulgence. Unused even to the scents of perfume, the congregation
subjected to Rev. Pulliam's long-winded sermon is almost overcome
during the wedding ceremony where the people experience, "the
voluptuous odor of mint and sweet william [wafting in through the
open windows]" (143).

Deek's affair with Consolata demonstrates his longing for
escape from the sterility of life in Ruby. The two initially encounter
each other during the festival the residents of Ruby celebrate to
commemorate the founding of their town. As Consolata and Mary
Magna come upon the merriment, the narrative voice comments
that "[s]omething *unbridled* was going on under the scalding sun"
(226, emphasis added). The carnivalesque atmosphere implies a
release from all constraint. During the few weeks of their tryst, the
narrative voice portrays the natural world with a glorious radiance:
"September marched through smearing everything with oil paint:
acres of cardamom yellow, burnt orange, miles of sienna, blue
ravines both cerulean and midnight, along with heartbreakingly
violet skies" (232). But Deek quickly recoups his more austere
self, rejecting Consolata along with the magnificent chamber she
provides for them in the basement of the Convent—a bed made up
with luxurious old linen, lit by candles in an antique candelabra.
While Connie believes her love bite that draws blood is the source

of Deek's abandonment, it is just as likely that his disquiet stems from luxuriousness itself—its intangible yet overwhelming force challenging the sober life expected of the citizens of Ruby.

It is not only Deek who deeply distrusts beauty. The first nuns to move into the embezzler's house quickly set about smashing pieces of sculpture and burning books. Admittedly, some of what they find abhorrent is pornographic, but the rigor of their demolition extends beyond items that would likely offend most women. One of the artifacts they preserve, or perhaps import, can itself be considered pornographic, but it has a larger meaning in *Paradise*. The painting is mislabeled as representing St Catherine of Siena, a martyr whose breasts were cut off. Gigi finds that the "I-give woman serving up her breasts like two baked Alaskas on a platter" (73) disturbs her sexual activities with K. D. The picture demonstrates that gender oppression has a long tradition in Christianity (Romero 416) since St Catherine of Siena was never martyred. St Catherine died of old age as a respected scholar in the church, famous for her intellect and learning. It was St Agatha who was mutilated after her refusal to marry. The substitution of Catherine for Agatha suggests the abhorrence the Catholic Church holds for intellectual women. Perpetual virginity, modeled by saints such as Catherine, provides the sole paradigm for female virtue. The model bespeaks control and restraint as strongly as it represents a denial of the reality of the body.

Morrison's novel forges an association between unrestrained, burgeoning nature and the jouissance available to those who find a way to disrupt the Symbolic Order, that is to say, the Law of the Father. That Law, operating in and through language, acts out of the principle of dualistic hierarchies. When we learn language, we learn to oppose "up" and "down," "light" and "dark," "man" and "woman," and, importantly for this text, "body" and "spirit." Outside of language, the boundaries of these categories blur and fuse—is dusk "light" or "dark"? Similarly, once Consolata rejects the teachings of the Catholic Church and the Law of the Father complicit with it, she recalls her very physical love for both Deek and Mary Magna, and adds, "So I wondering where is the spirit lost in this? It is true, like bones. It is good, like bones. One sweet, one bitter. Where is it lost? Hear me, listen. Never break them in two. Never put one over the other. Eve is Mary's mother. Mary is the daughter of Eve" (263).

Significantly, Consolata does not invert the hierarchy instated by
the Symbolic Order by claiming priority for the physical, the fleshly.
Morrison's portrayal of nature as it manifests in the physical world
and in the human practices of sex, birth, and death is not always
benign and often partakes of the excess that can be deadly. The story
of the blizzard demonstrates this. Sexuality can just as obviously be
exploitative and vicious (as every woman in the Convent knows—
Mavis is abused by her husband; Gigi is manipulated by K. D.;
Seneca is demeaned by Norma Fox; Divine is raped; and Connie is
abandoned by Deek) even as it can, if allowed to flourish naturally,
be a vital force in the construction of a healthy subjectivity.

For the men of Ruby, however, such understanding is
inconceivable. They are uncomfortable with women who are too
beautiful, gardens that are excessive, and even their own sexual
desires because the only power they recognize stems from the rigid
binaries of the Symbolic Order. The will to create—whether to create
art or life—falls outside of that control, hence the absence of any
living children of either Deek or Steward. Billie Delia's realization,
when she and Arnette are planning the wedding bouquets, that there
was "[n]o baby's breath anywhere" (149) in Ruby highlights this
absence of regeneration. The latent hostility toward both Fairy and
Lone, who have served as midwives at virtually every birth since the
founding of Haven, stems from the men's awareness that, during the
act of childbirth, they wield no authority and are actually forbidden
access to the birthing rite. Significantly, as Candice Jenkins points
out, in their one opportunity to intervene in the process of birth—
when Delia Best is attempting to deliver her second child—the men
"overrule the women and allow Delia to die" (278). Lone speculates
that her demise will not dismay the husbands of Ruby, who will
prefer their wives to give birth in hospitals "where other men were
in charge" (Morrison 272).

The figure of Lone is emblematic of the lack of insight among the
men of Ruby. Just as they are unaware of her presence at the Oven
the night they plot their brutal attack on the Convent, they are
unaware that she contains within herself that which they would
destroy *out there*. In her insightful article on the women and the
domestic in *Paradise*, Justyna Sempruch maintains that if the
housewife is not rigidly controlled, she can easily transition to "a
witch, the symbolic anti-housewife figure, responsible for disorder,
hysteria, and other processes of contamination" (99). Lone, who

never married, has never been subject to control by the men of Ruby, even though she is one of their community. Ironically, when Lone overhears the men label the Convent Women "[b]itches. More like witches" (276), she has been gathering mandrake root, an herb used by witches to increase male potency. Lone is a healer, and it was she who introduced Consolata to the magical arts (Tsai 190). However, since Lone, adopted by Fairy DuPres, has legitimately become one of the original founding families, the men of Ruby must tolerate her even as they choose to ignore her powers. The anxieties her powers stir within them become projected onto the Convent Women, who function as scapegoats for what the men cannot control within their own community.

The men of Ruby are fighting a battle they will lose. Their desire for dominance is flawed in part because of the magnitude of what they attempt to control. Their disallowal of the private goes hand in hand with their rejection of the natural and the beautiful. Their terror of the sexual impulse reflects their anxiety about the overwhelming forces of the natural world. They hasten their own end with their massacre at the Convent. When the bullet pierces Consolata's head, the mirror into which Steward and Deacon gaze and which confirms their authority, cracks. Seeing Consolata, even as an old blind woman, Deek realizes the deep love he has retained for her, and the memory of that uncontrolled, *unbridled* space ruptures his union with Steward. Deek has experienced castration, and now he experiences "an incompleteness, a muffled solitude, which took away appetite, sleep and sound" (300). The experience prompts him, for the first time in his life, to seek counsel and solace from another. Now subject to the law himself, his fracturing will allow him the possibility of moving into mature adulthood, aware of all his flaws and limitations.

Uniting the spheres

It is impossible to write about *Paradise* without weighing in on what exactly does happen at the novel's end. I have written about this elsewhere, insisting that the women do die and that they will be reincarnated after their encounter with the originary mother who sings but never says a word (Stave 228). Effectively, the women have achieved the Real, the third stage in Lacan's matrix, outside and beyond language and inaccessible by language. Having so thoroughly fused body and soul through their ritual, these women cannot be divided again, so a paradise where the soul thrives apart from the body is not a place at which they will arrive. Rather, "they will rest before shouldering the endless work they were created to do down here in paradise" (Morrison 318). However, the nature of Morrison's perception of paradise must be interrogated, especially given the multiple renderings of that conception teased out of the text—from the original Haven, to Ruby, to the beliefs of the Christians in the text in an otherworldly paradise, to the paradise achieved by the women at novel's end. As Morrisette points out, "Morrison's novel shows how Paradise is itself created out of God's grammar, and that grammar is therefore exclusionist" (146). Effectively, the traditional concept of paradise is predicated upon another kind of separate spheres—the saved and the damned. As Tsai points out, "The massacre is . . . triggered by the Ruby men's exclusive view of paradise" (197).

Integral to the Morgan twins' presumption of authority is their claiming the license to label, which is based on a sense of themselves as the chosen and all others as ultimately inconsequential. Hence, upon entering the Convent, they label the women there "detritus" (4). It is important to recognize, however, that while, in the case of the Convent Women, the men manufacture evidence of their victims' moral shortcomings, ultimately, for them, the divide between those saved and those unworthy is not based upon any theological hypothesis. Therefore, Steward labeled Pat Best's mother "dung" (201), not because of her behavior, but simply for her skin color. Essentially, Steward and Deacon have no profound connection with any deity; Rev. Misner reflects that they act "as if God were their silent business partner" (143), and in response to their own parents' belief that God would take care of them, the twins suppose ". . . He did, safe to say, until He stopped" (16). The twins' own state of belief—or, more to the point, unbelief—notwithstanding, it is imperative to remember that traditional Christianity has embraced and continues to embrace the distinction between the saved and the damned, a separation into spheres that are ultimately cosmologically far removed from one another—those of heaven and hell. Paradise, according to this theological model, becomes a place to which the saved ascend after death, a site of endless bliss in the company of God, far removed from the inferior, fallen earth.

To return to the Lacanian model that has driven this chapter, any of the dualities constructed by human subjectivity—man:woman, white:black, sufficiency:excess, saved:damned, heaven:hell—exist only in the Symbolic Order insofar as they are constituted by language. As we have seen in the cases of Zechariah, Dovey, and Consolata, true connection with the spiritual ruptures the Symbolic, opening up the possibility for momentary access to the Real. Hence Consolata admonishes her charges to resist separating Eve from Mary, but rather to fuse the duality of what these theological figures represent. As Romero points out, "patriarchal control defines who and what is Good and Evil, which women are Mary, which are Eve. It divides women from each other and their bodies" (417).

The theological implications of such a schism are immense. Categorizing and pigeonholing people within linguistic constructs foreclose the possibility of accessing the Real, or, in other words, of a paradise not predicated on exclusion and separation. The Real, incapable of being spoken in language, can, I think, be identified with the state achieved by the true mystic who comes to grasp, if only momentarily, the unity of all. The massacred women achieve a true paradise through their fusion with each other, but the text suggests that Deek also may arrive at a similar state of what we might consider redemption, given that he has opened himself up to vulnerability and uncertainty. In speaking to Misner, Deek's "language" approaches the semiotique: "His words came out like ingots pulled from the fire by an apprentice blacksmith— hot misshapen, resembling themselves only in their glow" (301). Furthermore, Deek now despises himself for having become "the kind of man who set himself up to judge, rout and even destroy the needy, the defenseless, the different" (302). In relinquishing the power to which he had believed himself entitled, in foregoing judgment, Deek may find himself capable of fusing the spheres he had once perceived as incompatible.

As Romero claims, *Paradise* "views 'paradise' not as the transcendent realm of normative Christian traditions, but as more flexible, inclusive communities on earth" (423). As Consolata is comforted by Piedade's song, on an island replete with "sea trash" (Morrison 318), a ship arrives bearing passengers both "lost and saved" (318), since that distinction is rendered insignificant once spheres have unified to become one whole beyond language, the ineffable that constitutes the Real.

3

The Working Through of the Disconsolate: Transformative Spirituality in *Paradise*

Gurleen Grewal

Toni Morrison's unfolding trajectory as a novelist situates her as a novelist-healer whose abiding subject is the healing of self and community. Her writings perform the archival and restorative work of redress that is at once social and political. A genuine "historical understanding," according to historian Dominick LaCapra, involves engaging in two forms of "working through" traumatic experience: a "discourse of mourning" and of critique (178). To such "historiography as working through," Morrison's *Paradise* adds a crucial third dimension, one that transforms the consciousness of mourning and critique: the spiritual. What distinguishes *Paradise* is its exploration, via the figure of Consolata, of the transformative role of spirituality in the process of working through and effecting ethical agency. Skillfully naming the ills and diagnosing their causes in sociopolitical terms means also challenging and changing the limiting discourse of race, gender, and class as it has historically circumscribed black experience.

Recovering from trauma: "Acting out" and "working through"

Paradise shares with Morrison's previous novels a disturbing opening scene of violence, which, as readers later recognize, constitutes acting out. The scene of violence is a symptomatic enactment of intergenerational trauma by the victimized. Trauma theorist and historian LaCapra applies the terms "acting out" and "working through" to the subjectivity of trauma survivors, following Freud's distinction between mourning (a "working through" of traumatic loss) and melancholia (an "acting out" that reveals a fixation upon traumatic loss). The compulsion to act out and the saving impulse to work through is a thematic constant in the repertoire of Toni Morrison's fiction. In all her novels to date, Morrison has the reader undertake the work of integrating the disavowed, the repressed, the other. She makes this difficult work palatable through the use of language that sings and dips in sensory rhythms. Awash in the intimacy of a seductive lyricism, we forget just how much psychic violence we have borne throughout the text. The violence, however, is no secret, it being the subject of each novel's exposition: incest, madness (*The Bluest Eye*); destruction of a friendship and a community (*Sula*); suicide, racial violence, and retribution (*Song of Solomon*); "man" and nature as fugitives of a destructive civilization (*Tar Baby*); the beating back of a ghost in *Beloved*; the shooting of a girl and the disfiguring of her corpse in *Jazz*; the hunting/shooting of women by nine black men (*Paradise*); a gang rape in the second chapter of *Love*; and an opening reference by the narrator to "blood . . . and bare teeth" (*A Mercy* 3). The narrative goal of the story of violence is reconciliation, catharsis, truce in the psyche brought about by the work of assimilating difficult memory. It is also political, demanding individual and collective reappraisal of the meaning of black identities in America. With her self-questioning narratives of symbolic recompense, Morrison seems to fulfill, via the novel, the role that LaCapra envisions for the historiographer.

While Morrison's novels seem to offer resolution, in fact, the trauma remains to take on new forms in succeeding novels. In the insightful study, *Quiet As It's Kept: Shame, Trauma, and Race in the Novels of Toni Morrison*, J. Brooks Bouson contends that while Morrison "seems bent on effecting a cultural cure," the "precariousness of that cure is revealed not only by her repeated depictions of the intergenerational transmission of victimization and shame but also by her constant restagings of familial and cultural scenes of shame and trauma in each successive novel" (5). To be sure, the process of working through is not linear. Morrison's novels evade "closure," and violations resurface, each successive novel returning to issues unresolved in the previous works. *Paradise* takes up what is only partially resolved in *Jazz*—the issue of the murdered-denigrated feminine and its relationship to a wounded and wounding masculinity. Representing these in *Paradise* are the symbolic spaces of the cellar, a private/domestic feminine space where "the stories rose" in release of the traumatic, and the Oven, a public domain of the black masculine that commemorates and perpetuates rather than heals trauma—here "the voices rose" in a scapegoating of the women (264, 274). Far from healing, the men's injured egos and wounded masculinity (loss of pride and control, fear, greed, and rage) lead them to cold-blooded murder. Magnifying the intergenerational reliving of trauma and its unwholesome defense mechanisms, *Paradise* underscores LaCapra's insight: "it's via the working-through that one acquires the possibility of being an ethical and political agent" (144).

Thus, Morrison's oeuvre comprises the ongoing history of a traumatized social group. Giti Chandra has identified Morrison's fiction as a "unique subcategory of the contemporary novel—a form that "revisits sites of extreme or intense violence in the lives of both of its protagonists and of the collective to which they belong in the process of defining the identity of that collective" (*Narrating Violence* 1). One critic has described *Paradise* as "a novel about black nationalism and its discontents" (Jenkins 274). Indeed, *Paradise* interrogates the hold of racist and sexist ideology within African American conceptions of nationalism spanning the two periods of Reconstruction (from the 1880s to the 1970s). Black nationalism's discontents are staged in *Paradise* through the controversy about the Oven and the signification of its motto, the conflict between the young civil rights militants and the old separatists of Ruby (represented by Rev. Richard Misner and Rev. Senior Pulliam, respectively), and through the "disallowing" of the permissive mixed-race Convent Women who defy the notions of both racial and sexual purity. *Paradise* challenges racial purity as a blighted nationalist idea acquired from the master narrative of race in America. Intraracial and class tension between underprivileged dark-skinned blacks and light-skinned privileged blacks is a theme with a long history in Morrison's novels. We see it on a personal level between Maureen Peal and Claudia McTeer, and between Geraldine and Pecola Breedlove in *The Bluest Eye*; between Ruth and Macon Dead, and between Milkman Dead and Guitar in *Song of Solomon*; between Son Green and Jadine Childs in *Tar Baby*); and between the narrator and the figure of Golden Gray in *Jazz*.

In its account of the 8-rock men's fixation on policing the color line in the 1890s and in its critique of the defended identity of the New Fathers in the 1970s, *Paradise* also highlights the "interesting paradox" that LaCapra identifies:

> how something traumatic, disruptive, disorienting in the life of a people can become the basis of identity-formation. If you think about it, this probably happens in the lives of all peoples, to a greater or lesser extent. All myths of origin include something like a founding trauma . . . indicating that through a trauma one finds an identity that is both personal and collective at the same time. Again, this is understandable, but it also should be questioned; the trauma should be seen as raising the question of identity, rather than simply founding an identity. (161–2)

Annulled by fair-skinned colored men who had "disallowed" them a home in the township of Fairly, the dark-skinned founders of Haven establish "the blood rule" that holds the residents of Haven and Ruby hostage to skin color. Instead of eradicating the malaise at the root, they privilege the very identity bequeathed to them by their victimization and mirror the exclusivity of the oppressor. We learn that the Morgans "carried the rejection of 1890 like a bullet in the brain" (109). Such is the reactive nature of most human response to suffering: victimhood becomes identity, and tightly held grievances perpetuate the state of war within and without. Morrison's original title for the novel *Paradise* was "War." The notion of home-as-paradise, an ideal safe space built upon exclusion, a defended space—whether called Fairly or Haven or Ruby—is of course a notion that supports war.

The meaning of home

In *Paradise* Morrison recounts the intergenerational memory of racial violence that, for African Americans, lends emphasis to the idea of home as safe space:

> Ten generations had known what lay Out There: space, once beckoning and free, became unmonitored and seething; became a void where random and organized evil erupted when and

where it chose. . . . Out There where your children were sport, your women quarry, and where your very person could be annulled. (16)

Every Morrison novel is also an exploration of what it means to be at home or not at home on American soil. In the argument between town-chronicler Patricia Best and Rev. Misner, intellectual priest, Morrison lets Rev. Misner have the last word on home/paradise:

But can't you even imagine what it must feel like to have a true home? I don't mean heaven. I mean a real earthly home. Not some fortress you bought and built up and have to keep everyone locked in or out. A real home. Not some place you went to and invaded and slaughtered people to get. Not some place you claimed, snatched because you got the guns. (213)

Here Morrison is alluding to European and American colonial past that dislocated so many from home. But she has Misner go further:

back past the whole of Western history, past the beginning of organized knowledge, past pyramids and poison bows, on back to when rain was new . . . back when God said Good! Good!— there right there. . . . Imagine that, Pat. That place. Who was God talking to if not to my people living in my home? (213)

Misner is evoking a primordial home unalienated by history— perhaps the very origin of life in edenic Africa ("Who was God talking to if not to my people living in my home?"). In the essay "Home," Morrison acknowledges but dismisses "nostalgia for the race-free home" she has "never had" and "would never know" (4). Perhaps Misner is asking the congregation to imagine what it would be like to feel naturally and completely at home within themselves in this world.

In the parable in Morrison's moving *Nobel Lecture*, the young ones urge the blind woman, who is "the daughter of slaves . . . and lives alone in a small house outside of town," to tell what only she can tell: "What moves at the margin. What it is to have no home in this place. To be set adrift from the one you knew. What it is to live at the edge of towns that cannot bear your company"

(*Nobel Lecture* 206). These lines apply equally to the disallowed, the Founding Fathers of Haven, Oklahoma, and to the five women of the Convent scapegoated by the New Fathers of Ruby.

Paradise identifies the 8-rock men's yearning for a safe home in the African American history of dislocation, terror, and the recurrent "disallowing": first, in the revictimization of blacks during the failed Reconstruction era that propelled migrations West; then, in the "rejection" of post-World War II or "the Disallowing, Part Two," described as equivalent to "watching a parade banner that said WAR-WEARY SOLDIERS! NOT WELCOME HOME!" (194). The wound of the forefathers is not allowed to heal, and the 8-rock descendants become the "New Fathers" who "did it again" by moving farther west, founding Ruby (194)—a town whose name also commemorates a death (that of the Morgan brothers' sister Ruby, whose illness goes untreated by racist doctors). The Oven the Old Fathers had built in 1890 as Haven's communal kitchen measured their ability as men to take care of their women, who need not work in the dangerous (sexually violating) space of white men's kitchens. Representing the achievement of black masculinity (the ability of black men to protect black women), the oven "monumentalized what they had done" and when the descendants leave Haven, the phallic sign, "[r]ound as a head, deep as desire" cannot be left behind (6–7). The men of Ruby were proud that "its people were free and protected" and that the women were safe: "Nothing for ninety miles thought [a woman] was prey" (8). It is, thus, doubly ironic that the Convent Women, 17 miles away from them, become prey to these protective fathers. It is in the public sphere of the Oven that the representatives from all three churches hold a secret meeting to plot against the women of the Convent.

The women who find a haven in the Convent are each alone and homeless, either fleeing a dangerous home or searching for refuge. In this regard, they have an affinity with the descendants of the Disallowed. That the men feel threatened by the women's autonomous coexistence says much about the normative constructions of masculinity and femininity. The New Fathers are determined to cleanse Ruby of the menace posed by the "loose" women because Ruby's social order is based on women knowing their place. The imagined purity of the remembered "nineteen Negro ladies," with waists "not much bigger than their necks" posing for the male gaze—the cherished memory of the Morgan

twins (Deacon and Steward)—and the domesticated "tippy-tap
steps of women who were nowhere in sight" in the Fleetwood
home are both bourgeois constructs of femininity that black men
such as Steward and Deacon Morgan endorsed in their own quest
for power and upward mobility (61). When the Ruby men invade
the Convent's cellar where the women have worked through their
pain, what the men "see is the devil's bedroom, bathroom, and his
nasty playpen" (17). The men's paranoia and virulent scapegoating
evoke the Puritan witch hunts of the seventeenth century in Salem,
Massachusetts, as well as the Inquisition in medieval Europe.

The lives of the four women—Mavis, Gigi, Seneca, and Pallas—
offer a contrasting picture. Each is a victim of a social order that
privileges masculine power and permits violence against women and
children. Feminist inquiry into sexual abuse and domestic violence
has exploded the sentimental idea of home as a space of safety for
women. Feminist analysis has shown how patriarchal definitions
of the women's roles as wives and mothers, along with women's
stunted sense of their own possibilities, makes them collude in their
own subjection. Witness Mavis's internalized self-hatred when she
affirms her abusive husband Frank's judgment of her—"he had
been absolutely right about her: she was the dumbest bitch on the
planet" (37). She takes all the blame for her twin babies' suffocation
to death in the car while she is buying groceries for her husband who
will not take the time to attend them. Unwed or teen mothers, such
as Arnette and Seneca's 14-year-old mother Jean (who may be white
or black), bear both the stigma of illicit sexuality and the burden of
child rearing. Unwed Arnette mutilates her womb in an effort to be
rid of the fetus, while men such as K. D. roam unaccountable. By
leaving ambiguous the race of the four women Morrison challenges
any attempt to find meaning in racial stereotypes and highlights the
oppression of women as an experience that cuts across race and
class.

Morrison complicates the understanding of patriarchal oppression by holding women as well as men accountable: Seneca,
abandoned by her teen mother, is later preyed upon by Norma Fox, a
married rich woman, who uses Seneca for her own sadomasochistic
pleasure. Seneca subsequently cuts herself in order to feel the
pain she is numb to. Runaway Mavis is let down by her mother
who informs Frank of her whereabouts. Pallas is betrayed by her
mother Dee Dee, who seduces or is seduced by Pallas's boyfriend,

leaving her daughter heartbroken and prey to sexual violence by strangers. Pallas is rendered speechless: "for soundmaking power she couldn't rival the solitary windmill creaking in the field behind her" (173); "the words to say her shame clung like polyps in her throat" (179). Hers is the loss of self often experienced by those who have been sexually violated:

> Pallas touched her throat and made a sound like a key trying to turn in the wrong lock. All she could do was shake her head. Then, like a child alone in a deserted playground, she drew her name in the dirt with her toe. Then slowly, imitating the girl's earlier erasure with the vomit, she kicked her name away, covering it completely with red dirt. (175)

Just as Haven and Ruby were once safe havens from racist violence, for Pallas the Convent "felt permeated with a blessed malelessness, like a protected domain, free of hunters but exciting too. As though she might meet herself here—an unbridled, authentic self" (177). Liberated from the pressures and agendas of defensive masculinity (both black and white), the women are free to heal within a safe space. Connie shares with Mavis two principles that inform the healing process: "Lies not allowed in this place. In this place every true thing is okay" (38); "Scary things not always outside. Most scary things is inside" (39). Led by Consolata, the women's traumas are ritually and somatically acknowledged and tended. The four women emerge no longer haunted.

The spiritual healer's journey

The novel charts Connie's growth and transformation from a wounded woman to healer-elder, Consolata Sosa. Originally constructed and furnished by the illicit wealth of an embezzler, the Convent embodies the split between body and spirit that is characteristic of patriarchal culture. *Paradise* interrogates these ideas of God and heaven. And Connie's spirituality is the synthesis of two mentors that shape her as thesis and antithesis: Mary Magna, the Catholic nun who shuns the body in favor of spirit, and Lone Du Pres, the aged midwife and intuitive healer of

Ruby, who represents the tradition that the Catholic Church has historically charged with witchcraft and magic. Midwife, healer, a witch "harvesting mandrake" from the streambed at night and able to "read the minds of men," and prolong the life of the body, Lone represents folk healing traditions of women, European as well as West African, marginalized by the Church and the medical establishment (Ehrenreich 272–3).

Connie is able to integrate the best of both teachers, combining reverence for the way of the spirit with respect for the carnal life of the body. The ascetic vision of the Catholic nuns is found wanting—even as Connie is counseled to repress the body's "[s]ha sha sha" by Mary Magna's "[s]h sh sh" (241). Consolata urges her pupils: "Hear me, listen. Never break them in two. Never put one over the other. Eve is Mary's mother. Mary is the daughter of Eve" (263). She has taken Lone's advice to her: "You need what we all need: earth, air, water. Don't separate God from His elements. He created it all. You stuck on dividing Him from His works. Don't unbalance His world" (244).

Herself open to inspiration from sources deemed paranormal or transrational, Morrison has integrated Christian mysticism with the West African cosmology of the New World ancestor. In the "loud dreaming" healing sessions in the Convent cellar presided over by high priestess Consolata, the novel gestures toward shamanic sacred ritual and practice. Scholars such as La Vinia Delois Jennings and K. Zauditu-Selassie have noted allusions to Yoruba and Brazilian *Condumble*, New World black rituals of cleansing, healing, or making whole. David Servan-Schreiber, in a book about healing cancer, identifies the essence of these rituals as a concern about the "will to live":

> In all cultures and in every period—up until the beginning of modern times—the art of guiding the sick back to health has been practiced by exceptional individuals called medicine men [*sic*] or shamans. . . . Since time immemorial, at the heart of this teaching one invariable principle is found: *the patient's treatment is focused on rekindling his or her life force.* Each shamanic tradition uses particular methods destined to free the patient of the "demons" threatening his will to live. (145)

Connie, whose own will to live weakens, is the classic wounded healer who must heal herself before she can effect genuine transformation in others. The role of grace is evident in this healer's journey: from her loss of sight and the development of her "bat vision" we learn that "Consolata had been spoken to" (241). Her sensual vision is gradually being replaced by a spiritual one. When Connie is abandoned and heartbroken by Deacon, she can only say "[b]ut he, but he. . . . Sha sha sha, she wanted to say, meaning, he and I are the same" (241). She had desired to fuse with Deacon, like the "two fig trees growing into each other" but their passion proved unfruitful like the trees with "the agonized trunks." Seared as the "burned-out farmhouse" in which they made love, she confesses on her knees, "Dear Lord, I didn't want to eat him. I just wanted to go home" (240).

Mourning the loss of her surrogate mother, Mary Magna, at 54, Connie experiences "resignation, self-pity, muted rage, disgust and shame"—the all-too-human emotions (250). She undergoes deep despair as "her rope to the world had slid from her fingers" (247). The path to wholeness is a difficult one—but it is what Connie-Consolata has chosen for herself. She experiences a prolonged and classic dark night of the soul, in her small room in the cellar, "a space tight enough for a coffin" (221). Connie dies a metaphoric death before Consolata the spiritual healer/transformer can emerge. In a paradox well recognized in spiritual literature, she must *empty* herself before she can be filled with spirit: "Facing extinction, waiting to be evicted, wary of God, she felt like a curl of paper—nothing written on it—lying in the corner of an empty closet" (247–8). Eli Jaxon-Bear writes, "[a]t its root, every ego has unexperienced despair" which is "based on the recognition of mortality and the inevitability of death. Death is the gatekeeper at the threshold to immortality" (260).

After a description of the sky colors "strutting like requited love on the horizon," Consolata encounters her spiritual paramour when she emerges sober from the cellar into the "winter-plagued garden" (251). The stranger in the green vest, red suspenders, and white shirt visiting her claims she knows him. She discovers that he and she are indeed *the same*; in his presence she experiences what she had longed for with Deacon: a coming home to herself. Only this homecoming is spiritual, not physical:

> She felt light, weightless, as though she could move, if she wanted to, without standing up. . . . Suddenly he was next to her without

having moved—smiling . . . flirtatious, full of secret fun. Not six inches from her face, he removed his tall hat. Fresh, tea-colored hair came tumbling down, cascading over his shoulders and down his back. He took off his glasses then and winked, a slow seductive movement of a lid. His eyes, she saw, were as round and green as new apples. (252)

The mysterious encounter with the guest represents the intimate and ineffable moment of spiritual awakening for Consolata. The reference to the apples of Eden implies the state of wholeness or undivided selfhood symbolized by the prelapsarian garden. After she encounters this androgynous (or unified), numinous reality of her spiritual being, Consolata prepares a feast and addresses the women with a new demeanor: "I call myself Consolata Sosa" (262). A "new and revised Reverend Mother," she takes charge and guides the lost women to recovery. Later when the rain falls, Consolata "fully housed by the god who sought her out in the garden" (283), dances in celebration. She is killed soon after, leaving in her wake a series of visible transformations among those whose lives she touched.

Rev. Misner reaches a breakthrough in his own unconventional understanding of Christianity following the postmurder visit to the Convent garden where he and Anna "sensed" rather than saw ("for there was nothing to see") an opening (305). Each of them described it differently. Anna "later" identified it as a door, while Rev. Misner called it a window. Yet they both sensed the power of Consolata's garden: a vision of the continuity of spirit beyond life's apparent termination in death. At little Save-Marie's funeral, "when he bowed his head and gazed at the coffin lid he saw the window in the garden, felt it beckon toward another place—neither life nor death—but there, just yonder, shaping thoughts he did not know he had" (307). Spiritually inspired, he articulates with clarity an understanding new to him: that "HE is with us always, in life, after it and especially in between, lying in wait for us to know the splendor"; that there is no sinner in need of saving, "since there never was a time when [Save-Marie was] not saved" (307). Through him, the novel affirms nothing less than the unbroken divinity of life—life eternally expressing itself through the life of the body and beyond it.

In the light of this understanding, the conventional Christian discourse of damnation, of heaven and hell, of saving sinners, is rendered as redundant as the discourse of superstition earlier rejected by Connie: "Her safety did not lie in the fall of a broom or the droppings of a coyote. Her happiness was not increased or decreased by the sight of a malformed animal. She fancied no conversation with water" (244). When Connie dies, "Soane and Lone DuPres closed the two pale eyes but can do nothing about the third one, wet and lidless, in between" (291). While "wet" refers to blood from the bullet wound in the forehead, the word "lidless" also refers to the subtle third eye that in Connie's case is awakened. In Hindu yogic literature, the word yoga connotes the union of individual self-awareness with the limitless and deathless divine consciousness pervading all life. In this tradition, the location of the third eye is the subtle energy center between the brows (*ajna chakra*). It is said to become energized in those who have opened to higher consciousness. The open third eye represents being "awake" to the beauty and unity—or in Rev. Misner's words, "the splendor"—of divine life.

No wonder then, given this transcendent and transrational realm of the spirit, where borders of life and death are rendered permeable, the novel treats the death of the women in a manner that is unperturbed. Redemptive rain falls on dry land and we witness "the rapture of holy women dancing in hot sweet rain" celebrating the end of the women's haunting the night before the murder (283). Brilliant light illuminates the Convent's rooms on the day of the sunlit murder. The assassins are led through "occasional rainbows to the front door" (285); as the mist clears it is "[g]lorious blue. . . . Sun follows [Steward] in, splashing the walls of the foyer" (285). The sisters Dovey and Soane, married to the assassins, drive to the Convent "through glorious dawn air" (288). Consolata's passing imbues the events in the Convent and its garden with the miraculous. The five women have vanished along with the Cadillac.

The fact that the vanished or dead women reappear to their loved ones while remaining invisible or incorporeal to others suggests that they have indeed passed on. Gigi appears to her father: "Armed guards strolled the road above them. None gave sign that they saw her" (309). Gigi connecting with her absent, jailed father and Mavis with her once-tormenting daughter Sally demonstrate reconciliation with their painful pasts. And both move on. Gigi, companioned, is swimming in a lake with "upright trees" (310), rather than the

longed-for lake where "two trees grew in each other's arms" (66).
She seems to have been liberated from an earlier sexual fixation.
Mavis, when asked by Sally if she is okay, replies, "I'm perfect, Sal"
(315). The two living mothers Dee Dee and Jean have a harder
time connecting with the apparitions of their daughters, Pallas and
Seneca respectively. But "the smile on Pallas' face was beatific"
(311), and Seneca has a friend who openly tends to Seneca's cut
hand, suggesting that the "under garment life" of cutting herself is
behind her (260).

But the one whose transformation is radical is Deacon Morgan.
Both Deacon and Connie jolt each other to transformation—
Deacon, by leaving her, and she, by finally leaving him (dying
in his arms). His "hands trembled" after he lays her down and
we learn that he is shaken to his core (290). Shaken by his
brother's hate-filled shooting of the woman he had once loved,
his transformation has begun. He walks barefoot in humility to
Rev. Misner's house and bares his soul. Unlike Steward, his twin,
Deek is penitent and teachable enough not to repeat the error of
his grandfather Coffee/Zechariah, who shunned his brother Tea
when the latter surrendered to the racist demand that he dance
for his survival rather than take the bullet in his foot. Deacon
chooses to examine the shame in himself. In contrast to Steward's
repudiation of blame for the deaths in the Convent, Deacon
asserts: "My brother is lying. This is our doing. Ours alone. And
we bear the responsibility" (291).

Lastly and happily, Anna Flood and Rev. Misner prove worthy
of receiving all that Consolata offers. Anna alone sees on the
Convent's cellar floor "the turbulence of females trying to bridle,
without being trampled, the monsters that slavered them" (303).
She with her unstraightened hair and insight, and Rev. Misner
with his depth and sincerity become the recipients and custodians
of Consolata's wisdom. They inherit the legacy of her garden with
its "faded red chair." The five fresh eggs in Anna's hands and the
"long pepper pods in his" symbolize the renewing fecundity of life
in the physical garden of "blossom and death," while the emergent
vision of the door and window "as they stood near the chair" imply
their capacity to receive the spiritual understanding that informed
Consolata (304–5). They are the ones who will remain in Ruby and
work for the community "shouldering the endless work they were
created to do down here in Paradise" (318).

Conclusion: Paradise at home

The novel's last scene frames an earthly vision of paradise/home. The scene has both aural and visual elements: Piedade, "black as firewood," with "[r]uined fingers" is singing a song, while in her lap rests the head of a younger Connie with the emerald eyes and tea brown hair. The setting conveys the ambiguous nature of paradise: "Around them on the beach, sea trash gleams. Discarded bottle caps sparkle near a broken sandal. A small dead radio plays the quiet surf." Their varying skin color reflects the turbulent mingling of races in the New World. Piedade and Connie, crone and maiden, are two aspects of the feminine psyche united and at peace here:

> There is nothing to beat this solace which is what Piedade's song is about, although the words evoke *memories neither one has ever had*: of reaching age in the company of the other; of speech shared and divided bread smoking from the fire; the unambivalent bliss of going home to be at home—the ease of coming back to love begun. (318, emphasis added)

However, the "solace" in Piedade's song bears a meaning much larger than the "unambivalent bliss of going home." We read the scene with knowledge of the violence that has frequently sundered the two women, and their union immediately follows Jean's partial and unsatisfactory reconnection with her long-lost daughter Seneca. In the larger space of Morrison's oeuvre, the scene contrasts with the absence of any sense of communion at the end of earlier novels, such as *Beloved*, and it anticipates the disconsolation in *A Mercy* of Florens and her slave mother whose memories are of separation and homelessness. In his *Postcolonial Narrative and the Work of Mourning*, Sam Durrant makes the interesting observation that although some degree of working through takes place within Morrison's novels, enabling individuals to come to terms with their personal histories, a "racial memory" of an "ungovernable" loss prevents her novels from offering closure (122). According to Durrant, the repetitive intergenerational trauma in each text is traceable to a founding violation, a prodigious loss that can never be fully articulated. Jennifer Lee Jordan Heinert cautions, Morrison's fiction is "not supposed to provide answers for readers"; it is their responsibility "to determine the answers to the questions

her novels raise" (11), and Jami Carlacio reminds us later in this
volume that a Morrison narrative "invites no easy interpretation.
Readers are expected to work at it, to struggle over its meaning, to
read (into) it."

In fact, the figure of Piedade creates a greatly expanded context
for this scene. The name Piedade means compassion or mercy in
Portuguese, and Piedade functions as the patron deity and spiritual
guide of the displaced and sundered in the Americas. As a deity,
she evokes Yemanja, the Yoruba divinity (orisha) and mother of all
life whose realm is the ocean, and who, in the various Afrocentric
syncretic religions of the New World from Cuba to Brazil (Santeria,
Shango, Candomble), oversees the survivors of shipwrecks as
their patron deity. The African orisha fuses with the Virgin Mary,
Stella Maris, Our Lady, Star of the Sea, as a guide and protector of
seafarers:

> When the ocean heaves sending rhythms of water ashore, Piedade
> looks to see what has come. Another ship, perhaps, but different,
> heading to port, crew and passengers, lost and saved, atremble,
> for they have been disconsolate for some time. Now they will
> rest before shouldering the endless work they were created to do
> down here in paradise. (318)

As she looks at the ship of passengers brought to port in "rhythms
of water," "disconsolate" and "atremble" (an allusion to the slave
trade), this Black Madonna-Black muse seems poised and at peace,
observing the pattern of "rest" and "endless work" that this earthly
paradise demands of them.

This final scene of three paragraphs is in itself a masterful cameo
of reconciliation where the tension of absence/presence, home/
not home, solace/disconsolation, ship/port, crew/passengers, lost/
saved, rest/endless work is encompassed by the soothing song and
transcendent vision of Piedade. It is the most elegant of Morrison
endings, one that does not claim to transcend all loss, nor does it
claim an attachment to it. Rather, consoled and consoling, it affirms
the endless work of humanity working through our place in the
world-as-home, world-as-paradise.

4

Reclaiming the Presence of the Marginalized: Silence, Violence, and Nature in *Paradise*

Aoi Mori

Introduction: Historical excavation

Toni Morrison's work attempts to reveal the voices and presences of African Americans who have been made invisible by mainstream American society. Her fiction serves to recover these marginalized presences through the act of remembering submerged and fragmented stories. According to one critic, remembering, or "rememory," means "to make an act of the moral imagination and to shape the events of one's life into story" (Jones 616). In constructing fictional narratives of marginalized people, Morrison creates characters that reconstruct an oppressed past and rescue their experiences from historical oblivion. Morrison expressed her passion for rescuing these suppressed stories in the following comments:

> There is no place you or I can go, to think about or not think about, to summon the presences of, or recollect the absences of slaves. . . . There is no suitable memorial, or plaque, or wreath,

or wall, or park, or skyscraper lobby. There's no 300-foot tower, there's no small bench by the road. There is not even a tree scored, an initial that I can visit or you can visit in Charleston or Savannah or New York or Providence or better still on the banks of the Mississippi. And because such a place doesn't exist . . . the book had to. ("A Bench by the Road" 36)

In expressing her regret for the lack of space in which to remember and ponder her ancestors, Morrison makes it clear that it is her mission to commemorate the forgotten people and historic sites relevant to African American history.

This chapter considers the ways in which Morrison weaves African American history into her accounts of two fictional all-black towns, Haven and Ruby. Through the voices of nine female narrators, Morrison makes the invisible visible by reversing the conventional value systems embodied in male dominance and modern commodity culture. I will explicate this process of reversal by analyzing gender relationships and the relationships between individuals and the natural world in *Paradise*. Looking from this reversed perspective enables readers to discern the nature of a paradise that Morrison envisages in this novel.

Rewriting history

By situating her novel in an all-black community in Oklahoma, the name of which means "red people" in the Choctaw language, Morrison directs the attention of the reader to the history of that future state. Historians such as Jimmie Lewis Franklin, Hannibal B. Johnson, Kenneth Marvin Hamilton, and John G. Van have conducted extensive research into the history of African Americans in Oklahoma. The region was designated as Indian territory when the Cherokee, Chickasaw, Choctaw, Creek, and Seminole were relocated there under the 1830 Indian Removal Act. At that time, most parts of the Oklahoma territory were still wilderness, yet they were fertile and well suited for farming. Since the white population in the territory was rather small in those days, and since the price of the land was relatively cheap compared to other regions, it became the ideal home for African Americans who had been exposed to discrimination and violence following the end of Reconstruction in 1879 and 1880. Kansas politician Edward P. McCabe, an African American, became a leading figure in the effort to establish Oklahoma as a state for blacks because their population exceeded that of whites. McCabe and other leaders proposed a bill providing that one-third of the territory be given to African Americans who had been enslaved in the South. Although the bill did not pass, McCabe and other leaders encouraged African American migration to the region through advertisements in newspapers and handbills. As a result of such calls, at least 30 all-black towns were founded in that territory between 1890 and 1916. In fact, Langston City, the first all-black town was founded in 1890, the year in which Haven, the fictional town in *Paradise*, is constructed.

Violence as the flaw of historical exclusiveness

Official histories of Haven, the dream town of ex-slaves, and the relocation of the town to Ruby after Haven's decline, are repeatedly told in *Paradise* by the Morgan brothers, Deek and Steward, who are prominent members of the community and descendants of the town's original families. They maintain respect for their ancestors, who wandered in the wilderness to find their promised land, by mythologizing them. Their genealogy is preserved in the name "8-rock," a term that derives from "a deep deep level in the coal mines" (*Paradise* 193). While the official histories of Ruby and Haven circulate among the townspeople as a heroic epic of founding fathers, the Morgans use the story to preserve their dominant status in the community. They assert themselves as the heirs of a legend of male dominance, ostracizing outsiders who do not belong to their genealogy and controlling marriages and the lives of women. Their elitism is epitomized in their surprise attack on the women sheltered in the Convent, whose independence becomes a threat to the male leaders.

The assault on the women in the Convent is the shocking opening sequence of the novel. The remoteness of the Convent, located "seventeen miles from a town which has ninety miles between it and any other" (1), signifies the displacement and marginality of the women who live there. This isolated place has begun to serve as a shelter for battered women, attracting the homeless and the helpless. When its self-sufficiency becomes discernibly influential on the women in Ruby, the men become terrified of losing control. Claiming the right to evict the Convent's "loose," transgressive inhabitants, the men act out their male supremacist fantasy in a brutal assault. Through the violence inflicted on the women in the Convent, Morrison depicts the terrible flaw of a self-righteousness that excludes the powerless.

Disallowing

The superior attitude of the men of Ruby is itself a curious form of reversal of values. It originated from their ancestors' heroic establishment of Haven after having been "disallowed." "Disallowing" is an insulting form of rejection perpetrated by local people in the all-black community. The founders of Haven were disallowed from other African American towns because they were dark-skinned. The shared shame and anger from this humiliating event galvanized the rejected people who "carried the rejection of 1890 like a bullet in the brain." It also intensified their sense of justice. When they later learned that some of the African American towns had failed, "They simply remarked on the mystery of God's justice" (109). Although they do not openly rejoice in such failures, they smugly accept them as God's vengeance against those who denied them the right of settlement.

Gradually, the male heirs of the founding fathers assume authority and identify themselves with the power of God. By juxtaposing the story of Genesis with the history of Haven and Ruby, these heirs authenticate the accounts of their ancestors' wandering to find their Canaan by equating themselves with the chosen people. The story fosters a solidarity rooted in the so-called racial purity of the original 8-rock families. Their history of exclusion becomes the basis for the exclusivity and arrogance of the town leaders.

Exposing the family tree

While *Paradise* can be seen as a project of reconstructing lost history, the novel directly critiques the manipulative creation and use of history in the narrative of schoolteacher Patricia Best, who laboriously tries to document the genealogy of Haven and Ruby. She intends to make a collection of family trees as a gift to the citizens of Ruby, supplementing the town's official public history with contemporary interviews. Since Patricia is suspicious of the oral histories told by the male leaders, she collects information from her students' autobiographical compositions and from conversations with other local people. She also examines church records to support the stories she collects.

While surveying people who do not appear in the official history of Haven and Ruby, Patricia notes that the history hides a secret practice of "takeover," a somewhat incestuous relationship among the members of the 8-rock families. The families maintain this practice in order to preserve the purity of their bloodline and lineage. She discovers that her mother-in-law was involved in such arrangement:

> Fawn, born a Blackhorse, was taken over by his grandmother's uncle, August Cato. Or, to put it another way, Billy's mother was wife to her own great-uncle. Or another way: my husband's father, August Cato, is also his grandmother's (Bitty Cato Blackhorse's) uncle and therefore Billy's great-granduncle as well. . . . Since Bitty Cato married Peter Blackhorse, and since her daughter, Fawn Blackhorse, was wife to Bitty's uncle, and since Peter Blackhorse is Billy Cato's grandfather—well, you can see the problem with blood rules. (196)

Fawn marries her great-uncle August Cato, and they have a son, Billy Cato, who is the only heir of the Cato family. At the same time, Billy's birth becomes good news for the Blackhorses because Peter's eldest brother, Thomas Blackhorse, has only two daughters (Soane and Dovey, married to the Morgan brothers). Billy's presence assures the Blackhorse family that their bloodline will not be terminated. August's "takeover" of Fawn, approved by the Blackhorse family, implies that their marriage benefits both families, but it also means that Fawn does not have the choice of finding a husband she loves; instead, she is "taken over" and forced to marry a man of advanced age. This practice not only limits the freedom of women but also ensures the exclusion of outsiders.

Patricia, who has grown up feeling this sense of exclusion, is now certain that she has not been accepted as a member of the community because her father Roger Best married a woman with lighter skin, violating the blood rule of Ruby. Patricia also realizes that the purity of the town is made possible at the cost of women and is completely dependent on male dominance. She then abandons her research and burns all of her papers, symbolically denouncing collaboration with the men who represent the "holy" families. Her act is not only a repudiation of the official history, but also a declaration of independence from male rule.

The reversal of binary oppositions

The witch and the healer

Morrison counters the official history of Haven and Ruby by juxtaposing the conventional standards and values of a hierarchical society with the fragmented and discredited narratives of the women, especially those who live in the Convent. In this juxtaposition, the flaws of chauvinistic history are undermined through the nullification of the dualistic concepts of founding fathers/outsiders, Virgin Mary/Fallen Eve, sacred/vulgar, and good/evil.

The polarized concepts of women as asexual/sexual or virgin/whore signify the power relationships between men and women. In effect, they manipulate the image of a woman in order to limit her personhood. The idea of "witch," for example, has a specific meaning, according to the *OED*, as "a female magician, sorceress; in later use esp[ecially], a woman supposed to have dealings with the devil or evil spirits and to be able by their co-operation to perform supernatural acts." It was the fear of the devil or evil spirits that promoted the notorious Western witch hunts of the thirteenth through eighteenth centuries. Although the connotations of "witch" vary greatly according to region, religion, and culture, Adele Getty, who has examined the witch hunts of medieval Europe, associates the brutal practice of exorcism with the fear of capable women who healed and nurtured people. According to Getty, the historical background of the witch hunt indicates male fear of women who competed with male authority. Those women were deliberately expelled from male-dominant societies. Getty explains the origin of the witch hunt as follows:

> The people of Europe had never given up "the old ways" [indigenous folk culture], and women in particular had kept the

folk-magic tradition alive through the making of charms, the wearing of laurels, by offering food to the spirit of the hearth and bread to the holy wells. Though the women were no longer able to be priestesses, many still served the community as mid-wives and healers. But soon the power of these wise women came to be perceived as a threat. In the 13th century, the first witch trials began, and they continued until the 19th century. (*Goddess* 27–8)

Getty's description of witches fits the Convent Women in *Paradise*, who help the needy, act as midwives, and live outside the power of the male town leaders. The Convent Women provide unconditional assistance to those who come to them in need. They deliver and nurse the baby of the teenage Arnette, the girlfriend of K. D., the Morgan brothers' nephew, who had intended to abort the baby. They also take in Pallas, a victim of rape, and Seneca, an orphan who expresses her vulnerability by secretly mutilating her own body. Their hospitality and kindness earn them the epithets witches and "Bitches. . . . [who] don't need men and they don't need God" (276).

Fairy and her adopted daughter Lone sense the jealousy that men feel toward them while they serve as midwives in the community. Fairy makes house visits to most of the families in the community. In performing her duty as a midwife, protecting mothers and babies from death, Fairy empirically learns that men are not comfortable with her presence and warns Lone to be aware of their hostility concealed behind words of gratitude:

Don't mistake the fathers' thanks. . . . Men scared of us, always will be. To them we're death's handmaiden standing as between them and the children their wives carry . . . the midwife is the interference, the one giving orders, on whose secret skill so much depended, and the dependency irritated them. (272)

Through their own experiences as midwives, Fairy and Lone have perceived male unease and resentment toward them as midwives, who preside over life and death and threaten male power, especially at the crucial moment of birth where men are irrelevant. The midwives' way of life and self-dependence parallel the Convent Women's autonomy. In other words, Fairy, Lone, and the Convent Women belong to the lineage of witches who have historically been feared and denigrated by men.

Retrieving the lost narrative: The *Nag Hammadi* and the pagan goddess

Despite their ostracization, women who have been condemned as witches do not remain on the margins of society. This is most notably presaged by the epigraph to *Paradise*, which is taken from "The Thunder, Perfect Mind" in the Gnostic library *Nag Hammadi*, a collection of Gnostic texts unearthed after centuries of oblivion. Notably, *Paradise* is a sequel to *Jazz*, which also opens with an epigraph taken from the same Gnostic text. Although Morrison does not reveal the source of the epigraph in *Paradise*, considering its significance can help readers understand the context of the novel.

The *Nag Hammadi* is an important text for the purpose of understanding Gnosticism, since most documents belonging to the sect were destroyed when the movement was banned by the clergymen in the Orthodox Church around the fourth century AD. These clergymen found Gnostic doctrine challenging to the conventional ideas and the hierarchical order in the church and thus accused Gnostics of heresy. Hence, the Gnostic text had literally been buried underground. James M. Robinson notes that in 1945 the documents of twelve codices plus eight leaves hidden in a jar were unearthed by local peasants travelling on camels in the Nag Hammadi region of Upper Egypt (Robinson 22–3). Although, as Elaine Pagels writes in the *Gnostic Gospels*, followers of Gnosticism were relegated to "a suppressed current, like a river driven underground" (150), they have secretly survived. In his introduction to *The Nag Hammadi Library*, utilizing the banned text as a prelude to the overall landscape of *Paradise*, Morrison underscores the resistance of the oppressed and the recovery of silenced stories.

Morrison's allusion to Gnosticism, moreover, suggests a challenge to men's power over women. Unlike the male-dominant Orthodox Church, Gnosticism treated women and men as equals. One crucial detail is the inclusion of the Gospel of Mary Magdalene in the *Nag Hammadi*. Although it is difficult to validate her identity, Mary Magdalene is often described in the New Testament as a reformed prostitute with no significance as a disciple of Jesus. Yet, in his introduction to "The Gospel of Mary," Douglas M. Parrot describes Mary Magdalene's close relationship to Jesus and her superior position to the other disciples:

She is the Savior's beloved, possessed of knowledge and teaching superior to that of the public apostolic tradition. Her superiority is based on vision and private revelation and is demonstrated in her capacity to strengthen the wavering disciples and turn them toward the Good. (524)

Morrison's epigraph, taken from the Gnostic text, links Mary Magdalene with the women in the Convent: both are regarded as "whores" or "bitches and witches" in an attempt to destroy the women's personal power and authority.

It is worth noting that the narrator of "The Thunder, Perfect Mind" is a goddess. According to Rose Horman Arthur, this goddess derives from Isis (158), the goddess of wisdom in ancient Egyptian mythology, whose magical power brought her murdered husband back to life (*The Facts on File Encyclopedia of World Mythology and Legend*). Morrison's use of a citation attributed to a pagan goddess reinforces the significance of the novel as a form of retrieving a forgotten and heretical narrative from the history of women.

Pagan as Isis may be, her impact on the Western world is unquestionable. Anthropologists Leonard W. Moss and Stephen C. Cappannari, who have examined images of Black Mary, find in those images the influence of Isis on Christianity. They introduce the observation of the art critic Anna Brownell Jameson, who postulates that Isis has inspired the representations of Black Mary or Black Madonna in Europe. From the perspective of fine art, Jameson asserts the affinity between Isis with Horus and the Virgin Mary with Christ as follows:

The earliest effigies of the Virgin and Child may be traced to Alexandria, and to Egyptian influences; and it is as easily conceivable that the time-consecrated Egyptian myth of Isis and Horus may have suggested the original type . . . a fact which does not rest upon supposition, but of which the proofs remain to us in the antique Christian sculptures and the paintings in the catacombs. (*Legends* 58–9)

In examining substantial examples of the images of Madonna and Christ, Jameson historically traces their prototype to the Egyptian myth of Isis and her son Horus (see Figure 4.1).

Incorporating Isis into *Paradise* allows Morrison not only to call attention to suppressed stories, but also to revise the Eurocentric

FIGURE 4.1 *"Isis Suckling a Young Horus"* Encyclopedia Mythica Online *<www.pantheon.org/areas/gallery/mythology/africa/egyptian/isis-horus. html>*

myth of white supremacy. In *Paradise*, Isis's power over life and death is reflected in Connie's ability to "step in" or revive the dead: at the deathbed of Mary Magna, the nun who adopted her, and in the scene of the car accident that killed Soane Morgan's sons. The narrator in the epigraph from the *Nag Hammadi* challenges binary thinking, proclaiming the link between the whore and the virgin:

> I am the whore and the holy one.
> I am the wife and the virgin.
> I am (the mother) and the daughter.
>   ("The Thunder, Perfect Mind" 297)

That Connie and the other Convent Women are "whores" is a fait accompli as far as Dovey Morgan is concerned, even though her sister Soane reminds her that "[t]hese are women, Dovey. Just women." Dovey counters, "Whores, though, and strange too." Dovey's conviction is based on her husband's pronouncement, "That's what Steward says, and if he believes it" (288). Dovey's unfinished statement implies that her husband's word is not to be questioned. The Convent Women, on the other hand, are more aligned with the Virgin Mary. Connie herself echoes the narrator of "The Thunder, Perfect Mind," claiming: "Eve is Mary's mother. Mary is the daughter of Eve" (263). She specifically emphasizes the link between Eve and Mary, who have been polarized by conventional religion. To the women of the Convent, the distinction between the Virgin Mary and black Eve becomes totally irrelevant.

Revisions of Pieta

Piedade, the goddess-like figure that Connie dreams about, also challenges dichotomies. The character evokes the Pieta, the image of the Virgin Mary lamenting Christ's death with his body in her arms. One of the most famous, of course, is Michelangelo's 1499 sculpture in St. Peter's Basilica in the Vatican (see Figure 4.2).

FIGURE 4.2 The Pieta *in St. Peter's Basilica (Permission from St. Peters Basilica Organization <www.saintpetersbasilica.org>)*

The last scene of *Paradise*, in which Piedade holds a younger woman's head on her lap, echoes this popular Christian iconography. However, Morrison reverses its Eurocentric origins by making Piedade "black as firewood" (318). In fact, Mary, the mother of Christ, was from Nazareth, a city in Lower Galilee, and would therefore not have been white. Thus, Piedade, Morrison's black Pieta, corrects the Eurocentric myth of a Mary with a pale complexion, clearly defying the tradition of Western aesthetics.

Piedade even transcends the limitation of the Virgin Mary, who is rather confined as an icon of lamentation by the male gaze. The girl whom Piedade is holding is not dead, and she is tenderly comforting her as her fingers "troll the tea brown hair" (318). The reference to "tea brown hair" hints that the injured woman might be Connie, whose hair was described earlier in the novel as "tea-colored" (223). Although she was fatally shot during the Convent massacre, Connie/Consolata is resurrected in the last scene. This scene, in which the power of Piedade rescues the marginalized woman, dramatically connects Piedade to the images of Isis and Black Mary. She predicates the presence of the black pagan goddesses that possess the power to heal and nurture, revising the passive image of the Pieta.

Referring to Michelangelo's later *Pieta in Duomo*, Florence, completed in 1559, adds depth to our understanding of Morrison's use of the image of Pieta. This sculpture in Duomo includes the figures of not only Jesus and Virgin Mary as seen in the *Pieta* in St Peter's Basilica but also of John the Apostle and Mary Magdalene, based on the Gospel of John 19. 25–7 (see Figure 4.3).

This sculpture looks much more humane and realistic than Michelangelo's first *Pieta*, which represents a feminine ideal of angelic purity. The inclusion of Mary Magdalene has a significant relevance to recovering the silenced and oppressed. According to the *Historical Dictionary of Feminism*, the lack of reference to her as an apostle in the New Testament is due to her confrontation with Peter, the chief of the 12 Apostles. Peter did not approve of the authority of women to teach and identified her as a prostitute in order to deny her position as an apostle. The conflict between Mary Magdalene and Peter devalued her position despite her significant role in delivering the news of the resurrected Christ.

Morrison's reversal of the power structure also expands the interpretations of the Pieta that allude to Yemanja, a Brazilian sea goddess. Morrison, according to Denitia Smith, took a trip to Brazil

FIGURE 4.3   The Pieta in Duomo, *Florence (Permission from ALIMDI. NET/Raimund Kutter)*

in the 1980s and heard a rumor about black nuns who practiced Candomble, an Afro-Brazilian religion. According to the rumor, the nuns were murdered by a posse of men. Although the story turned out to be false, it inspired and motivated Morrison to write *Paradise*. As Naomi Katz observes in her article, "For Love of a Sea Goddess," Yemanja has been worshiped by African Brazilians whose ancestors transported their sea goddess to Brazil during slavery in the early sixteenth century. The Portuguese authority tried to suppress the African religion, but they could not prevent the Africans from worshipping the goddess. Eventually, the image of Yemanja was conflated with the image of the Virgin Mary (Katz 40). But she is rather similar to a Black Mary who is much more powerful than the Virgin Mary, since Yemanja controls the sea and offers a source of strength and hope in times of despair. Yemanja has survived the purge of the pagan goddess by the oppressors in the same way as a Black Mary.

As the story of Yemanja displays the defiance of colonized people against an imposed religion, Morrison's use of the name "Piedade" implies the unyielding spirit of the oppressed through the power of language, and in Portuguese it means "pity." Morrison's use of the Portuguese word implies the appropriation of the colonizer's language. Those Africans who were taken to Brazil during slavery were forced to assimilate into a new environment and they had to give up their mother tongue and appropriate a new language, Portuguese. Thus, the symbol of Yemanja and the name Piedade represent the potential for the oppressed to develop new cultural identities by merging colonizing and indigenous cultures into an original heritage.

Recovery of transgressive women and ecocritical reading

Ecocriticism and power structure

As gender-based criticism enables recovery of the voices of the oppressed, the recent scholarship of ecocriticism similarly exposes the problematic power relationship between the oppressor (human beings) and the oppressed (nature). Toni Morrison has been aware of the danger of environmental deterioration, and her critique of this issue is substantial although, as scholars Wallace and Armbruster have observed, little attention has been paid to Morrison's "profound engagement with the natural world" (211).

The field of environmental criticism is known to have originated in nonfiction nature writing, which was predominantly a white genre. However, as Adamson and Slovic note, it also originated in the abolitionist movement, which shares the mission of saving a subordinate group. They also point out the connections between colonization, conquest, slavery, resource exploitation, and capital. Thus, many of the most successful strategies of early environmentalists were borrowed from the abolitionist, civil rights, and women's movements, as well as the American Indian Land Claims lawsuit (Adamson and Slovic 7–8). By incorporating strategies from movements that seek equal civil and human rights for oppressed people who struggled to gain an autonomous identity, ecocriticism has evolved and expanded through multiple "waves" to include gender and ethnicity, in order to discuss the relationship between literature and nature.

Morrison's descriptions of nature and its abuse direct her readers to rethink the imminent environmental crisis. For instance, Morrison claims, in an interview with Christine Smallwood, that *A Mercy* was inspired by William Cronon's *Changes in the Land* (2003). In this book, Cronon, an environmental historian, studies the history of colonial New England from the perspectives of nature and the lifestyles of the settlers, which significantly influence the ecosystem. Cronon emphasizes the importance of the conversation between human beings and nature for the survival of both.

Morrison's explicit concern with nature in *A Mercy* is also embedded in *Paradise*. Piedade, for example, identifies pleasure and peace with nature and the environment. She first appears in Connie's dream, in which "white sidewalks met the sea and fish the color of plums swam alongside children" (263). Connie continues to speak nostalgically of "scented cathedrals made of gold where gods and goddesses sat in the pews with the congregation. Of carnations tall as trees. Dwarfs with diamonds for teeth" (263–4). In this beautiful, peaceful location, Connie remembers that Piedade "bathed her in emerald water" (284). Yet these representations of a colorfully harmonized place contrast with the change of landscape in the last scene of the novel, which depicts a beach full of trash: "Around them on the beach, sea trash gleams. Discarded bottle caps sparkle near a broken sandal. A small dead radio plays the quiet surf" (318). It is no longer safe for children to walk on the sidewalk or swim with colorful fish because of the potentially harmful debris. The scene suggests that the sea is polluted by the garbage of commodity culture.

Nature, violence, and gender

It is worth noting that ecocriticism—or more specifically, gender-oriented ecofeminism, which ecocritic Cheryll Glotfelty defines as "a theoretical discourse whose theme is the link between the oppression of women and the domination of nature" (*Ecocriticism Reader* xxiv)—explores the power structure between the oppressor and the oppressed in society and nature. Morrison echoes the relationship between the men and women of Ruby in the relationship between people and nature in the novel. For example, Deek Morgan flaunts his pride in game hunting as a fulfillment of his male, chauvinistic, egotistical desire to dominate animals and nature. In contrast, Soane, who is not so enthusiastic about hunting, seems to feel some empathy with the quail that Deek is chasing:

> Look out, quail. Deek's gunning for you. And when he comes back he'll throw a sackful of you on my clean floor and say something like: "this ought to take care of supper." Proud. Like he's giving me a present. Like you were already plucked, cleaned and cooked. (100)

Soane accepts Deek as a brave, capable breadwinner, literally bringing food to his wife; still, she finds it a burden to clean, cook, and prepare food for him as he expects. His fondness for hunting reinforces the gender roles between them, imposing on Soane the domestic responsibilities of handling the fowl whether she likes or not.

Furthermore, in Ruby, "hunting game was a game" (103). The men's arrogant assumption that they can hunt animals as game, not simply to sustain themselves, reinforces their belief that they can subjugate human beings as well. The Ruby men apply this attitude toward game hunting and to their assault on the Convent Women. As predators on the women of the Convent, the men are armed with "rope, a palm leaf cross, handcuffs, Mace and sunglasses, along with clean, handsome guns" (3). A palm leaf cross, symbolizing Christianity, is used by the men as a sign of their alliance with God and justification for their violence. Their attack is motivated by their desire to confiscate the Convent property. They blame the Convent for their own losses and failures: the decline of the retail business belonging to the Fleetwoods, one of the original families, and the absence of a legitimate heir to the Morgan brothers. Subjugating the women alleviates the men's frustration and allows them to retain their pride.

Although the Convent becomes the victim of violence, the ultimate survival of the Convent Women is implied in their ecological lifestyle. Connie uses herbs and plants for nurturing and healing. In the Convent's garden, she "discovered the wild bush heavy with stinging-hot peppers" (225), one of the popular bits of produce that pleases the palates of many of her customers— including Steward, who cannot differentiate between fresh garden peas and store-bought canned ones because of his heavy smoking habit. Connie also prescribes a special tonic, comprised of rosemary, bran, and aspirin, to relieve the sorrow of her friend Soane, who lost her beloved sons in the Vietnam War (although Soane's husband Deek, who once was Connie's lover, does not approve of the folk remedy). In addition, Connie takes in and shelters homeless women who suffer from physical and psychological problems, feeding them with vegetables and herbs fresh from her garden. No matter how desperate or oppressed they may be, their identities and sensitivities, as well as their appetites, are recovered by her tasty, nourishing homemade food.

Organic farming and the transcendence of dichotomies

The novel does not specify the Convent's farming method, but implies that organic farming is employed in the Convent garden. The women lead a self-sufficient life without the modern conveniences of electricity or telephones. Thus, it seems unlikely that they use fertilizer or chemical components, which promote the efficiency of industrial farming production but eventually impoverish the soil. Instead, the women let nature take its course, following the cycle of nature without using technology to conquer it. Connie is particularly aware of how nature is exploited, as she learned the relationship between nature and humanity while performing chores for the nuns at the Convent. She herself is oppressed: she works as a servant who "slept in the pantry, scrubbed tile, fed chickens, prayed, peeled, garlanded, canned and laundered" (225). Placed in a situation of lifetime indenture, she understands the sensitivities of the silenced and is capable of discerning the inaudible sounds of nature.

The philosophy of organic farming and its secret of savory taste is depicted in *Epitaph for a Peach*, by the third-generation Japanese

American farmer David Mas Masumoto, who decided to grow peaches in a way that adheres to the old-time farming method of "doing nothing" or "accept[ing] the cruel reality of natural forces" (147). Masumoto avoids the use of fertilizer and pesticides, farming organically so that he can harvest the most delicious peaches. He discovers that the agricultural industrialization that his parents' generation was encouraged by the government to employ during the 1960s eventually impoverished the farm. The orchard could no longer yield peaches as delicious as those raised by first-generation farmers who farmed before agricultural industrialization. Masumoto therefore returns to old-fashioned farming, letting nature take its course. Shiuh-huah Serena Chou explicates Masumoto's farming method as follows:

> By foregrounding organic nature's uncontrollable irregularities and particularities, Masumoto in fact presents the organic as the antithesis of an industrial landscape of uniformity, order, and mechanistic control. . . . The logic through which Masumoto underwrites nature as chaos parallels that which essentializes nature and culture and dichotomizes them into a simple good-versus-evil binary. (161–2)

One characteristic of organic farming is to accept chaos, transcending the dichotomizing value system based on industrial control. Lone and Connie are among Morrison's women who utilize the vegetation surrounding them without altering its natural state.

Conclusion: The Convent garden and rebirth

The condition of the Convent garden after the attack implies the cycle of nature that transcends the boundaries of life and death. Rev. Richard Misner, a newcomer to the Ruby community, goes to the Convent with his fiancée Anna Flood after the massacre in order to confirm the rumor that all of the corpses of the Convent Women have disappeared. They observe the juxtaposition of life and death in the garden as follows:

At the edge of the garden a faded red chair lay on its side. Beyond was blossom and death. Shriveled tomato plants alongside crops of leafy green reseeding themselves with golden flowers; pink hollyhocks so tall the heads leaned all the way over a trail of bright squash blossoms; lacy tops of carrots browned and lifeless next to straight green spikes of onion. Melons split their readiness showing gums of juicy red. Anna sighed at the mix of neglect and unconquerable growth. (304–5)

The garden epitomizes transcendence beyond the polarities of life and death and embodies the natural cycle, accommodating contradictory images to create a salutary sense of autonomy and future potential. Though chaotic and devastated, it suggests rebirth and the creation of a new generation, hinting at the possibility of resurrection and hope. And, although the women undergo a brutal massacre, they will transcend the dichotomies of life and death, good and evil, oppressor and oppressed.

The openness of space in *Paradise* is underscored by the changes of the capitalization of the last word in *Paradise*, from "Paradise" with a capital "P" in the first edition to "paradise" with a lowercase "p" in the second edition. Morrison explains the necessity of the change to Dinitia Smith, "The whole point is to get paradise off its pedestal, as a place for anyone, to open it up for passengers and crew" (Smith E3). "A paradise" does not imply the final destination for the homeless and the devastated, but it offers a glimpse of hope, like that witnessed by Misner and Anna at the Convent garden in the last scene. The chaotic cycle of nature that parallels the lifestyle of the "uncontrollable" women of the Convent foregrounds the possibility of uniting diverse voices in order to seek survival as a whole.

Throughout *Paradise*, Morrison reconsiders the traditions of able women, revealing the fragmented narratives of women such as Isis, Mary Magdalene, Black Mary, Yemanja, the midwife, bitches and witches, and the women in the Convent. Their stories may be unspoken—neither officially passed on nor widely circulated. Their stories counter the narratives of mainstream discourse. Isis recovered the dismembered body of her husband and came to control both life and death. Similarly, Connie resurrects the dead, while Piedade signals life beyond death. Those women eventually encompass marginalized voices, resisting the insatiable desire of the dominant authority to exploit others for profit and power. These women refuse to submit to male power. Thus, *Paradise* brings the powerful message that respect for the marginalized might be the key to refuting violence and countering the monolithic values of patriarchy.

PART II

Love

Chronologically, *Love* is a fitting sequel to *Paradise* in terms of both time and themes. While *Paradise* covers the post-Reconstruction migration and settlement of former slaves in Oklahoma up to and including the civil rights struggles of the 1960s and 1970s, *Love* fills in some important gaps—the struggles of African Americans elsewhere in the nation through most of the twentieth century. Unlike *Paradise*, however, *Love*, is concerned with African Americans living within a de jure and de facto segregated country. One of *Love*'s central themes is the development of black enterprise under segregation and its demise after integration. And while both novels focus on raw economic and political power and solidarity, *Love* poses the complicated choices and ethical dilemmas for blacks seeking access to better opportunities in a desegregated society.

Love, like most of Morrison's fiction, is also about family dynamics and interpersonal relationships. James M. Mellard has observed that "[a]ggressiveness displaces care" when Bill Cosey marries 11-year-old Heed and "throws the girls into narcissistic competitiveness" and unleashes events that prove to be "disastrous in just about every aspect of life around the Cosey family and its livelihood, as disastrous for Cosey's resort as for various personal relationships" (707). The most jeopardized relationship and the one that in/directly and sometimes negatively affects all other relationships in the novel is the developing friendship between Heed and Christine. When Cosey marries Heed, he effectively changes the way Christine views him as a grandfather and Heed as a friend. The marriage simultaneously elevates Heed to the status of woman/wife and creates an ever-widening fissure between the two young friends—a fissure that May, his daughter-in-law, is keen to exploit.

Equally important is the relationship between Cosey and the young Heed, whose status as wife is undermined by her age and by Cosey's disrespect for her that is quietly mimicked by others.

Carolyn Denard uses the leitmotif of silence to examine the role of secrets in the novel and, coextensively, in African American culture. Denard foregrounds the novel's opening passage, the character L's embrace of silence, "as wilful resistance and cultural decorum—as agency rather than disempowerment." She argues that silence can serve both good and harmful purposes. She observes that L's silence about the secret she holds is important because it is intended to save a family of women from total financial ruin. Bill Cosey's secret regarding his pedophilia, by contrast, is destructive to Christine's and Heed's characters as well as their friendship.

Building upon Denard's exploration of the strategic uses of silence, Evelyn Schreiber stresses the destructive nature of secrets. She reads the novel through psychoanalytic theories of identity and is keen to expose the psychological trauma induced by intergenerational exploitation and parental abandonment. Looking at adults who ignore the needs of children and exploit them for personal gratification and economic gain, among others, Schreiber highlights the traumatic consequences to Christine and Heed at the moment their inchoate friendship begins to solidify.

Following on Schreiber's analysis of trauma induced by power and dominance, Herman Beavers offers an expanded reading that focuses on positive adult behavior that inculcates values in young people. Using Cosey and Romen as representative models, Beaver examines the undercurrents of excessive pleasure that masquerades as reality and fulfillment. He focuses upon choices characters face to surrender to an immediate need for gratification or to forego pleasure for ethical and moral reasons; to seek pleasure through dominion and betrayal or to behave selflessly for a higher purpose. In the end, Romen, as a consequence of the values instilled by his grandparents, stands out as the one character whose growth is noteworthy and whose values are worth emulating.

5

"Some to Hold, Some to Tell": Secrets and the Trope of Silence in *Love*

Carolyn Denard

In African American literary criticism, the primary trope, the definitive marker in the identification of a distinctive, culturally black text has, since its beginnings, been black language. While there are other tropes within the culture that have received varying degrees of attention from writers and critics—escape, migration, the city, the ancestor, the trickster, freedom—black language, or black orality more broadly, continues to hold a singular place. Largely because of the historical necessity of verbal forms of cultural transmission, the tropes of black vocal expression—dialect, folktales, signifying, testifying, work songs, spirituals, blues, and jazz—have been the perennially reliable cultural resources that both critics and artists have mined in order to write and establish critical paradigms for a literature that could be distinctively identified as black.

Because of the critical and creative attention given to the trope of orality in African American culture, most clearly evident in language and music, it is not surprising that silence as a trope of cultural difference has received little critical attention. But like storytelling, signifying, talking, laughing, singing, and other oral forms of expression, silence, as both a sign of wisdom and resistance, has also had a distinctively expressive place in African American culture. Whether it was in the coded messages of the drums during slavery or the directions for escape silently embedded in domestic crafts or in the words of the spirituals, whether it was in the cunning but often forgotten role of the "she-don'-say-nothin" tar baby character in black folktales, or in the powerful political protest evident in the Silent Parade down Fifth Avenue in Harlem to protest race riots in East St Louis, Illinois, in the summer of 1917, or in the too-cruel-to-be-spoken secrets kept for both the physical and psychic survival of slavery and the racial segregation that followed, or, finally, in the "you-didn't-hear-it-from-me" disclaimers of gossipers, keeping quiet has also been a persistent and complex form of cultural "expression" in African American community life.

The absence of attention given to the trope of silence in African American culture stems largely, I believe, from the difficulty of analyzing what might be considered the oxymoronic quality of "expressing silence." The lack of critical attention might also exist because silence runs counter to the historical emphasis on the political power implied by the *spoken* expressive voice in African American culture. When critics have addressed silence in African American literature, they have largely treated silence as disempowering, as a moment of protest and lament for the voice that cannot be heard particularly among black women.

Broader interpretations of the meaning of silence in literature by women have come from, among others, critics of Asian American literature such as Trinh T. Minh-ha (*Women, Native, Other: Writing Postcoloniality and Feminism*), King-Kok Cheung (*Articulate Silences*), and Patti Duncan (*Tell This Silence: Asian American Women Writers and the Politics of Speech*). These critics have begun to explore the multiple meanings of silences in the works of minority women writers and are now demonstrating how such meanings and functions can vary with individuals and cultures. They are finding, as Cheung concludes in her introduction to *Articulate Silences*, that it is important for critics to remember that the "modalities of silence need to be differentiated." Cheung finds in these works that:

> Silence can be imposed by the family in an attempt to maintain dignity or secrecy, by the ethnic community in adherence to cultural etiquette, or by the dominant culture in an effort to prevent any voicing of minority experiences. . . . the works also challenge the blanket endorsements of speech and the reductive perspectives on silence. These writers question the authority of

language . . . and speak to the resources as well has the hazards of silence. (3)

The analyzes of these critics are opening the way for a closer look at the trope of silence—not just as evidence of erasure and oppression, but as willful resistance and cultural decorum—as agency rather than disempowerment. As Duncan concludes, "silence, too, operates as a form of discourse and a will to 'unsay'" (ix). In African American life, silence has indeed had continued expressive power, and literary and cultural critics would be well served to do more to study its meanings and its uses as a cultural trope.

Morrison's treatment of silence

In her works, Toni Morrison has generously embraced black language as a major cultural sign of blackness, and her novels are especially rich with music, folk tales, lyrical dialogue, and jazz rhythms that emanate from black vocal expression. But for all of her focus on the vocally expressive forms of music and language, Morrison has also been, subtly and progressively, becoming more attentive to the presence of silence as a trope within African American culture as well. The narrative strategy in most of her novels, even as they embrace and articulate black language and black musical forms, involves acknowledging— even while breaking—a code of silence. As *meta* texts, Morrison's narratives are often framed as documents that tell a secret that the community had kept quiet. In this way, the novels themselves have been the "silence breakers"—the vehicles through which her narrators could share with her readers, go behind the veil as it were—to tell what people do not tell, to say what they have not told. And thus while she at once interrupts the cultural silence by the very telling of the story of the novel, Morrison has also found sophisticated ways to signify the trope of silence in her writing.

From the very beginning of her career, precisely because the secret keeping was so embedded in the culture, Morrison has been keenly aware of the strong revelatory value in finally telling what everyone has been, as a matter of cultural expectation, quiet about. And she has embraced that silence-breaking design in most of her novels.

In her first novel, *The Bluest Eye*, the opening sentence "Quiet as it's kept" signals that posture of "secret telling" that will be the subtle narrative frame that all of her works will take. She was very deliberate about the opening of *The Bluest Eye* and its implied cultural meaning, as she explained in her Tanner Lecture, "Unspeakable Things Unspoken," at the University of Michigan in 1987:

> The opening phrase of this sentence, "Quiet as it's kept," had several attractions for me. First, it was a familiar phrase, familiar to me as a child listening to adults; to black women conversing with one another; telling a story, an anecdote, gossip about someone or event within the circle. . . . The words are conspiratorial, "Shh, don't tell anyone else," and "No one is allowed to know this." It is a secret between us and a secret that is being kept from us. (20)

Morrison explains that "[t]he conspiracy is both held and withheld, exposed and sustained," and thus the writing of *Beloved* represents "the public exposure of a private confidence" (20).

Morrison further explains that it is necessary to consider the "immediate political climate" in which she wrote *The Bluest Eye* between "1965–69, during great social upheaval in the life of black people." She adds that "the writing was the disclosure of secrets 'we' shared and those withheld from us by ourselves and by the world outside the community" (20–1).

In her subsequent novels, while the trope of silence and secret keeping is not the major focus, as it is by implication in *The Bluest Eye* (and more deliberately in *Love*), silence does figure repeatedly—sometimes as a strategy of plot, and sometimes in the development of character. In *Sula* the movement of the plot and the intrigue of the characters are often a result of what one of the characters—Shadrack, Sula, or Nel—overhears or sees but does not tell to someone else. In *Song of Solomon* the work of the Seven Days is the pivotal secret of the novel that exacts group revenge but which also emotionally destroys those who commit the secret acts. In *Song of Solomon* there is also the presence, like the shell-shocked Shadrack in *Sula*, of characters who are defined by saying nothing—like Empire State, "who just stared and swayed." In *Tar Baby* there is Thérèse, the inimitable maid whose hatred of America and American Whites drew her to a *willful* pledge of silence. Thérèse is not mute as her employers believe; she simply *chooses* not to talk to them. As Morrison points out in the novel, silence becomes Thérèse's personal (cultural, political) victory over her white employees: "What they took for inattentiveness," the narrator explains "was, in fact, a miracle of concentration" (111). *Beloved*, a story so horrifying that it "stops the blood," is a secret kept far too long; the horror of slavery, like the horror of the middle passage, as the narrator repeatedly acknowledges "was not a story to pass on" (274). And more metaphorically in *Beloved* there is the presence of the bit as a profound signifier of the silence imposed upon slaves. In *Jazz*, it is what Dorcas does *not say* that gets Joe and Violet into that self-inflicted lament and misery that they experience in Harlem in the 1920s. In *Paradise*, there is a trunk load of secrets which Patricia Best exposes—secrets that become the motivations and the lamentations of nearly everyone in Ruby, Oklahoma. And, of course, in *Paradise*, there is also the cunning, and—we can now say—culturally deliberate narrator, who, for the life of us, will *not* tell us which of the Convent Women is the "white girl" that the men shoot first.

Clearly, the issue of verbal restraint, of keeping secrets in African American discourse, has continued to be of great interest and intrigue in Morrison's novels and a source for the construction of character and narrative play. In her critical works, most notably in the Tanner lecture as noted above, Morrison also addresses the issue of silences in African American culture. In that lecture, she addresses secret keeping as cultural practice directly—the writing was the disclosure of secrets, secrets shared, and those withheld from ourselves and from the world outside the community. But she has also spoken about the silences less directly, as in her 1987 interview with "London Weekend" broadcaster Melvyn Bragg, recorded as *Profile of a Writer: Toni Morrison*. In a discussion of the Middle Passage, a subject she addresses in *Beloved*, she points out that this historical moment in African American culture is shrouded in silence: "There are no stories, no tales, no jokes, no blues about the Middle Passage." As a writer, Morrison feels that she must fill that silence with her own imagination—a position she echoed in 1989 about the silence in this country's public remembrance of slavery in an interview, "Bench by the Road": "There is no suitable memorial or plaque or wreath or wall or park or skyscraper lobby . . . there's not even a tree scored, an initial that I can visit or you can visit in Charleston or Savannah or New York, or Providence or, better still, on the banks of the Mississippi" (4). And because of this historical silence (by the country and those who were enslaved), the novel (*Beloved* in this case) had to be written to tell the story that others have not been able to articulate in language or by a historical marker.

More recently, in her 2005 Baccalaureate Address at Princeton University, Morrison again spoke about silence. In that address, she characterized silence, or "stillness" as she calls it, as one of four viable responses to the "chaos of the modern world." The first three, she explains, are "awe," "violence," and "naming." A fourth, Morrison asserts, is "stillness": "It can appear to be passivity or dumb-foundedness," she explains, "but its quiet does not have to diminish its power." As both her novels and her critical analyses reveal, the notion of the power of silence—the power of the nonvocal, seemingly passive, though potentially profound—is one that Morrison has been progressively considering with a keen interest and transforming potential in all of her works. But it is only in *Love* that she fully engages the cultural, psychological, emotional, artistic meanings of silence within the black community itself.

Silence in *Love*

Love is set in one of the small preintegration black beach resort communities of the 1940s and 1950s. The story focuses on the life and the family of the black entrepreneur, Bill Cosey, who is the owner of Cosey's Hotel and Resort, the "best and best known vacation spot for colored folk on the East coast" (6). As the richest black man in the town, Bill Cosey assumes a kind of godfather, benefactor role in the community. He is, as such, both "a *good bad man*" and "a *bad good man*" (200)—who provides jobs to locals, offers financial bailouts for families, and pays for burials and college tuition. He is also a good husband to his first wife Julia and an adoring father to his son Billy (102–3). But all the while he freely engages in extramarital affairs, pays off the cops to sell liquor, and most shockingly of all, after his wife's death, he marries his granddaughter's best friend, an 11-year-old from the part of the community that he feels is only worthy enough to work at his resort—perhaps to save her from the poverty of her family, but perhaps more to satisfy his abhorrent fetish for young girls. It is a *pro forma* relationship for the most part—Heed the Night Johnson, the child bride, is Cosey's toy, not his wife. When the novelty of the marriage wears off, Cosey keeps up appearances but focuses on the clandestine love he has for the one woman who does not include marriage in the bargain—a "sporting woman" named Celestial.

Aside from his own disappointment, Cosey's marriage to the 11-year-old Heed also wreaks bitter havoc on the rest of the women in his family. His daughter-in-law, May, now a widow, vehemently opposes the union, and Christine, May's daughter and Cosey's granddaughter, suffers great psychological damage because she and Heed are best friends. When their relationship has to move abruptly from love-struck best friends to step-grandmother and granddaughter with all of the attendant adult implications of marriage—sex, hierarchy, control—Christine is shipped away to boarding school to soften the blow. When she returns 20 years later, she and her mother become the venomous enemies of Heed, acting out their revenge in any number of ways. Not able to realize his true love for Celestial and saddened by the double loss of his wife and his son, Cosey grows old and dejected. He decides secretly to leave everything he owns, not to the women in his family—Heed, Christine, or May—whose only home is the Cosey household, but to Celestial, his mistress. His long-time housekeeper and cook, L, who has admired Cosey and worked for him since she was 14, sees the potential damage of this arrangement and decides when Cosey is 81 and in ill health to poison him and tear up the Will in order to save his family.

Love is the novel that comes after the grand revisionist trilogy of slavery (*Beloved*) and migration (*Jazz*) and integration (*Paradise*) has been written. With the grand stories written, Morrison is free in this novel to go back to the black community to mine the finer, more nuanced, less glorified elements of the culture that indicated the strength, depth, the layered complexity of the black community life of an earlier time.

In *Love*, Morrison also employs silence as a trope in the culture and explores what it means in the black community *not to speak*— either because one cannot or will not, or because one does not think that one should. She further reveals how black folks use silence and its variations—whether in keeping secrets, using coded language, or

not speaking at all—to demonstrate the power and value in black
communities. The novel poses the following questions: What does the
willful act of choosing not to speak mean in the cultural life of the
black community? What do such choices imply? What are its processes,
and what are the consequences? For Morrison, the practice of keeping
secrets becomes a kind of cultural site in the black community life
of an earlier time. And revisiting the motives, manifestations, and
implications of that act of secrecy and finding out what "love" has to
do with it become part of the novel's project.

Silence in *Love* is not the silence of resistance (a willful form of
protest) or the silence of repression (an unwillful sign of oppression).
It is a willful silence that members of the community choose largely
for protection and care. The trope of silence within the boundaries
of *Love*'s black community is evident in a number of ways, but it
primarily involves the telling and keeping of *secrets*. The ability to
keep secrets is implicated in the thematic lament of the narrator
who opens the novel; it is the number one job requirement for
Junior, the boarding school runaway, when she answers Heed's job
advertisement; it is the motive behind the coded language shared
between Heed and Christine and the humming of L. But finally,
and most importantly, secrets are the back stories of the major
characters—Christine, Heed, Cosey, and L—whose held-secrets
drive the plot and shape the cultural meaning of secret keeping
inside and outside of the novel.

The opening lament

The novel opens with a lament by the character known as L, whose
name is conjectured to be a foreshortened form of "*Eleanor or
Elvira*" (65), but, according to L, her name is really "*the subject of
First Corinthians, chapter 13*" (199). L narrates from the grave as an
older woman who has intimate knowledge of the community. She
is appalled by the barefaced revelations of this younger generation,
and she has decided that the best response to what she sees, the
gap-legged, wide-opened-mouth world of the 1990s, is to hum, a
closed-mouth if not totally silent response to the contemporary
situation (3). What she regrets about contemporary black culture is
that black women, the young ones at least, have lost the ability or

the complexity to keep secrets. Without wisdom and understanding of themselves and their power, these young women, the narrator laments, simply reveal too much:

> *The women's legs are spread wide open, so I hum. . . . Standing by, unable to do anything but watch, is a trial, but I don't say a word. My nature is a quiet one, anyway. As a child I was considered respectful; as a young woman I was called discreet. Later on I was thought to have the wisdom that maturity brings. Nowadays silence is looked on as odd and most of my race has forgotten the beauty of meaning much by saying little.* (3)

She decries the lack of privacy and secrecy that erupted in the 1970s, and she cannot get over the willingness of women to expose everything, including their bodies and their business:

> *Now tongues work all by themselves with no help from the mind. Still, I used to be able to have normal conversations, and when the need arose, I could make a point strong enough to stop a womb—or a knife. Not anymore, because back in the seventies, when women began to straddle chairs and dance crotch out on television, when all the magazines started featuring behinds and inner thighs as though that's all there is to a woman, well I shut up altogether. Before women agreed to spread in public, there used to be secrets—some to hold, some to tell. Now? No. Barefaced being the order of the day, I hum.* (3)

In *Love*, as in all of Morrison's novels, the first page is a foyer piece where almost always the entire plot, if not the thematic kernel of the novel, is revealed. This threshold presentation of "L's lament," focusing on silence and, in this case, lamenting the loss in the culture of women being able to keep secrets, and by implication, knowing their real power, will see various manifestations in the novel.

Significations on silence

After establishing both tone (loss) and theme (the power of secret keeping) in the opening lament by the narrator, Morrison plays aesthetically with secret keeping in small rhetorical strategies throughout the novel. The job advertisement that Heed writes in search of someone to help her with a "book about her family" indicates most importantly that the work is "Highly Confidential" and when Junior makes her case in her job interview of what she *can* do for Heed—read, write, type, fix her hair, give her a bath— Heed listens but only wants to know if she can do *one* thing: "Can you keep a secret?" (27).

Coded language is another rhetorical method through which Morrison foregrounds and improvises on the trope of silence. The relationship between Heed and Christine is characterized by their secret language. First the shared, coded message embedded in the phrase "Hey Celestial"—the greeting they'd heard an old man call out to a beautiful, fearless "sporting woman." The woman had ignored the man and winked at the girls and "made their toes clinch and curl with happiness". They were warned by their elders, however, to stay away from such a woman because "there is nothing a sporting woman won't do". Enamored of her fearlessness, Heed and Christine, name their playhouse after her, "Celestial Place," and from then on, to say Amen or to acknowledge a particularly bold, smart, and risky thing, they mimicked the male voice crying, "Hey CeLEStial!" (188). It is the 1940s equivalent to "You, Go Girl," but with an embedded, racy history that only Heed and Christine understand.

In addition to the coded refrain of "Hey CeLEStial," Heed and Christine also have their own private language—the Pig Latin[1] they call "idagay." Morrison's use of Pig Latin between Christine and Heed rightly takes on the same secret coding value that Pig Latin has served for children who have wanted to create a separate language that adults could not understand. In black communities, particularly in the South during and after slavery, Pig Latin was also used by adults to talk to each other without whites being able to understand. In Pig Latin, the first consonant letter of the word is dropped and added to the "ay" sound at the end as in "ig-pay [Pig] atin-lay [Latin]." For Heed and Christine, "Idagay" is for intimacy, gossip, telling jokes on grown-ups. Only once is it used to draw friendly blood: "Ou-yidagay a ave-slidagay! E-hidagay ought-bigaday ou-yidagay ith-widagay a ear's yigaday ent-rigaday and-idagay a andy-cidagay ar-bidagay! [You a slave. He bought you with a year's rent and a candy bar]" (188). The coded language of

Pig Latin allows Heed and Christine to keep their childhood secrets; it also contributes to the larger thematic focus of the novel of what is not said, coded, secret in black community life.

Finally, among the small significations on silence in the novel, there is L's hum. It is the meme that opens and closes the novel. The humming is a wordless, closed-mouth exercise that suggests knowledge and understanding that go deeper than the open-mouthed voicing of the words could reveal. It also has gendered overtones of being the "nobody-knows- the-trouble-I've-seen" refrain that black women have used to articulate sadness, displeasure, or shock. It is not surprising that Morrison's lead character, the woman of wisdom in the novel who knows the troubles and the trials of the Coseys and the community, hums. In vocal music, humming is what we do when we "don't know the words." But as Mari Evans's signature poem, "I Am a Black Woman," suggests, humming is also a distinctive trope of black women, who "can be heard humming in the night" (l. 6).

Morrison's use of humming here also shows the generational differences between how young black women and older black women record their sorrow. Celestial, the younger of the two, *"sings one of those down-home raunchy songs that used to corrupt everybody on the dance floor"* (202). But when L wants to share Celestial's sorrow, she joins in, not with singing, but with a hum: *"But once in a while her voice is so full of longing for him, I can't help it. . . . So I join in. And hum"* (201–2). Humming, Morrison seems to suggest, like the coded language, is a more sophisticated, complex way of making a statement than the barefaced, artless tell-all behavior that has become so much of the reality of young women of today. Something is communicated in humming that the words cannot achieve, and it is not surprising that humming becomes the signifying sound of L in this novel.

The silence of secrets

The significations of advertisements, of coded language, of humming are all the stylistic ways that Morrison foregrounds the larger focus of the novel, and they are clear manifestations of the cultural meanings that can be embedded in the trope of silence in African

American culture. There are also, however, the "real secrets" of the novel—the truths that are concealed or never spoken that cause pain or provide comfort and change the lives of both those who keep the secrets and those who eventually tell them. The choice to keep a secret by the characters in the novel is not always beneficial to the one who does not tell. There is much lost by the individual in this protective secret keeping, but the motive for such secret keeping never seems to be about self-gain—self-protection maybe—but more about what is perceived to be for the greater good of the community as a whole.

There are four major secrets in the novel—the secret that Heed and Christine keep from each other about Bill Cosey's sexual actions when they were girls in the summer of 1940, and the secret of their love for each other that, after Heed's marriage to Cosey, they refuse to admit until Heed is near death. There are also the more volatile secrets: that Bill Cosey has really left all of his property to his mistress, Celestial, and not to May, Christine, or Heed, and, finally, the secret that in order to keep the family intact, L poisons Bill Cosey and changes his Will. These secrets drive the plot of the novel and ultimately encompass the novel's theme. In their development, Morrison demonstrates both the destructive and the saving power in keeping secrets. And whether the secrets are ones that ought to be told, as in Heed's and Christine's secrets; or ones that ought to be held, as in the secrets involving Cosey and L, Morrison shows how powerful the trope of silence can be in the culture. The love, the restraint—sometimes the shame—involved in keeping secrets can, literally, save or destroy people's lives.

The four secrets in the novel can be divided into two ethical categories: between those that are held *to protect the self* and those that are held *for the greater good of the community*. Heed's and Christine's secrets are those kept to protect the self. Both girls are fearful that if they were to reveal Cosey's indiscretions, or if they were to disclose their love for each other, they will have to admit to something evil/sinful about themselves: "It wasn't the arousals, not altogether unpleasant, that the girls cannot talk about. It was the other thing. The thing that made each believe, without knowing why, that this particular shame was different and could not tolerate speech—not even in the language they had invented for secrets." Ultimately they fear and they question: "Would the inside dirtiness leak?" (192). Even their coded language cannot express the private sexual secrets that they consider self-incriminating. "Now exhausted, drifting toward a maybe permanent sleep, they don't speak of the birth of sin. Idagay can't help them with that." All that they can finally share in the end is their love for each other: "He took all my childhood away from me, girl. He took all of you away from me" (194). It is clear that in guarding their discrete secrets, they have both undermined and poisoned their love and friendship. And, until they "tell the secret that they have held"—a telling that comes too late for them to relish—Heed and Christine remain wrapped in a mutually destructive web of sadness, distrust, and anger because of the personal secrets they have kept from each other.

It is more than Christine's and Heed's secrets that drive the novel's plot; Bill Cosey's secrets underpin much of his character development. Understanding whether Bill Cosey is "a good bad man" (driven by the greater good) or whether he is "a bad good man" (driven by self-indulgence) comes from knowing what he has done in secret. Cosey's secrets held in the interest of the "greater good" (his altruistic communal gestures) and his self-indulgent secrets (his pedophilia and his clandestine "sporting woman"—neither wife nor kin but heir to his estate)—cause us to reassess Bill Cosey at every turn. Although it may be argued that Bill Cosey, in guarding his secrets, is driven both by self-indulgence *and* community love, it is clear that he can never openly confront his private self-indulgence. As a consequence, he, like Heed and Christine, leads a life of sadness and anger. Cosey, the man who marries a young girl from the slums of Up Beach in hopes of having more children, perhaps to protect her from poverty, but most likely for his own indulgence, is a man who never tells the rest of the world his biggest secret: his illicit relationship with a woman other than his young wife and his frustration with the bickering women in his household are enough to leave them all out in the cold. His willingness to acknowledge that secret only after his death, when it does neither him nor Celestial any personal good beyond sexual gratification, is a secret that denies him happiness and begrudgingly holds his family together in a jealous and rapacious bond that ultimately destroys them.

The other type of the secret, the one that comes on the heels of Cosey's decision regarding the heir to his estate and the one that L keeps, is the secret held for the "*greater good.*" In the culture, such

a secret maintained for the "greater good" must be kept in order
to do the least damage to the greatest number. The ability to keep
that kind of secret, when so much hangs in the balance, exposes
the true emotional power of this kind of silence. The willful silence
that L maintains while the Cosey household—if not the whole
of Silk and Up Beach—are torn down around her is the decision
to alter his Will. In L's mind, her decision to *change* Bill Cosey's
official Will and write a more ambiguous one was done for the
benefit of the aging women (May, Christine, Heed) who had been
dependent upon him for most of their lives. Convinced that Cosey's
decision is unbridled self-indulgence, L feels compelled to defy him,
"*Regardless of what his heart said, it wasn't right*" (201). So she
intervenes for the "greater good"—thereby controlling Bill Cosey
after his death and protecting the Cosey women as well. L avers,
"*Whether what he believed was true or no, I wasn't going to let him
put his family out in the street.*" Besides, at "*sixty-one . . . what was
[May] supposed to do?*" At "*forty-one*" Heed could not return to
her estranged family. And there was Christine, who was dependent
upon her grandfather as an income source, "*whatever she was into
was not going to last. . . . He wasn't fit to think, and at eighty-
one he wasn't going to get better.*" So L decides to hasten Cosey's
demise by poisoning him (201) with foxglove and destroying his
Will in order to save his female kin. It is a hard choice. But a choice
L believes is the right choice and one she is willing to make because,
as she contends, "*I had to stop him. Had to*" (200). The strong will
of the quiet woman who has the courage to make the hard choice
and the iron will to keep silent about it is the kind of fortitude
that Morrison examines and seems to celebrate in this novel. From
the minor significations of silence to L's final and crucial choice,
Morrison illustrates the great range of silence as a trope—from the
rhetorical to the moral—in the novel as well as in African American
culture of an earlier time.

Conclusion

Although vocal expression has become the well-known and
celebrated marker of what is distinctively African American in
literary, historical, and anthropological discourse, silence, too has

a profound place in African American culture. Silence has been enforced by oppression, resulting in blacks not being able to speak; silence has been used as a form of resistance to make a "statement" in response to oppression. But within the black community, keeping silent, as Morrison demonstrates in *Love*, is also a form of protection emanating from an ethic of care.

Love is, then, Morrison's full-fledged exercise in what secret keeping specifically and silence generally have meant for the African American community. In *Love*, Morrison plays along the periphery with the rhetorical discourse that silence suggests—coded language, confidential notices, and closed-mouth humming—and she also brings the necessity of secrets and silence to front and center stage. The plotline is filled with the shocking, the ugly, and the distasteful secrets that often determined behavior in black communities like Silk and Up Beach. But this novel, ultimately, is not about the content of the secrets that were kept; it is, more importantly, about the motivation and the outcomes involved in the hard choice of keeping them. Morrison suggests that often the motivation for the hard choice of secret keeping—whether to prevent self-discovery or to save the community—is love.

Meditating on the tell-all contemporary world in *Love*, Morrison encourages us to consider again the power, the sacrifice, and the wisdom involved in *not* telling all so that we can understand not only the deep dark and salacious stories that may be harbored in black beach towns of the 1940s, but also the restraint, the fortitude, and, yes, the love involved in keeping the details of those dark and salacious stories at bay. Different historical circumstances call for different cultural responses. But Morrison, like her narrator, seems to believe that black women today may well consider how black women of another generation were able to wield power. The restraint, fortitude, and iron-will engendered by love are values, she believes, worth remembering in a contemporary culture where too many believe that power resides in revelation, not in silence.

6

Power and Betrayal: Social Hierarchies and the Trauma of Loss in *Love*

Evelyn Jaffe Schreiber

In her foreword to the 2005 edition of *Love*, Toni Morrison brings attention to the vulnerability of children. Before we have an idea of our own identity, she writes, an adult, "someone we trusted our lives to could, might, would make use of our littleness, our ignorance, our need, and sully us to the bone, disturbing the balance of our lives as theirs had clearly been disturbed" (x). That those who injure future generations were themselves violated by those who came before them is one concern that frames the narrative in *Love*. The perpetrators of harm in one generation were probably victims in the last one, and, as a consequence, parents and family members of subsequent generations often unconsciously bequeath their children lives of emotional pain. This chapter examines this process of intergenerational harm and its effect on the lives of characters in Morrison's narrative about a specific African American community, with particular attention to the family of Bill Cosey.

In *Love*, white-on-black racial dynamics frame the power relationships in the all-black community, where wealthy males dominate and all others take subordinate roles. Although Bill Cosey builds a space where black people can "walk in the front door" and hold their heads high, only wealthy and educated blacks have access (102). The social "othering" that occurs in the black community of Silk destroys youthful innocence, causes familial abandonment, and creates fragile psychological health. Bill Cosey's assertion of parental and social authority both abuses his family and engenders the ongoing battle between his child-wife Heed and his granddaughter Christine. Alternative possibilities, however, are suggested by the lives of L, Sandler, Vida, and Romen, whose conscious choices suggest that it is possible to alter behavior and create different and better conditions for future generations.

"Othering" and cultural hierarchies

Patriarchy, projection, and desire

Race has historically provided a fundamental basis for the psychological process of "othering." In Western culture, racial "othering" equates "whiteness" with agency, privilege, and power. In *The Souls of Black Folk*, W. E. B. Du Bois claims that blacks see themselves only "through the revelation of the other [white] world" that creates a "double-consciousness, [a] sense of always looking at one's self through the eyes of others [whites]" (3). Similarly, in *Black Skin, White Mask*, Franz Fanon describes the black man's objectification by white culture, where the "Other [whites] alone can give him worth" (154). As a result of this refractive gaze, blacks attempt to gain recognition by identifying with whiteness. Even within *Love*'s all-black community, characters mimic white culture through the "othering" of women and the impoverished. Such social hierarchies dominate the lives of many characters in *Love*.

Psychoanalytic theories of identity describe "othering" through the idea of projection, whereby "people attribute to others wishes and impulses of their own which are unacceptable to them and which they unconsciously try to get rid of, as it were, by the mechanism of projection" (Brenner 102). People project hatred, unconscious desires, and forbidden desires onto others. Projection on a cultural level results in targeting a group or in scapegoating, in which the "negative part of one's own psyche . . . is . . . transferred to the outside world and experienced as an outside object" (Neumann 50). Projection also functions within marginalized communities and families, where class and shade of skin lead to the "othering" of the poorest and darkest-skinned community members.

According to French psychoanalyst Jacques Lacan, what individuals desire reflects the expectations of society. Patriarchal culture—especially the white male Southern culture that is the backdrop in *Love*—defines individuals through the white male perspective. Hence, those defined as Other and denied access to opportunities often seek acceptance from the prevailing white male authority, desiring to become part of that power structure. The fact that individuals un/consciously practice the prevailing ethos of their ancestors strengthens this dynamic of personal desire by copying specific cultural practices. According to Volkan, survivors of traumatic events unconsciously "*deposit* into their progeny's core identities of their own injured self-images" (48). In this way, prior ideology lodges in one's unconscious, passing on customs like "othering," that direct one's current life. Only by reconfiguring one's relationship to cultural demands can one let go of a dysfunctional system and create a new personal ethical structure.

Love as an alternative to "othering"

Love—self-love, parental love, community support, and friend-ship—should serve to alleviate the abuse of "othering." To feel safe, children need stable parental figures to comfort them in times of trauma or distress. In *Love*, Morrison considers various forms of love that flounder: love for a spouse, a lover, children, and commu-nity. Characters in *Love* struggle to gain a positive sense of self in the face of familial and communal abuse. The novel's central nar-rative is built around the relationship between Christine Cosey and Heed the Night Johnson, who develop a close friendship despite their class differences. They also develop trust and a sense of secu-rity as their friendship deepens through innocent play. Bill Cosey, Christine's grandfather, destroys this bond of security by marrying 11-year-old Heed. The girls' friendship is shattered, and they are both traumatized at a crucial moment in their development and at a time when they are most vulnerable.

Heed and Christine illustrate what Joan Woodward has described elsewhere, how children with "insecure attachments [to parental figures] . . . can feel themselves deeply alienated from the rest of society," leaving them "highly vulnerable to further abuse, inflicted

either by themselves, or by others. . . . [S]uch people feel they are
to blame for what has been done to them and feel that they are of
no value" (16). Researchers Mauricio Cortina and Giovanni Liotti
explain that "[d]uring middle childhood and particularly during
adolescence, peer relationships (based as much in competition as in
cooperation) begin to have equal or sometimes greater importance
than family attachment relationships" (10). In fact, their research
shows that "the need to be recognized and valued by others becomes
both a biological necessity and a psychological imperative: the need
to be valued as persons" (26). Christine and Heed struggle for
recognition throughout the novel, first clinging to each other for
validation, then blaming themselves for misfortunes and doubting
their self-worth.

Love's community

Original ancestors

The relationships in the novel are a product of Bill Cosey's
manipulation of power and wealth in the black community of
Silk. Cosey inherits his prominent position from his father, Daniel
Robert Cosey, who made his money at the expense of the town
as "[t]he one police could count on" to snitch on other blacks for
his own gain. Besides his secret betrayals, Cosey's father stingily
"withheld decent shoes from his son and passable dresses from his
wife and daughters" and instilled dread in the community (68).
In service to the white power, Robert "Dark" Cosey, Bill Cosey's
father, is estranged from his family and his community. In selling
out to the white authorities, the elder Cosey psychologically abuses
and compromises the young Bill Cosey's innocence by "inducting"
him into his treacherous schemes. He asks his son to spy on a
neighboring house and report who comes out. When a man he
identifies is arrested, young Bill Cosey exhibits the compassion his
father lacks. He is especially affected by witnessing the scene in
which the arrested man's daughter, while running after the wagon
taking her father away, slips in horse manure. "People [whites]
laughed" at her shame, and Bill Cosey admits that he did "[n]othing
at all" (45). His repeated telling of the story as an adult leaves his

friend Sandler Gibbons wondering "*if Cosey laughed too*" (45). L points out that Cosey rehearsed the story "*every time he needed an example of heartless whites,*" while she "*supposed the point was he laughed too*" (139). She speculates that Bill Cosey's marrying Heed is reparation for his participation in his father's treachery. In the end, Cosey's participation in his father's treacherous behavior implicates him in activities that reinforce the power of white authority figures—"*some creatures called Police-heads*" (5)—that are out to punish and humiliate black people. By collaborating with the white power structure, Robert Cosey prospers economically but sets a bad example for and forfeits a nurturing relationship with his son and community. The father passes on a legacy of subordinating personal integrity to the demands of a hostile dominant society.

The patriarchal son

Through his father's actions, Bill Cosey learns to accept and embrace white power dynamics. His hotel and resort reflect the hierarchy of class, excluding uneducated and impoverished community members—especially those who relish Cosey's achievements and seem to accept their exclusion as part of the social order. Ironically, Cosey's success allows the black community of Silk to feel worthy and part of his success:

> It was enough to know Bill Cosey's Hotel and Resort was there. Otherwise, how to explain the comfort available nowhere else in the county, or the state, for that matter. Cannery workers and fishing families prized it. . . . [A]ll felt a tick of entitlement, of longing turned to belonging in the vicinity of the fabulous, successful resort controlled by one of their own. (41–2)

Cosey fully understands the depth of his father's villainy and attempts to compensate for it by altruistic gestures, such as paying for burials, getting people out of trouble with the law, and paying college fees. In contrast to his father, Bill Cosey praises his own son Billy and extends tenderness to his wife. L remembers first seeing Bill Cosey "*standing in the sea, holding Julia, his wife, in his arms*" and "*the sight of all that tenderness coming out of the sea*" leads L to work for him nine years later when she hears that Julia has died (64). While only 14 herself, L takes care of Cosey and 12-year-old

Billy because "*it was the most natural thing in the world*" for her to do (100). Vida also recalls Cosey's generosity. As his receptionist, she can wear sheer hosiery and

> a really good dress, good enough for church. It was Bill Cosey who paid for two more, so she would have a change and the guests wouldn't confuse the wearing of one dress as a uniform. . . . His pleasure was in pleasing. "The best good time," he used to say. That was the resort's motto and what he promised every guest. (33)

The community virtually worships Cosey for his altruism even though he remains separated from most of them by his elevated financial status.

The price Cosey must pay to give blacks an elite playground is the eventual loss of his property and power because he must pay off the police and other white officials. In the end, everything he has built and worked for goes back to the white power structure: his land goes to a developer with HUD money instead of to locals who want "some kind of cooperative: small businesses, Head Start, cultural centers for arts, crafts, classes in Black History and Self-defense" (45). Rather than uplifting his community, Cosey stalls, and when he dies, Heed quickly sells their property to a developer. Thus, Cosey, "the county's role model," ultimately does harm to the community that strongly believed that he was helping them (37).

His father's deficient parenting leaves Cosey with a void that he can never fill, and he ultimately replicates the hierarchy that enables those at the top to abuse their power. Neither family members nor employees dare to risk losing Cosey's approval for fear of material or psychological abandonment: they "were court personnel fighting for the prince's smile" (37). From his elevated position, he is free to make the perverse choice of taking young Heed as his second wife, buying her from her father for $200 and a pocketbook for her mother. Heed has no voice in the transaction, and, as Saidiya Hartman suggests about subjection, because she is "legally unable to give consent or offer resistance, she is presumed to be always willing" (81). In their financial transactions, Cosey and Heed's parents exercise the patriarchal power that determines Heed's future. Their decisions prematurely initiate her into an adult world, disrupting her growth into a mentally and socially adjusted adult.

Cosey's selection of Heed is a bold assertion of dominance and power over the community. His choice ignores Heed's needs as well as those of his granddaughter Christine. While the community is shocked, no one openly challenges his choice of a prepubescent girl or calls it for what it is—child abuse. Christine thinks of Cosey as, "the Big Man who, with no one to stop him, could get away with it and anything else he wanted" (133). Catherine Clinton has observed that in the "rituals of domination and submission," dominance is proven by docile submission (216). In marrying defenseless Heed, Cosey, who has slept with other women in the town, carries out a ritual that asserts his patriarchal authority over the personal lives of nearly everyone in the community—including the women and children. So the "fairy tale" of Cosey's power lives on in the community after his death (42). Yet Heed, Christine, and May, his daughter-in-law, all suffer as a consequence of his selfish acts. Heed is a Johnson from Up Beach—poor, trifling, and presumed "loose." Her family, as well as May's, belong to what Walter R. Allen has described as a "black underclass mired in poverty and possibly at risk of permanent exclusion from full participation in the wider society" (49). The people in Up Beach represent the element that might bring down Cosey and his middle-class family. However, in order to maintain his position of power, Cosey himself has created an "other" within his community by treating blacks at the bottom of the economic heap much like whites treat him and other blacks: by asserting control over them. Billy Cosey's marriage to May and his father's marriage to Heed serve to highlight the status of the Up Beach community as a despised, inferior group that finds its status elevated by these men of social standing. As a consequence, May and Heed cling to their new status because it would be social death to lose the Cosey name and position.

Ignorant of the life that Cosey and his family lead, Heed must learn about manners and the finer things in life from L. In fact, Cosey purchases Heed in order to mold her as he wishes. And he tries to assuage his conscience or cover his "crime" by paying for her brothers' funerals, buying her mother gifts, and paying her father enough to keep him happy. In the end, however, Heed is forced to sever ties with her family and the rest of the Up Beach crowd who want to use her for their own ends. She becomes totally dependent on Cosey for all her material and psychological needs, but she loses her friendship with Christine, who becomes a rival for Cosey's affection rather than an ally she can grow up with. L wonders if Cosey married Heed to atone for the humiliation he caused by reporting the black man whose daughter slipped on horse manure. But in his effort to make amends for his father's sins, Cosey passes the harm along to another generation. L explains:

> It was marrying Heed that laid the brickwork for ruination. See, he chose a girl already spoken for. Not promised to anyone by her parents. That trash gave her up like they would a puppy. No. . . . [S]he belonged to Christine and Christine belonged to her. (104–5)

When Cosey severs the bond between Christine and Heed, he destroys their future.

The ineffectual mother

Cosey's choice of spouse upsets a girlhood friendship as well as another relationship between mother and daughter. Ideally, the mother-child relationship provides protection and a sense of security. As the mother in Cosey's household, May fails this responsibility. Like others in the community, May understands the need to placate Cosey in exchange for his protection. Insecure in her role as daughter-in-law, she views Heed as well as her daughter Christine as obstacles to her own safety, and so she withholds support from both. Having grown up the daughter of an impoverished minister, May devotes herself to "*making sure those Cosey men had what they wanted. The father more than the son; the father more than her own daughter*" (102). L describes how May's "*ladylike manners,*" despite her childhood spent in poverty, proves to be an asset to Cosey's enterprise from the start (137). A real business woman, May was "*bred to hard work and duty*" (103). When her son Billy dies, May and L run the hotel to Cosey's satisfaction. However, her insecurities lead May to fear that Heed will supplant her and Christine, leaving them to a life of poverty.

In her mission to please Cosey, May is haunted by her early years in poverty and cannot parent Christine effectively. She sends Christine "away rather than confront [Cosey]. Put her in a faraway school and discouraged summer vacations at home" (133). After Cosey's death, May and Heed fight because Cosey leaves the Hotel to

May. Both women, raised in precarious financial circumstances, try
to hold on to the material manifestation of the homes they created
through marriage. The quarrel over the hotel is petty, especially
since Heed has been running it for years. Yet May, "frantic with
worry that the hotel and everybody in it are in immediate danger,"
hoards and buries silver to protect what resources she has from
rioters (80). Ultimately, May succumbs to insanity: "The world
May knew was always crumbling; her place in it never secure. A
poor, hungry preacher's child, May saw her life as depending on
colored people who rocked boats only at sea" (96).

The foreclosure of friendship and the birth of rivalry

In self-defense, May encourages a rift between the girls, transforming
her daughter into her own ally by disrupting her friendship with
Heed. When Heed, the child-bride, returns from her honeymoon,
eager to share the experience with her friend Christine, she finds
that avenue of communication closed forever. After the wedding,
playing together is impossible because each waits for "the other's
insult" (133). Heed returns to "May's scorn" and "Christine's sulk"
(127). "Her friend's eyes were cold, as though Heed had betrayed
her, instead of the other way around" (128). Heed, who cuts out
dolls and colors while Cosey visits friends on business, cannot
understand why her friend would reject her rather than share stories
of her new adventures. But new battle lines are drawn, and Heed
and Christine can react only as children, sulking and fighting over
who can be the "chosen one" and get the most from the adults who
should protect them (75). When Heed, in a gesture of playing dress
up, offers to let Christine wear her wedding ring, Christine betrays
their friendship by running away in tears and yelling at Heed in
their secret code. Simon Clarke explains this process of envy: "We
perceive others as possessing something good that has been stolen
from us; ways of life, jobs, even culture; we try to take it back, but
we cannot have it all so we destroy it in envy" (166). The girls fight
for the position of "favorite."

   To placate Cosey and to separate Christine from the
inappropriate adult sexual world that Heed now inhabits, May
moves her daughter from her bedroom to a smaller one in the

attic. Christine reacts by running away, and as a consequence, is shipped off to Maple Valley School. Remembering how she had fought with her mother to keep Heed as a friend, to give her clothes and enjoy picnics, Christine must come to terms with her unfair banishment. Her exile will cause her to hate the three she leaves behind—Heed, Cosey, and May. Powerless to protect themselves, Christine and Heed are moved from one place to another, with Cosey (and May on his behalf) manipulating them, and ignoring the emotional toll of their actions.

While Christine is away at school, Heed assumes the role of wife and hostess, and when Christine returns four years later, the distance between them is too deep to repair: "Heed had not seen her used-to-be friend in four years. The Christine that stepped out of Papa's Cadillac was nothing like the one who, in 1943, had left home rubbing tears from her cheeks with her palm. . . . They did not pretend to like each other and, sitting at the table, hid curiosity like pros" (125). Still relating to each other as competing children, Heed and Christine bicker over proper grammar and etiquette. May reinforces the competition by exchanging "glances with her daughter" to acknowledge Heed's picking up the water glass rather than the champagne one for the toast (126). Heed, embarrassed, responds by throwing her glass at Cosey, who, in turn, responds as the patriarch by spanking Heed and dismissing her from the table. Although he privately admits to L that he made a mistake in doing so, he refuses to apologize.

Relating through hatred and trauma

Christine suffers another exile from her family when Heed sets fire to Christine's bed. But it is his granddaughter that Cosey banishes: "they threw her away, because by then Heed had become grown-up-nasty. Mean enough to set her on fire. . . . It should have been different. She meant it to be different" (133). Heed and Christine are still locked in a preadolescent relationship. Their interpersonal dynamic remains fixed, even as they themselves age. Even though Christine realizes that she needs to leave her childhood home forever in order to change her life, the choices she makes prove to be self-destructive. Having internalized a self-image based on rejection, she puts herself in situations that cause her to relive that experience. And while she looks for love, she finds abandonment. Her quick marriage to Ernest Holder ends with Holder's infidelity. When she dedicates her life to working with the civil rights activist Fruit, he discards her when her services become obsolete. Ironically, she describes her years with Dr. Rio, a married man inaccessible to her full time, and the years with her grandfather Cosey as her best ones. "[H]aving men meant sharing them" (165) is the lesson she learns from Cosey. Thus, Christine's pattern of recreating the relationships from which she has escaped can be seen as both a learned behavior and a repressed trauma that "involves continual reliving of some wounding experience . . . in a compulsive seeking out of similar circumstances" (Erickson 184).

Early trauma becomes so fixed in memory that it is "re-experienced over years and decades, seemingly without modification" (van der Kolk 244). Christine relives her abandonment—by her grandfather, mother, and friend—throughout her life away from Silk. Ultimately hitting rock bottom, Christine "was as lonely as a twelve-year-old watching waves suck away her sand castle" (91). Her only recourse is to return home, under the guise of "taking care of her ailing mother, and a noble battle for justice—her lawful share of the Cosey estate." Resigned to living in a house with someone who "was willing to burn it down just to keep her out," Christine takes refuge in L's old apartment next to the kitchen (86). She chooses to return to fight for her inheritance, even at the price of forever looking over her shoulder out of fear of what Heed might do.

Even after May and Cosey are gone, Christine and Heed coexist in an unending battle of wills. At Cosey's graveside, they fight, Christine armed with a switchblade. L, always the concerned caregiver, quits her job at the hotel the day of the funeral but steps in to end the fight between Christine and Heed. The women continue their physical fights through the years, mostly for their cathartic value: "drawn annually to pant through an episode that was as much rite as fight." This fighting allows them to touch and hold each other, as "they punched, grabbed hair, wrestled, bit, slapped." But over time they accept the fact that they are somehow inextricably linked together and declare a truce: "Along with age, recognition that neither one could leave played a part in their unnegotiated cease-fire" (73). So Christine accepts this prison of wills for 20 years, cooking, cleaning, shopping, and taking care of their disputed house filled with mutual hatred.

It is clear, despite their endless battles, that Heed and Christine share a closeness based on mutual love and enmity. Their dark thoughts about each other link them in a bond that they cannot escape. They are "connected—by the darkness between them" (25). In their love-hate relationship, Heed knows that Christine will serve her the shellfish she does not eat, but abides the insult. Christine, for her part, dutifully makes dinner for Heed while hoping that she chokes on it. They continue to fight "*as though they were champions instead of sacrifices*" (141). Both women have wasted most of their years with a childish projection of their resentment toward each other rather than toward the real villain—Bill Cosey.

The rebirth of love and the naming of desire

Christine will forever think of her grandfather as "The dirty one who introduced her to nasty and blamed it on her. . . . The powerful one who abandoned his own kin and transferred rule to her playmate" (165). Christine recollects waving good-bye to a confused Heed going off on her honeymoon and relives the moments of fear and abandonment: "Neither one understands. Why can't she go too? Why is he taking one to a honeymoon and leaving the other? They will come back, won't they?" (170). The old feelings, ever ready to surface, come too easily. But these emotions have kept them both alive. When Heed falls from the attic at the novel's close, "the feeling of abandonment loosens loneliness so intolerable" that Christine rushes down the ladder to cradle Heed in her arms. As they search each other's face, the "holy feeling is still alive, as is its purity, but it is altered now, overwhelmed by desire. Old, decrepit, yet sharp" (177). Rather than relive their hatred, they now experience a renewal of their childhood love.

Coming to terms with what should have been

In Heed's dying moments, she and Christine share their true feelings of jealousy and lack of power. Christine muses that "May wasn't much of a mother to me"—giving her away much the same way Heed's parents had sold her to Bill Cosey (184). Christine realizes that they were too young to make life decisions and the people who should have protected them failed to do so. May "was the mama. She wanted me gone because he did, and she wanted whatever he wanted" (184). This abandonment of parental responsibility, unfortunately, engenders a cycle of abuse from which neither Heed nor Christine can escape: "we started out being sold, got free of it, then sold ourselves to the highest bidder" (185). Their years of embattled rivalry reflect the trauma imposed by others. As Dominick La Capra explains, they are "possessed by the past and performatively caught up in the compulsive repetition of traumatic scenes—scenes in which the past returns and the future is blocked or fatalistically caught up in a melancholic feedback loop" (21). They have become attached to their trauma with what LaCapra calls "a more or less unconscious desire to remain within trauma" (23). In other words, they find it difficult to give up something that has not only controlled their lives, but in some sense it may also explain or justify their lives. Allan Young explains this behavior on a bodily level when he defines memory as the reactivation and acting out of prior sensory-motor experiences:

> [V]ictims of traumatic memory seek out circumstances that replicate their etiological events . . . [because] endorphins . . . are released . . . [that] produce a tranquilizing effect by reducing the feelings of anxiety, depression, and inadequacy. . . . Over time, such people would become *addicted* both to their endorphins and to the memories that release these chemicals. (95)

Ironically, repeating trauma also brings pleasure on a biochemical level.

At the novel's end, Heed and Christine realize that with better guidance, they might have lived different, more fulfilling lives that would have preserved their friendship. They confess to each other that they felt lost, "[t]rying to find a place when the streets don't go there. . . . We could have been living our lives hand in hand instead of looking for Big Daddy everywhere" (189). With hindsight, they realize that they were just defenseless children: "There's virgins and then there's children" (132). They had their childhood stolen from them by adults seeking to satisfy their own desires.

The unspoken trauma

Beneath these layers of memory lies the original abuse that neither girl has been able to verbalize. The shame connected to their unacknowledged budding sexuality, dirtied by Cosey's adult demands, finally emerges. Cosey inappropriately fondles Heed, "touch[ing] her chin, and then—casually, still smiling—her nipple, or rather the place under her swimsuit where a nipple will be if the circled spot on her chest ever changes." When Heed runs to tell Christine what her grandfather has done, she finds Christine puking behind the hotel: "She looks sick, disgusted, and doesn't meet Heed's eyes" (191). Believing that she has ruined their relationship, "Heed thinks Christine knows what happened and it made her vomit. So there is something wrong with Heed. The old man saw it right away so all he had to do was touch her and it moved as he knew it would because the wrong was already there, waiting for a thumb to bring it to life" (191–2).

But Christine experiences her own shame at witnessing her grandfather "in her bedroom window, his trousers open, his wrist moving with the same speed L used to beat egg whites into unbelievable creaminess" and cannot explain her shame to Heed because she is "ashamed of her grandfather and of herself." Each girl feels an "inside dirtiness" and "the birth of sin" (192). Only now, years later when Heed is dying, can they admit that Cosey was at fault: "He took all my childhood away from me. . . . He took all of you away from me" (194). Cosey sexually traumatized the girls, and that trauma compounded, undermining their close attachment and diminishing their self-esteem.

Throughout the novel, both girls verbalize their experience of rejection, their desire to be the one most loved, and their unfulfilled lives. Yet, neither one ever verbalizes to the other the shame and hurt prompted by Cosey's molestation—his tweaking of Heed's nipple and his masturbating in Christine's bedroom. Because the girls never articulate the abuse, it is reexperienced in their acting out of hostilities toward each other. Both girls, victims of sexual abuse and parental desertion, have warped personalities. Rather than the self-esteem and the sense of security that children should expect from their parents, Heed's and Christine's parents psychologically damage them for life. Joyce McDougall has argued that a "mother's unconscious [is] the earliest traumatic reality with which the child

[has] to cope" (151). May's and Heed's parents respectively pass on their fears, abjection, and disrespect for children to Christine and Heed.

Their vulnerabilities lead Christine and Heed to their special childhood connection. Jean Wyatt claims that Cosey's destruction of that vital friendship leads to the "radical discontinuity of Heed's and Christine's lives—the irreparably damaging break with their childhood love from which they never recover" (213). Ruled by the desire of others, Heed and Christine, at the novel's end, voice their own desire for their innocent girlhood friendship that could have sustained them throughout their lives in troubled times. The closing scene of Heed's fatal injury yields access to the underlying source of the girls' trauma. This forced encounter unleashes the language of their pain. Revisiting the childhood bedroom with its wallpaper and the revival of their secret language releases the shared shame, and they are finally able to validate each other's trauma.

Conclusion

The interpersonal dynamics in *Love* point to the damaging narrative of patriarchal power in American culture. The small, all-black community of Silk provides a controlled environment in which Morrison explores the dynamics of power in terms of race, class, and gender. The members of Cosey's family and community enact repeating patterns of cultural behavior that control and restrain individual choices. Morrison states in her foreword to *Love* that the "terror of social arrangements" can turn individual vulnerability "into shame, into loneliness—the clear sense of having no one on whom one can safely rely." So she searches for the "weapons [needed] to survive them" (xi) and for the "raw material of reconciliation." Finding an alternative path based on love and personal integrity rather than on conformance to social hierarchy and division has "to be cultivated to know what and how to defend; what and how to cherish" (xii). Thus, *Love* becomes the narrative through which Morrison conducts and fulfills that search.

7

The Power in "Yes": Pleasure, Dominion, and Conceptual Doubling in *Love*

Herman Beavers

The attributes of power

I wish to begin with two quotations that provide a productive frame for my discussion. The first is from an interview with Michel Foucault, where he states,

> What makes power hold good, what makes it accepted, is simply the fact that it doesn't only weigh on us as a force that says no, but that it traverses and produces things, it induces pleasure, forms knowledge, produces discourse. It needs to be considered as a productive network which runs through the whole social body, much more than as a negative instance whose function is repression. (119)

And the second is from *Love*, specifically L's assessment of Bill Cosey, "*You could call him a good bad man, or a bad good man. Depends on what you hold dear—the what or the why. I tend to mix them. . . . He didn't have an S stitched on his shirt and didn't own a pitchfork. He was an ordinary man ripped like the rest of us, by wrath and love*" (200). To my mind, the first quotation speaks to the social utility of power, while the second outlines an emotional landscape against which power is foregrounded.

In the foreword to her eighth novel, *Love*, Toni Morrison states, "People tell me that I am always writing about love. Always, always love. I nod, yes, but it isn't true—not exactly. In fact, I am always writing about betrayal. Love is the weather. Betrayal is the lightning that cleaves and reveals it" (ix). If betrayal can be thought of as an instance where what begins as shared purpose is compromised or sundered, then *Love* represents the dialectic that inheres between acts motivated by self-interest and those aimed at the collective good.

I would like to suggest that *Love* dramatizes Foucault's description of how power relates to pleasure. Though *Love* is set in a Southern town, where discrimination and racial animus are part of the landscape, what proves interesting to Morrison is the system of understanding blacks fashion to negotiate it. An instrument in this collective act of fashioning is power, and as a consequence, pleasure becomes a means through which to express it. Nowhere is this truer than in the novel's central and abiding presence: Bill Cosey. Early in the novel, as the reader is becoming acquainted with his legacy, Cosey is described as a man "whose pleasure was in pleasing" (33). However, he is a man of vast contradictions; a good neighbor to his fellow inhabitants of the black community in Silk, but also a man who consciously eschews intimate connection across class lines, opting instead to service the Talented (and moneyed) Tenth. Though this should create enmity, it has the ironic effect of making the black inhabitants of Silk value and admire him all the more.

One of the people who see through Cosey's illusion of generosity is Sandler Gibbons. Having been taken into Cosey's confidence as a young man, Sandler accompanies Cosey on their early morning fishing excursions where he is forced to conclude "the more [he] learned about the man, the less he knew." On the one hand, Cosey is a man who refers to the circumscription of black progress by insisting that "every law in this country is made to keep [blacks] back" (44). But Sandler juxtaposes this declaration against Cosey's unwillingness to sell land to local people, his polite refusals to host their celebrations, his tendency toward melancholy in the face of widespread admiration from women and men alike, and he concludes that he is "of two minds about Cosey. Knowing him, watching him, was not so much about changing his mind; it was more like an education" (45).

Sandler's assessment recalls Foucault's notion that "if power is strong this is because . . . it produces effects at the level of desire— and also at the level of knowledge" (59). Sandler's "education" represents his introduction to the ways power, placed in the hands of Bill Cosey, can be used to rationalize the establishment and maintenance of dominion over one's surroundings, making it part of the common sense of being a "race man" but showing such a designation, when applied to Bill Cosey, to be bankrupt. Sandler knows that the illusion Cosey is able to create has as much to do with his ability to disguise his appetites as racial uplift. So that what appears to be his resistance to the racism in Silk (which he manages by paying bribes and entertaining the town Sheriff) is more aptly explained by Cosey's mistress of many years, Celestial, who represents the counterbalance to Silk's racial hierarchy and his marriage. Cosey's decision to channel his power through the fulfillment of desire means that Sandler's "two minds" indicates the necessity of unraveling the relationship between power and pleasure, as it likewise serves as a metonym for Morrison's deployment of conceptual doubling in the novel, her intimation that *Love* is an occasion for understanding that power's seductiveness is located in the ways it says "yes" rather than "no."

As Foucault points out, "the notion of repression is quite inadequate for capturing what is precisely the productive aspect of power." According to Foucault, power is anything but repressive, [concluding that] "if it never did anything but to say no, do you really think one would be brought to obey it?" (119). Morrison proposes, therefore, that it is not enough to view the misery of her characters, particularly Heed and Christine, solely under the aegis of suffering or repression. As I will argue in the pages below, Morrison's novel is an extended rumination on the ways pleasure connotes the instantiation of power and the betrayals synonymous with the dominion of privilege.

This is by no means to suggest that *Love* is lacking in characters that function as counterpoint to Bill Cosey. One of the novel's principal narrators, simply known as "L," is the best example. Given that her name is the first letter of the word "love," she functions as an emotional analogue, since she is the character most consistent in her rejection of self-serving behaviors and her enactment of a posture that is reconciliatory and redistributive. But L is not so much an active agent as a redolent one, for it is her role to narrate the past with an eye to reminiscence, though this should not be confused with nostalgia. That is to say, the role she plays in the narrative is, for the most part, connotative. Morrison signals this by putting all of L's narration in italics, as if to suggest that her comments lie outside the purview of the characters in the narrative present, even as they demonstrate her close proximity to the novel's main occurrences.

Love and the critique of pleasure

Toni Morrison's fiction demonstrates her recurring interest in how people in the African Diaspora pursue pleasure. She does not propose that pleasure, in and of itself, is wrong or dangerous. Through its ability to transform how the individual understands her place in a society contingent on hierarchies of race, gender, and class, pleasure can function as the companion of human suffering. As such, pleasure complicates human relations, obscures the path to truth, and masquerades as liberation. The role of pleasure recurs in Morrison's fiction in various guises that inform the dynamics of power on a personal level and in social relationships.

It would be an oversimplification to suggest that *Love* turns on the distinction Freud makes between the pleasure principle and the reality principle in *Beyond the Pleasure Principle*. However, it is useful to note that, according to Freud, resolving the "strong tendency towards the pleasure principle" in the tension between pleasure and reality is not a matter of nullifying pleasure. Rather, the reality principle "demands and carries into effect the postponement of satisfaction, the abandonment of a number of possibilities of gaining satisfaction and the temporary toleration of unpleasure as a step on the long indirect road to pleasure" (7). A number of Morrison's novels have provided examples of what it means to experience pleasure. As she presents it, pleasure is distinguished by its ability to transform noble intentions into acts characterized by debasement and excess. As simplicity of purpose becomes overwrought, pleasure dispatches tranquility in favor of strife.

Song of Solomon's Guitar eschews the pleasure of sweets after his father is killed in a sawmill and the boss brings compensation in the form of a bag of candy. But Guitar's disavowal of "[c]andy, cake, [and] stuff like that" (61) becomes transmuted into the violence he enacts as retribution as a member of the Seven Days, a group who seek to "balance" the losses created when blacks are killed by whites. Guitar's acceptance into this society of assassins requires that he pass up the quotidian pleasures of a wife, children, or fun with his best friend, Milkman. For if pleasure can be understood as a quickening of the senses, a state in which the elapse of time is intensified, accelerated, the Seven Days are characterized by their resistance to haste, which emphasizes taking "the time to last." But in opting for such a profile, they elucidate the lure of pleasure by constructing lives overdetermined by the effort to redirect it to different ends. Indeed, by equating sweets with "dead people . . . and white people" (61) all Guitar has done is catalyze the transience of pleasure into a sustained penchant for racial violence.

Food plays an equally compelling role in Morrison's fifth novel, when Stamp Paid goes into the woods and returns with a bucket of blackberries "that tasted like church" (136). But the joy and thrill the berries create lead Baby Suggs "to do something with the fruit worthy of the man's labor and his love." Creating a feast that harkens back to Christ's feeding of the multitudes, where what began as a small repast turns into enough food to feed 90 people, the opulence of the feast—a celebration of Sethe's escape from slavery—leads to anger rather than satisfaction. The feast is evidence that pleasure often resides in the interstitial space between joy and excess. Baby Suggs's generosity spurs her neighbors to the malevolent conclusion that their suffering during slavery was on par with Baby Suggs and Sethe's. The insatiability of pleasure insists that it has greatest consequence when it generates a system of comparison in which scale is distorted. Hence, the berries "that tasted *like* church" lead the community to confuse thanksgiving with hubris.

Morrison therefore takes the bifurcation of self that Freud describes, whereby an individual learns that deferred gratification in no way signals the end of pleasure, and uses it as a conceptual pivot. She creates a set of conceptual doubles, at the level of both characters and situations. The doubling consists of characters whose actions reveal the deeper motivations of characters in earlier circumstances or in recurring events that generate different outcomes. When a character opts for self-discipline and eschews immediate satisfaction, we come to understand that pleasure can be antithetical to control. Moreover, because the thrill of pleasure relies on stimulation, it represents an alternative to the kinds of speculative circumstances that grow out of the deferral of pleasure, as if what is most palpable about pleasure is the fear that deferring it is foreclosing upon the possibility of ever finding it.

Pleasure thus convinces us that our imperfections can be expunged or nullified in favor of the attributes we value most in ourselves. In *Jazz*, the narrator comments that when Southerners arrive in the city, "they feel more like themselves, more like the people they believed they were" (35), led to feel "not so much new, as themselves: their stronger, riskier selves" (33). In *Sula*, Hannah Peace "ripple[s] with sex" (42) and thus functions as a constant source of pleasure for men living in the Bottom. Unlike her mother, Eva, who leaves men "feeling as though they have been in combat," Hannah "rubbed no edges, made no demands, made the man feel as though he were complete and wonderful just as he was—he didn't need fixing—and so he relaxed and swooned in the Hannah-light that shone on him simply because he was" (43). The language Morrison uses to describe Hannah's carnal attributes exposes pleasure's ability to substitute adequacy for aspiration.

At a level that might seem counterintuitive, then, pleasure can represent an important instrument of power, for it camouflages power relations. After Sandler Gibbons accompanies Bill Cosey on one of his boat parties, he promises himself "that he [will] never go again" (111), because he finds himself uncomfortable fraternizing with the town's most powerful white men and well-to-do black men. The boat party points to the ways that pleasure can forestall social and legal disciplinary systems, masking the effects of social inequality. So that even as Sandler finds the "laughter was easy enough" during the party, he realizes it was the talk, its tone, its lie that he couldn't take. Talk as fuel to feed the main delusion: the counterfeit world invented on the boat; the real one set aside for a

few hours so women could dominate, men could crawl, blacks could insult whites. Until they docked. Then the sheriff could put his badge back on and call the colored physician a boy. Then the women took their shoes off because they had to walk home alone. (111)

In the carnivalesque atmosphere of the boat party, social conventions are turned upside down; where blacks are equal with whites and women dictate men's behavior, pleasure's transience is on full display. What appears to be the abandonment of social convention in favor of *communitas* is finally a social fantasy meant to serve as a release valve for the pressures that, if allowed to mount, might lead to demands for political and social equity. Though the black men on the boat are given temporary access to the privileges of dominance, the speed with which this access disappears leads us to understand pleasure as a way to suspend both disappointment and its inverse, purpose. Morrison does not mention alcohol as the primary intoxicant—rather it is the atmosphere pleasure creates, in which sobriety is deemed inappropriate and lack of restraint is a sign of belonging.

The experience of Sandler's grandson Romen at a house party provides the conceptual double of Sandler's rejection of the pleasures available around Bill Cosey. Romen finds himself in a room at a house party, standing "next in line," with his "belt unbuckled, anticipation ripe." Having been invited to participate, with six other boys, in the gang rape of a girl at a house party, he feels, in a reprise of language from *Jazz*, that he is "about to become the Romen he'd always known he was: chiseled, dangerous, and loose" (46). The intensity of perception and suspension of reason lead Romen to conclude that participating in the gang rape is a necessary step to self-authentication. He links pleasure with masculine privilege and its sense of entitlement.

Surprisingly, though, when Romen steps up to take his turn, he opts to untie the girl's hands from the bedpost and carry her out of the room. In opting out of his right to "have his way" with Pretty-Fay in favor of rescuing her, Romen eschews the illusion that manhood relies on acts of domination. What is more noteworthy is the fact that Romen acts not out of a deep concern for Pretty-Fay but rather because he is caught between two conflicting notions of himself.

The sense of Romen's double self is emphasized by its juxtaposition with an earlier scene involving Romen's grandfather and Bill Cosey, in which Sandler Gibbons remembers the portrait of Bill Cosey that hung behind the registration desk of the hotel. The portrait was created from a photograph in which Cosey was looking at his lover, Celestial. Sandler knows what his wife refuses

to acknowledge—that what has been captured in the painting
is not Cosey's enduring charm and affability, but rather his self-
indulgence and unfaithfulness. The doubling of Cosey's image—first
as photograph and then as portrait—indicates the people of Silk's
inability to see Cosey as he is. According to the narrator, Cosey
presented two different personalities to people in the town: "Cosey
didn't mix with local people publicly, which is to say he employed
them, joked with them, even rescued them from difficult situations,
but other than at church picnics, none was truly welcome at the
hotel's tables or on its dance floor" (41). Because the photograph
does not capture the object of Cosey's gaze, its transmogrification
into a portrait means that the place where Cosey is aiming his
look—the object of his desire—becomes a mysterious instance
where no one in Silk "know[s] who he [is] looking at" (45).

The contrasting attitudes of Sandler and Vida highlight the
contours of Bill Cosey's two faces. Vida remembers Bill Cosey as a
man whose "pleasure was in pleasing" (33); her memory is linked
to what she interprets as Cosey's generosity after he purchases three
dresses, "good enough for church," for her to work behind the
registration desk. She sees "a powerful, generous friend gaz[ing] out
from the portrait hanging behind the reception desk." But Sandler's
fishing trips with Cosey, allow him to see "Cosey's wealth not as a
hammer wielded by a tough-minded man, but more like a toy of a
sentimental one" (45).

Hence, Romen's actions with Pretty-Fay are the inverse of
Cosey's self-indulgence, for his act of compassion is likewise an
instance of tough-mindedness. However, he believes, wrongly, that
he has allowed sentimentality to get in the way of the camaraderie
and bravado pleasure should create. But the clear-headed decision
to remove Pretty-Fay, in such close proximity to his grandfather's
revelations regarding Cosey's true motives, intimates that the
"chiseled, dangerous, and loose" self Romen sought to occupy is
an artifice.

The act of [mis]naming that follows, where the narrator never
repeats the slur (but which we can assume is either "faggot" or
"punk"), renders swift judgment. As he walks away from the girl
and her friends, having left her without saying a word, Romen's ears
are assaulted by "the trumpet blast of what Theo had called him:
the worst name there was; the one word whose reverberations, once
airborne, only a fired gun could end" (47). Even when he hears his

"name" on the basketball court, he declines to fight them because he reasons if "he fought back, he would be fighting not for himself, but for her, Pretty-Fay, proving the connection between them—the wrong connection" (48). Believing that the many and not the one, self-interest and not concern for a stranger, dictate the path to manhood Romen duplicates Cosey's sustenance of the status quo, which is symbolized by his infidelity, not only to his wife, but also to the black community of Silk.

Love pays strict attention to the black community's presumption that racial progress can only occur when someone in its midst replicates the hierarchy and exclusivity found in the white community. And because the pleasure associated with Cosey's Resort is read through a hermeneutic of racial possibility, the inhabitants of Silk's black community, rather than being critical of Cosey's strict adherence to separatism, are instead, "Proud of his finesse, his money, the example he set that goaded them into thinking that with patience and savvy, they could do it too" (40). If this idea sounds familiar, it may be because it is reminiscent of the message trumpeted by John H. Johnson; founder of the Johnson Publishing Company and publisher of *Ebony* magazine, that conspicuous consumption is a necessary handhold in the black community's climb toward respectability. Hence, in the character of Bill Cosey, who uses his financial wherewithal to create what appears to be open doors and new opportunity, Morrison explicates the cost of upward mobility as pleasure for its own end. For if racial possibility is predicated on a man whose "pleasure was in pleasing," it also means that the community is configured around a chiasmus from which it can extricate itself only by decoupling pleasure from progress.

Love and the dynamics of dominion

The parallels that Morrison draws between naming and systems of order suggest that names are shadows of the deep structure that informs the African Diaspora's search for wholeness. According to Elizabeth T. Hayes, naming "is an act of creation" and thus the act of naming anything (a child, an animal, an estate) "is also to claim dominion over it" (669). The conscious attention to naming across the African Diaspora is, as Kimberly Benston puts it, "inevitably genealogical revisionism" (3). As an act of asserting cultural agency, naming seeks to counteract what Nathaniel Mackey declares is "the normativeness, brought about by the slave trade, of Africans bearing European names throughout the Americas that has given rise to the preoccupation with (and complication of) the relationship between naming and space among African Americans" (184). Morrison shares with numerous other African American writers the sense that acts of self-naming are essential to the acquisition of what Booker T. Washington termed our "entitles."

But as Benston insists, the politics of naming can reside as easily in acts of unnaming, where a former name is exchanged for one signifying a liberated self, as we see with Frederick Douglass, William Wells Brown, or El Hajj Malik El Shabazz. Morrison's portrayal of systems in crisis suggests that the act of learning our true names is inseparable from understanding our place in those systems. In Morrison's fiction, characters often seek to discern their "place" in situations where conditions are anything but stable and outcomes are difficult to predict.

Love explores the relationship between claims of dominion and the nature of pleasure. Because these two concepts turn on radically divergent principles, we can reconcile them only by imagining that they are synonymous. Pleasure and dominion come together in Cosey's Hotel and Resort if one does not look beneath the rhetorical surface Bill Cosey erects in order to obscure the unconscionable behaviors that lead to its establishment. By inviting the reader to breach this surface, *Love* reimagines naming as an unstable practice—signifying that the spatial dominion naming makes possible is equally unstable. Both literally and figuratively, Bill Cosey has built his fame and his estate on sand.

Events in the novel reveal that the act of claiming dominion over a set of spatial coordinates is by no means liberating. Like Morrison's *Beloved*, *Love* presents us with "a named house (in the form of Cosey's Hotel and Resort) and . . . nameless women (women whose subjectivity is bestowed upon them through their relation to men)" (Hayes 669). The unique twist in *Love* arises when Bill Cosey's widow, Heed, and his granddaughter, Christine are in danger of becoming "nameless." Each seeks to prove that Cosey's Will has *named* one of them as the legitimate heir to his estate. Lacking such a designation, they are trapped in limbo, occupying the Cosey house but unable to claim sole ownership. Unlike *Song of Solomon*'s portrayal of the transformation of genealogical knowledge into a new form of cultural capital, *Love* portrays the disequilibrium created when individuals seek to equate the economics of naming with emotional capital. If such an equation intimates an inversion of scale, a confusion of registers, it proffers that in the replication of complex structures like property, acts of naming signify beyond the confines of family, the consequences felt by the whole community.

The place to begin is with the history of the Cosey family, which appears to be synonymous with the history of the Southern town of Silk. As the son of a father nicknamed "Danny-Boy" by whites and "Dark" by blacks, Bill Cosey validates the idea that patriarchy is a system whereby sons are compelled to reprise the lives of the fathers that preceded them, even as they establish a legacy to pass on to their own progeny. Dark Cosey generates capital through his willingness to turn his gaze onto the black community, when he becomes the "*one police could count on to know where a certain colored boy was hiding, who sold liquor, who had an eye on what property, what was said at church meetings, who was agitating to vote, collecting money for a school—all sorts of things Dixie law was interested in*" (68). The conceptual doubling of Bill Cosey's father, as both Danny-Boy and Dark, dramatically demonstrates the double consciousness of a black man who uses his position in the black community to satisfy whites' desire to police black behavior.

Hence, Dark Cosey is like Ralph Ellison's Lucious Brockway, "the machine inside the machine," through whom every move the black community makes toward integration and equality, is checked by white supremacist control. The purpose he serves, as the "regulating" mechanism holding black progress at bay, makes Dark Cosey the embodiment of conservatism. Knowing that he cannot defeat white supremacy, Dark Cosey opts to take the energy generated by white supremacy (which is of a piece with the racial anxiety whites experience) and transform it into capital, which continues to circulate in and around the town of Silk.

Consider, then, L's characterization of the progression from the elder Cosey to the younger:

The son decided to enjoy his share. Not throw it away exactly, but use it on things Dark cursed: good times, good clothes, good food, good music, dancing till the sun came up in a hotel made for it all. The father was dreaded; the son was a ray of light. The

cops paid off the father; the son paid off the cops. What the
father corrected, the son celebrated. The father a miser? The son
an easy touch. (68)

Though it might seem that as a man whose "pleasure was in
pleasing," Bill Cosey has devoted himself to redressing the sins of
the father by putting Dark Cosey's 114,000 "resentful dollars" to
beneficial use, when viewed from the standpoint of capital, Bill Cosey
has increased his inheritance, but he has done so by exchanging
one form of service for another without in any way disrupting the
negative feedback loop that holds the black community in limbo.

Whereas his father generated capital by transforming information
about the black community into a commodity, Bill Cosey uses
capital to create a fantastical image of the black community. While
favoring light skin over dark, rich over poor, and leisure over labor,
the hotel is viewed as a source of both race pride and social progress.
Bill Cosey was known for his generosity of spirit, his willingness
to help a neighbor in need, and Vida remembers Cosey's Resort
as "more than a playground; it was a school and a haven where
people debated death in the cities, murder in Mississippi, and what
they planned to do about it other than grieve and stare at their
children." The resort carries the motto "The best good time," amidst
Cosey's promise that a stay at his resort is "The best good time
this side of the law" (33). But in declaring it to be "this side of the
law," the motto reprises Dark Cosey's position *on the side of the
law.* As Figure 7.1 demonstrates, Cosey's Hotel and Resort remains
intricately linked to Dark Cosey's legacy.

Though L has characterized Cosey as the antithesis of his father,
it is perhaps more apt to suggest that his variation on the theme
of betrayal is to focus it inward, to enact a brand of hurting that
is aimed more precisely, not at the collective, as we see with Dark,
but on a personal scale, at his granddaughter, daughter-in-law, and
second wife, Heed.

Cosey's position takes on a special significance in the evening
hours, for it is in the darkness that Cosey's inheritance from his
police-informant father takes form. For all the political chatter
between guests fretting over US race relations, Cosey's Hotel and
Resort specializes in the art of diversion. Just as the patrons begin
to imagine how they might address the growing racial unrest in the
South, to see themselves as the purveyors of a new racial legacy,

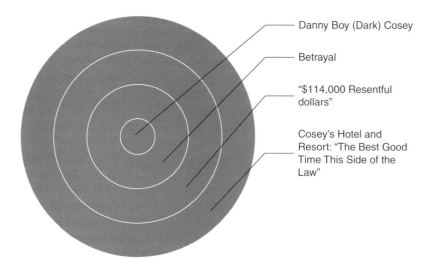

FIGURE 7.1

we note that in the sentence following Vida's observation quoted above, Morrison writes: "Then the music started, convincing them they could manage it all and last" (35). Hence, what might have begun as disenchantment with the social order ends with music that induces them to dance their troubles away, to embrace the idea of endurance rather than upsetting the order of things. Though it cannot be said that the resort is a den of iniquity, the chiasmus mentioned above, embodied in a proprietor whose "pleasure [lay] in pleasing," replicates a social gaze that turns in on itself to become narcissism, which feels better perhaps, but which leaves white supremacy wholly intact.

Here, Morrison holds up for critique our propensity to misinterpret hedonism as racial progress. Because pleasure leads us to understand ourselves in terms of how we would like to be rather than who we are, it does not lend itself to acts of resistance because these require individuals to defer gratification, to endure hardship, and thus to remain optimistic about the prospects for change, even in the face of disappointment and failure. Further, because hedonism is so often associated with escapism, it cannot function as a means of engagement. Many of the patrons at Cosey's Resort are likely to see their interests apart from those they deem less fortunate. As Morrison presents it, pleasure is problematic because it leads one to assume that dominion inheres, even though that dominion is transient.

Cosey's Resort is a chiasmic space, created within the dominion of white supremacy by the intersection of pleasure and betrayal. The Coseys' prosperity rests on the presumption that blacks will always opt to pursue pleasure rather than confront the realities of segregation and discrimination. The system is a product of white supremacy—not of the assets of the black elite. Dark's accumulation of assets relies on the assumption that the place blacks hold in the racial hierarchy is a product of the dominion whites enjoy at the expense of blacks.

Dominion and the politics of conceptual doubling

The importance of the role Junior Viviane plays in the process of conceptual doubling in *Love* is evident the first time Junior looks at Cosey's portrait. The narrator observes, "As soon as she saw the stranger's portrait she knew she was home" (60). By naming the character "Junior," Morrison performs two important gestures. First, she signifies on the propensity of men's naming their sons after them as an act that is both self-tribute and blueprint. By bestowing their names on their male children, fathers place them in a straitjacket and trap them in a temporal loop, where their actions are not read as their own, but are viewed as a reprise of the father's exploits. Secondly, Morrison challenges the assumption that dominion, especially under patriarchy, is a male prerogative that depends on women's subservience. Junior's dream after her arrival at One Monarch Street immediately calls attention to the relationship between the two sexes. "She had dreamed him the first night, had ridden his shoulders through an orchard of green Granny apples heavy and thick on the boughs" (60). The dream suggests a revision of the story of the Garden of Eden in which the man and woman are coconspirators staging the theft from the tree of knowledge. However, it is equally compelling to think of the well-worn aphorism, "The apple doesn't fall far from the tree," and to consider the ways that Junior's position on Cosey's shoulders ensures that the proverbial apple will not fall, but will, by contrast, be plucked in a gesture of entitlement. The dream signals the manner in which patriarchy can "deputize" women as surrogates for male power, where their main purpose is to further the interests of men.

For all her attention to the personal habits of Heed and Christine, Morrison's description of life in the Settlement reveals that Junior Viviane's life has been one of deprivation and abuse. It manifests in her penchant for rough sex and her ability to discern and exploit people's motives. Junior and Cosey are alike in the way they fetishize their original hunger, leading them to reject the idea that it can ever be satiated, understanding "Christine's generosity and Heed's stinginess as forms of dismissal" (119). Junior's "hunger" is symbolic of what happens when the quest for sustenance becomes a self-justifying practice, an end-in-itself. Thinking of Cosey's portrait, Junior sees a future of "hot, tasty food" (30), and more importantly, she feels "a peculiar, new thing: protected" (28). In Cosey's case, this insatiability makes him appear larger than life—as a man who sees that his lot in life is to "*contradict history*" (103) and function as a counterweight to the pull of discrimination and racism. But, in lieu of using his wealth as a hammer, Cosey aims nonetheless to maintain control over it. As the son of a father who "worshipped paper money and coin, withheld decent shoes from his son and passable dresses from his daughters" (68), Bill Cosey is imbued with the same hunger as Junior Viviane, which makes her—not Heed or Christine—his "rightful heir."

Thus, we can understand Cosey's production of two "Wills" as a sign of his aversion to chance. Morrison's description of Junior suggests a similar bent:

> Unlike what people thought, in the daily grid of activities, *to plan was fatal*. Stay ready, on tippy-toe. And read fast: gestures, eyes, mouths, tones of speech, body movement—minds. Gauge the moment. Recognize the chance. *It's all you. And if you luck out, find yourself near an open wallet, window, or door, GO! It's all you. All of it. Good luck you found, but good fortune you made.* And her Good Man agreed. As she knew from the beginning, *he liked to see her win.* (118, emphasis added)

This sentiment is underscored in Junior's strategizing in the scene in which she pulls on a pair of Cosey's underwear, and as she does so, realizes Cosey's "happiness was unmistakable. So was his relief at having her there, handling his things and enjoying herself in front of him." Feeling "flooded" by Cosey's "company," Junior moves swiftly past the idea of being Heed's employee and begins to work to assume her place in a home she can call her own. "Everything was becoming clear. If she pleased both women, they could live happily together. All she had to do was study them, learn them" (119).

But juxtaposing Junior's cunning with her sexual trysts with Romen not only reveals the extent of her alienation from social convention, it also points to Bill Cosey's earlier pedophilia (revealed when he molests the 11-year-old Heed). Junior Viviane is between 18–20 years old, and Romen is only 14. Junior's sense that Romen is her reward for becoming Cosey's "right hand," is exemplified in her sense upon seeing him that the "gift was unmistakable," leading her to couch her declaration of dominion as an invitation, but which serves nonetheless as a projection of Cosey's code of behavior onto Romen.

For his part, Romen interprets his sexual play with Junior as an opportunity to discover an authentic self. Ensorcelled in the sexual transgressions Junior occasions, Romen concludes that all "of his impulses were right, now" (113). Sex with Junior erases the episode with Pretty-Fay, concluding that the boy who opted against pleasure is gone. "Who was that wuss crying under a pillow," he asks himself, "because of some jive turkeys?" and he concludes that he has "no time for that sniveling self now." He knows his "score" with Junior to be "big time," so much so that he has "new eyes that [appraise and dare]" (114), and he concludes that sex induced by alcohol, domination, or herd behavior is for boys whose behavior is equal to that of a "punk." But if the narrator offers us a framework through which to critique hegemonic masculinity when it assumes the form of herd behavior, what we realize is that Romen is enacting a form of manhood enshrined in Hollywood cinema, where the "hero" gets the girl for doing the right thing, a version of masculinity that, when linked to "manifest destiny," is equally catastrophic.

The notion that Junior is Romen's "prize" for acting decently requires us to heed the fact that Morrison's narrator withholds judgment on Romen's actions. The effect of this deferral of judgment is that we are equally hesitant to judge Bill Cosey. Romen's "look"— which mirrors the one in Cosey's portrait—declares dominion over his surroundings. Though this sentiment does not center on the acquisition of property, it nonetheless has spatial characteristics.

Junior's access to Christine's car, which is supposed to be used for
running errands and shopping, becomes a vehicle for extending what
appears to be Romen's sexual dominion across the whole town.
Junior's plan to "make it everywhere," with Romen, to "map the
county with grapple and heat" (115) suggests that Morrison opted
to give him that name because his liaisons with Junior are akin to
establishing an empire. The more locations he and Junior find to
have sex, the more "indelible" the town becomes. His sense that sex
with Junior is synonymous with the act of inscription recalls the
ways the pen, as a surrogate for the phallus, is an instrument of
dominion. This explains Romen's "ownership" of both Café Ria and
his former friend, Theo. The novel's use of free indirect discourse
implies that the spoils of heroic behavior are bestowed on him as
an individual. His dismissal of boys (or men) who need "a chorus
of each other to back them up," as if their sexual escapades are
unreal, "doing it, not to the girl but for, maybe even to, one another"
(115), intimates the role sexuality plays in the staging of self-made
manhood. Though it is possible to ascertain the merits of Romen's
position, especially since it has the effect of making him look mature
beyond his years, its deeper function is to provide a window into
the attitude Heed assumed as Bill Cosey's "child-bride." As I suggest
in Figure 7.2, Bill Cosey's transformation of his father's "resentful"
dollars is what fuels his ability to manifest power in the form of both
pleasure and dominion and which lead, in turn, to the conceptual
doubling portrayed through both characters and situations.

   The Junior/Romen dyad leads us to a more profound truth,
which Bill Cosey articulates when he says, "You can live with
anything if you have what you can't live without" (112). Junior's
"bottomless" desire for Romen is meant to evoke the legacy of Bill
Cosey, especially as it relates to his lover, Celestial. When Sandler
Gibbons looks at his grandson's face, he recalls Cosey's portrait and,
without fully realizing the circumstances, links the face that displays
"a look he would recognize anywhere," with "[o]ne that Romen
was acquiring: first ownership" (112). Hence, the intermingling
of pleasure and dominion relies on the failure of imagination, the
collapse of a quality of aspiration that seeks to be inclusive and
thus creates a sense of shared destiny. One of the errors of insight
we make, Morrison suggests, is to view the pursuit of pleasure as a
surrogate for selfhood. Hence, when Sandler tells Romen, "You not
helpless" (154) he does so as a way to insist that he is empowered

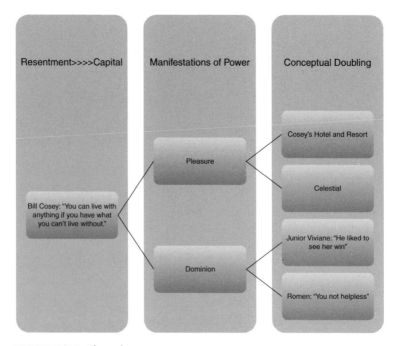

FIGURE 7.2 *Flow chart*

to resist the lure of pleasure, not realizing that Romen has already proven his ability to do so. But in the midst of enjoying his time with Junior, Romen pays scant attention to his grandfather's claim, believing that he has arrived at the place where he can become his authentic self. However, by novel's end, his decision to leave Junior in order to rescue Heed and Christine represents the instance when he truly arrives at an "authentic" self who selflessly defers pleasure.

Conclusion

If the events of *Love* have been fueled by betrayal and the quest for pleasure and dominion, their resolution lies in Heed and Christine's mutual decision to relinquish their adherence to *Eros* and return to *Agape*. It is the former that establishes the connection between body and property, and fuels the impulse to establish dominion. But this linkage is rendered bankrupt by Cosey's distortion of *Eros*. The "desire" Christine feels for Heed, as an expression of *Agape*, is undermined by the shame she feels when she discovers her grandfather's pedophilia. What confirms this conclusion is Romen's decision to leave Junior and find Heed and Christine at the hotel. When he breaks free of her, the "old Romen" is proven to be authentic because his selflessness replays what initiated the bond between Christine and Heed.

We come to understand the degree of devastation that accompanies the sundering of their bond in Christine's description of her friendship with Heed as one in which "one's dreaming was the same as the other one's" (132). The language recalls Sula's observance that she and Nel "were two throats and one eye and we had no price" (147) and it is likely what led *New York Times* critic Michiko Kakutani to declare that *Love* "reads like an awkward retread of *Sula* and *Tar Baby*." But my sense is that Heed and Christine's relationship *is meant* to recall the relationship between Sula Peace and Nel Greene. However, in reprising the earlier relationship, I would argue that Morrison seeks to create a new heuristic through which to examine its mechanisms. Though the narrator of *Sula* articulates the merits of the bond, no one in the Bottom understands. Eva Peace condemns Nel and Sula, insisting "never was no difference between you" (169). Hence, when L decides to poison Cosey rather than allow him to leave his widow and granddaughter with nothing, it is the character that opts not to pursue her own self-interest who proves to be in the best position to thwart Cosey's vengeful act and reserve the possibility of a reconciliation between Heed and Christine. In this, the letter "L" signifies *linkage* and it proposes that Morrison's decision to utilize L as the source of an "eyewitness account," from the "other side," anticipates the ways the connection between Christine and Heed will survive Heed's death. Hence, Morrison eschews the state of irremediable exigency in Nel's empty cry in *Sula* in favor of characters like L whose humming at novel's end indicates the efficacy of mediating our worst impulses and our best.

PART III

A Mercy

Karin Coddon cautions "that access to history is always partial—both incomplete and inevitably biased" (12). It is, perhaps, this notion of history that prompted Morrison to offer a fictional representation of the earliest period of Africans in North America. Morrison's novels, in many respects, are archives of four centuries of Africans and their descendants in America. Along that continuum, *A Mercy* marks the beginning of blacks in what would later become the United States of America. In this novel, Morrison takes us back to the "preracial" moment in American history and the emergent racism and class prejudices. The novel speaks to the dawn of twenty-first-century America, which some cultural critics describe as "postracial" and others view as the "Age of Obama." *A Mercy* depicts a moment when individuals—settlers and servants, free and indentured, regardless of color—worked cooperatively based upon similar economic and social status, but also the moment when emergent wealth and power differentiated one group from another. The novel demonstrates how quickly wealth and status alienate and divide even those who previously risked their lives and reputations for others with little regard to color or ethnicity.

In the opening chapter to this section, Jami Carlacio explicates Morrison's narrative strategies that enable her protagonist (Florens) and her readers to achieve certain knowledge through revelation and inquiry. Carlacio traces Florens's development as she gains knowledge and understanding of self through experiences that in the end represent the reader's epistemological maturation. Florens's "growth," Carlacio writes, "becomes our growth," and "her knowledge becomes ours." Florens achieves agency through developing knowledge of the world and self that results in her ability to inscribe her bildungsroman on the walls of her owner's unoccupied mansion.

Marc Conner, like Carlacio, begins with two pivotal issues raised by Florens at beginning of *A Mercy*: responsibility and literacy. However, Conner moves from character to landscape, from Florens's self-understanding through her ability to "read" other characters' perceptions of her to her ability to read and know her self. Conner is concerned primarily with what he reads in this novel as Morrison's urgent appeal to readers to focus on the landscape. For Conner, Morrison's "need to understand *how knowledge and geography speak to each other within narrative* form a defining concern" of *A Mercy*. Conner engages humans and their relation to the land: a desire to conquer and own it or live harmoniously with it.

Finally, Susan Mayberry begins with Conner's landscape and brings us back, in a sense, to Stave's focus on gender relationships. Mayberry's concern is masculinity and its manifestations in terms of power, class, gender, and sexuality. Building upon *Can't I Love What I Criticize?* a monograph on masculinity in Morrison's earlier novels, Mayberry argues that American masculinity originated in a patriarchal vision of ownership and enslavement. She further argues that *A Mercy* represents Morrison most developed "notions of homosexual masculinity . . ., associating its fluidity with sensitivity to women and children." She adds that Morrison "defines the free black man via his disruptive presence and the complex nature of freedom." By examining the developing class consciousness and racism at their originary moment, Mayberry offers an astute vision of American masculinity that entails a broad spectrum of gender and sexuality.

8

Narrative Epistemology: Storytelling as Agency in *A Mercy*

Jami Carlacio

Introduction: Narrative (as) *Ethos*

A substantial amount of literature on the fiction of Toni Morrison has focused on the author's narrative strategies, with particular attention to the dialogic relationship between reader and writer/narrator. Scholars have investigated the relationship between the good and the bad, between what is considered moral and immoral, and between the narrator's and the reader's (ethical) stance: in short, they have examined the implications of the situational conflicts within the lifeworld of the novel and the questions these conflicts pose for us as readers and participants in the world of the literary text. According to James Phelan, a basic definition of narrative involves both an author's description of a progression of events and "somebody telling somebody else on some occasion and for some purpose that something happened" (300–1). For Phelan and other narrative theorists, a rhetorical understanding of narrative ethics implies judgments on the text and/or on the characters themselves and their actions (see Newton 8–9; 295–6, n. 8; Nussbaum, *passim*). Phelan explains that "our values and those set forth by the implied

author affect our judgments of characters, our judgments affect
our emotions, and the trajectory of our feelings is linked to the
psychological and thematic effects of the narrative" (300).

Like Phelan, I regard what he refers to as the "communicative
situation of narrative—somebody telling somebody else that
something happened—[as] an ethical situation" (300), but somewhat
differently than either he or other theorists do. For example, Wayne
Booth writes, "I can think of no published story that does not
exhibit its author's implied judgments about how to live and what
to believe about how to live" and that "stories are our major moral
teachers" (26, 27). Similarly, in her quest to understand how one
should live, the philosopher Martha Nussbaum joins ethical inquiry
to literary criticism in an attempt to answer just that question
(172–3). That stories and narratives "spea[k] *about us*, about our
lives and choices and emotions, about our social existence and
the totality of our connections" (171) as human beings is for me
beyond question; however, I want to suspend for the moment the
idea that value judgments are implicit in literature or in characters'
narratives and actions. My project here is to consider other ways of
understanding the function of narrative.

Little attention has been paid to how exactly the characters
themselves, as agents, drive the narrative and craft their own
ethical stances in the classical Aristotelian sense of *ethos*. I use
ethos to mean not just the character and stance of the speaker/
storyteller but also the entire rhetorical situation of the story. In this
chapter, I examine specifically the character of Florens, *A Mercy*'s
primary narrator, as she develops throughout the novel. I discuss
how her ethical stance—not necessarily as a moral agent but as
an individual *persona*—changes and develops throughout the
novel to parallel the character's own mental and epistemological
maturity. By epistemological I mean a way of knowing (the self, of
arriving at self-consciousness) that is contextualized by experience,
not the Platonic notion that there is a certain knowable truth. To
further explain *ethos*, I borrow from rhetorical theorist Jimmie
Killingsworth's modern reconceptualization of the Aristotelian
definition of the term "as a cultural outlook or worldview that
characterizes a community" (251). As he explains it:

> The author's position is not simply a personal account of himself
> or herself. The author is a complex individual who selectively

reveals (or invents) aspects of character pertinent to the rhetorical work required at the moment. The author's position represents a particular communal outlook that points toward agreed-upon values and invites the audience to join (or return to) the community. We can also understand the author's position as a persona, the mask of "I." (251–2)

I base my analysis of the character Florens on three elements of Killingsworth's definition. First, I take his term "author" to include "character" as well since Florens may be read as the implied author of the novel even as she is the author of her own story. Second, Florens's narrative is a complex retelling of her personal experience. At the same time, however, this narrative encompasses the stories of a diverse array of individuals and groups: the Portuguese slave trader D'Ortega; the Dutch plantation owner and homesteader Jacob Vaark and his wife Rebekka; Native Americans collectively and as individuals, such as Lina, who serves as a mother-figure to Florens; a minha mãe, Florens's biological mother; the blacksmith, the object of Florens's desire and the ostensible Other with whom she must ultimately disidentify; indentured servants such as Scully and Bond, whose contractual obligations are seemingly never fulfilled; religious groups such as the Anabaptists vying for ideological supremacy; and the other enslaved and free characters who populate the novel.

Finally, in occupying that ethical position, the narrator "invites [us] to join (or return to) the community" in an implicit summons, signifying an intersubjectivity with her as well as a responsibility that is ours to shirk or take seriously. Put another way, as readers, we are intimately linked to Florens, identifying with her imaginatively, because we are beckoned by the command with which she begins her story ("Don't be afraid" [3]); we undertake the same epistemological journey that she does in an experience that transcends the boundaries of one life. Implied in and intertwined in this journey lies the whole of human experience.

In reading the novel as an epistemological journey in which the reader and narrator coparticipate, I am also framing this chapter in terms of "narrative ethics," a phrase coined by Adam Zachary Newton to mean a reciprocal relationship between life and fiction (8). Newton's approach entails a "doubling of reality" (19), in which life is story and story is life. His methodology implies that telling (saying, writing) is an intersubjective relationship between storyteller and reader, as well as an interpretive responsibility that is both "intimate" and "ethical" in the moral sense (19). As already noted, I am not reading *A Mercy* in the *moral* sense of ethical; insofar as I am using the term (and its derivatives), "ethical" refers to human beings who possess moral agency, not necessarily that every reading of a novel or of its characters must be read on ethical-as-moral grounds. What I am suggesting instead is that in reading the novel, we enter into the lifeworld of the characters and for the purposes of this chapter, into the lifeworld of Florens, and we participate in her epistemic development. Her growth becomes our growth. As her story unfolds, her knowledge becomes ours. From a hermeneutical or interpretive standpoint, we experience *vzhivanie*, a term Newton borrows from the Russian philosopher Mikhail Bakhtin that literally means "live-entering": "a mode of active engagement with the other which mediates between identification or empathy on the one hand, and objective respect at a distance on the other" (85–6). Regarding the latter part of this statement, we are necessarily the readers of the novel proper and thus regard the characters respectfully (and) objectively. Regarding the former part, we experience this "live-entering" at the moment we first encounter the lifeworld of the novel. We are cautioned with the words, "Don't be afraid. My telling can't hurt you in spite of what I have done and I promise to lie quietly in the dark—weeping perhaps or occasionally seeing the blood once more—but I will never again unfold my limbs to rise up and bare teeth" (3). Initially we do not know that our interlocutor is Florens; we do not realize that we are not (necessarily) the only ones to whom she is writing/speaking; and we do not know what she has done except that it involves blood and, ostensibly, violence. Is it a confession, as she suggests? A dream? A story? Are we being summoned? If so, why?

Of origins and stories

In typical Morrisonian fashion, the narrative is complicated in that it parallels the nonlinear nature of memory and recall and (intentionally) invites no easy interpretation ("Unspeakable" 24). Readers are expected to work at it, to struggle over its meaning, to read (into) it. More than this, we do not initially grasp the significance of the narrator's relationship to nature and to the wild(erness). We are given a hint of this early on, however, with the imagery of the phoenix. In classical mythology, the phoenix is described as a bird that rises up out of the ashes once every 500 years, the ashes being those of its parent, carried in an egg of myrrh. According to Roelof van den Broek, who interprets the myth according to the Christian tradition, the bird symbolizes renewal as well as, among other things, time, the sun, empire, and resurrection (9). As we see through the development of Florens's narrative over time, the character reinvents herself by dying to one self and rising into another, inscribing the story of her life—inscribing herself—on the walls of Jacob Vaark's dying empire. Born again, she is poised to relate a tale of atonement and renewal.

In describing herself as the one whose limbs will remain closed and whose teeth won't be bared again, Florens suggests several things. First, as narrator, she has at least a hand in the creation of this particular story. In her now-famous essay, "Unspeakable Things Unspoken: The Afro-American Presence in American Literature," Morrison states that "Stories are the vehicles we use to share, translate, and interpret the human experience, and are, in terms, part of the process of canon building" (8) and that "Canon building is Empire building. Canon defense is national defense. Canon debate . . . is the clash of cultures" (8). She explains:

> [N]ow that Afro-American artistic presence has been "discovered" actually to exist, now that serious scholarship has moved from silencing the witnesses and erasing their meaningful place in and contribution to American culture, it is no longer acceptable merely to imagine us and imagine for us. We have always been imagining ourselves. (8–9)

Morrison's claims here apply directly to how we may read Florens's narrative as well as the function of the narrative in the novel as a whole. Taking the latter first, we may regard the novel as a(nother) contribution toward alternative canon-building (with Morrison, many other African American authors have already demonstrated a strong tradition in black literature) insofar as it intervenes in the classical literary canon as well as in the dominant narrative of empire building. These are intimately tied together because so much of received (written down and published, taught in schools) history of the settling of the Americas is a part of the dominant narrative, which has only relatively recently—within the past few decades—been called into question. *A Mercy* inserts itself toward the beginning of that story. To wit, the novel is set in the latter part of the seventeenth century, when Maryland was still under the rule of the British Crown, Virginia under Papist Portugal, and the transatlantic slave trade in its infancy. As Morrison tells NPR commentator Lynn Neary in an interview upon the novel's release:

> I wanted to separate race from slavery, to see what it was like, what it might have been like to be a slave, but [. . .] without being *raced*. Because I couldn't believe that that was the natural state of people who were [. . .] born and people who came here . . . that it had to be *con*structed, planted, institutionalized. So I moved as far back as I was able, when what we now call America was fluid, *ad hoc*, a place where countries from all over the world were grabbing at land, resources, and all sorts of people were coming. ("Morrison Discusses")

As such, *A Mercy* tells a different story with a radically different narrator of the "founding" of America as well as offers another piece of the complicated history of slavery and the institutionalization of racism.

On another, more local, level Florens's narrative plays a significant role in this larger one for at least two reasons. First, she is a literate black slave, unusual insofar as she was taught to read and write "every seven days" by Reverend Father, who would have been imprisoned or fined if caught (6). It was de facto or statutorily unlawful to teach slaves how to read or write, though in some cases exceptions were made for Sabbath instruction. While slave rebellions were relatively rare until the late eighteenth century, slave owners believed that literate slaves were more dangerous (and therefore liable to organize a rebellion) than nonliterate ones (see Rodriguez). Second, this is Florens's story to tell. In that same NPR interview, "Morrison Discusses," she tells Neary that Florens's contributions are in the first person and present tense "to give it the immediacy" of a story being told here and now. The other characters' life stories are presented from the third-person omniscient point of view, not only adding layers to Florens's own history but also filling in the gaps left by the missing parts, splicing through the weave of her narrative fabric. That is, the narrative is structured in such a way that it necessarily impels the reader not just to participate but to fill in what the narrative ellipses leave out. Because the novel opens with the penultimate part of Florens's story, it is particularly important that the reader join in by imaginatively completing the narrative writ large as well as those aporias in Florens's personal knowledge by making subtle connections, particularly those that come from the third-person omniscient narratives of Lina, Jacob Vaark, and a minha mãe.

Self-consciousness divided

Before Florens is able to reconcile her divided self-consciousness and arrive at self-knowledge via the vehicle of narrative, she is incomplete, her storytelling technique mirroring this ontological status. By examining the narrative structure as well as the novel's dominant trope of shoes, we may gain insight into how the writing mirrors this cognition.

The journey toward a unified self requires self-reflection and the presence of an "other" in the face of which the speaker can distinguish herself. At the outset, Florens assumes an interlocutor, suggesting that her story might be taken as a "confession, if you like, but one full of curiosities familiar only in dreams" (3). She even apologizes in advance for possibly confusing her listener/reader, admitting that "bright omen[s] clou[d] up too fast" and that in trying to recall events she "miss[es] much" (4), implying that she relies on her interlocutor to supply some of what is missing. Her "confession" implies an atonement (broken down by syllable, this word signifies "at-one-ment") that both enriches this epistemological journey and creates an intimacy that it warrants.

Storytelling is often nonlinear when it functions as memory or recall; thus, it makes sense that the story begins in medias res and that bits and pieces of it are missing. Being privy to the others' narratives offers the reader the chance to participate fully in the story by filling in what Florens necessarily omits because she lacks access to certain information. She begins her story by explaining that "the beginning begins with the shoes" (4), the trope that defines her subjectivity throughout most of the novel. "When a child," Florens explains, "I am never able to abide being barefoot and always beg for shoes, anybody's shoes." Florens's unusual desire to wear "the throwaway shoes from Senhora's house" warrants her mother's admonishment about her "prettify ways," which render her feet virtually useless on wild terrain. Wearing shoes that not only belong to someone else but are also broken and do not fit signifies that Florens has no identity of her own—or, at best, one that is very confused: she has "the hands of a slave but the feet of a Portuguese lady." Lina remarks that Florens's feet "will be too tender for life and never have the strong soles . . . that life requires" (4). If shoes function as a trope for Florens's self, then the soles—the shoes' foundations—are the homonymic metaphors for Florens's divided soul. As a child, Florens's soul is divided between a foundation in slavery and a misplaced desire for freedom.

Unable to walk through life literally on her own two feet and recognizing that there are "too many signs" that she is unable to read clearly (4), an incomplete Florens can only relate an incomplete story. As a child, Florens identifies indirectly with her mother, to whom she refers as *a minha mãe*, an impersonal form of mother in Portuguese, and incompletely with her half-brother, to whom she refers as her mother's little boy (6). Treated as fungible property of a Portuguese slave trader, Florens cannot comprehend the motives of a mother who would seemingly willingly offer her daughter to a stranger (Vaark) as partial payment for her master's debt. Referring to her mother's choice as an "expel" (137), she believes that her mother rejected her.

This "abandonment" ultimately becomes the core of her personality and shapes her relationship to herself as well as with others. Whether abandoned or forsaken as her mother's daughter, Florens identifies initially solely as a slave, worth "twenty pieces of eight" (27). Even when she is visited in her dreams by a minha mãe, who "is trying to tell [her] something" (137), Florens refuses to try to understand. Her relationship with her mother is limited to the distant "figure" with whom she interacts only imaginatively or in dreams, not someone with whom she shares an intimacy characteristic of a mother and child. As Cathy Covell Waegner explains, "in her frequent re-sightings of what I have called her ur-trauma, Florens increasingly sees the image of her mother as a generic, often foreboding figure" (100). Second, as Waegner's comment suggests, a minha mãe's presence (or absent presence) is not a comforting one. Morrison's *Beloved* reminds us that the damage that the institution of slavery does goes beyond the destruction of personhood. It rips apart families and makes the mother/child bond virtually impossible, or at the very least, perverted. Recall the novel's opening, "124 was spiteful. Full of a baby's venom" (*Beloved*, 3), which signifies Beloved's deep resentment against Sethe for what the daughter perceives to be the mother's betrayal. Having escaped from Schoolteacher, the cruel slave master at Sweet Home Plantation in Kentucky, Sethe, along with her children, is discovered to be living at the home of Baby Suggs, her mother-in-law, on the outskirts of Cincinnati. When Sethe and her children are confronted by Schoolteacher and his nephews in the shed in which she had shut herself and children, she attempts to murder the children rather than have them forced to return to Sweet Home and be subjected to the same tortured life that she had experienced there. Succeeding in killing only one—Beloved—she is haunted by the child's avenging ghost for years afterward.

Florens cannot "punish" her mother in the same way that Beloved asserts herself on Sethe, but she can—and does—distrust her mother by refusing to understand her when she appears in the girl's dreams, and the malice she does bear is transferred to Malaik, the foundling taken in by the blacksmith. The boy becomes, in Florens's mind, a substitute for the brother her mother chose to keep. Moreover, unlike Beloved, whose ghost is ultimately exorcised from 124, Florens's subjectivity will become complete through the process of her epistemic and ontological journey in which she has gained self-determination and self-recognition. I theorize this process of self-determination and cognition through the lens of phenomenology. Above, I demonstrated how Florens essentially lacks subjectivity—she is not tied intimately with her mother, who she believes has abandoned her, and as a young girl, she wears the mismatched and broken shoes of her Portuguese mistress. Moreover, Florens presents readers with an incomplete and confused narrative that leaves us with more questions than answers. In a word, Florens lacks something fundamental to humanity: her confession-as-narrative is a search for at-one-ment. Lack may be couched as desire, a key concept in the philosophy of G. F. W. Hegel. In the words of the modern philosopher Judith Butler, in addition to being "*intentional* in that it is always the desire *of* or *for* a given object or Other . . .

[desire] is also a modality in which the subject is both discovered and
enhanced. . . . [D]esire is a tacit pursuit of metaphysical knowledge,
the human way that such knowledge 'speaks'" (25). Florens does
not, of course, realize that she is metaphysically incomplete given
her unself-consciousness, but this "lack"—symbolized by the tender
soles of her feet—becomes poignantly clear when she encounters
the blacksmith for the first time.

Though the protective and loving mother-figure Lina warns
against him, Florens is immediately drawn to the man Vaark has
hired to build the wrought iron gates whose "kissing cobras" signify
the mansion's Edenic paradise will be ultimately compromised by
greed and pride. Indeed, she will go to any lengths to lose whatever
self she possesses. Lina recognizes as much: "a bleating desire
beyond sense, without conscience. The young body speaking in its
only language its sole reason for life on earth" (60). Knowing that
Florens will inevitably succumb to the charms of a tall, handsome,
free black man, Lina tries unsuccessfully to protect Florens from "a
man that had not troubled to tell her good-bye" when he eventually
departed the Vaark patroonship and meant only "disruption" (61).
It is this "disruption," or external force, a point to which I return
below, that ultimately enables Florens to complete this journey to
self-consciousness.

Returning to the concept of the desire, we see how it awakens in
Florens her first significant conscious encounter with self. According
to Hegel, the self is explicitly aware of itself only when it confronts
another self. This process begins for Florens when at about age 16
she meets and falls in love (lust?) with the blacksmith. That moment
awakens desire in her, which from a Hegelian standpoint is critical
to an individual's self-recognition. As the philosopher Alexandre
Kojève explains:

The man [sic] who is "absorbed" by the object that he is
contemplating can be "brought back to himself" only by a Desire;
by the desire to eat, for example. The (conscious) Desire of a
being is what constitutes that being as I and reveals it as such by
moving it to say "I." . . . Desire is what transforms Being, revealed
to itself by itself in (true) knowledge, into an "object" revealed to
a "subject" by a subject different from the object and "opposed"
to it. It is in and by—or better still, as—"his" Desire that man is
formed and is revealed—to himself and to others—as an I, as the

I that is essentially different from, and radically opposed to, and non-I. The (human) I is the I of a Desire or of Desire. (3–4)

Florens's desire for the blacksmith offers the opportunity for transformation by recognition of her *self* as separate from a sub/ob/ject other than herself. It is important to note that the "desired thing" is not necessarily sexual desire. Fundamentally, it is recognition by oneself and by another. The self-recognition is accomplished through a process of negation and assimilation: an "I [that] will be its own product" and whose process of becoming and evolution will be intentional and deliberate (Kojève 5). Florens's desire is, as we see, initially sexual and is directed toward the blacksmith, but she must transcend this human-directed desire to bring together the parts of herself (animal and human) into a coherent and spiritual whole. In order to be complete, she must move from an (unconscious) slave "by choice" or as the blacksmith asserts, from a slave to herself and to her passion, to a person who can "own [her]self" (141). This is not to suggest that in doing so she must annihilate the other (the blacksmith); rather, she must be able to affirm herself through and by recognition of the other.

Becoming Florens

The awakening of desire signals the beginning of Florens's becoming. Upon her initial encounter with the blacksmith, Florens notices how "the shine of water runs down [his] spine," and she is "shocked" at the feelings of sexual desire that have begun to stir inside of her. "There is only you. Nothing outside of you," she decides (37). Without realizing it, Florens has already submitted to this man, who has yet to even recognize or notice her: "Before you know I am in the world, I am already kill by you. My mouth is open, my legs go softly and the heart is stretching to break" (38). Florens has willingly placed herself as the subordinate in this unequal relationship, which she must ultimately reconcile in order to achieve self-consciousness.

Florens's visit to the blacksmith one evening can be read as a description of her unself-conscious animal passion. She steals a candle by whose light she is able to navigate her way to where he is sleeping, and the candle's flame scorches her palm. The burnt palm may remind Florens that she is ruled more by passion than by reason. The hand that holds the candle, whose light guides her to the blacksmith's quarters, does so without any sense of self-consciousness. (However, this same marked hand later becomes the measure of Florens's agency.) At this moment in her development, Florens believes that she is not simply a leaf on the blacksmith's tree, as Lina suggests; rather, she asserts, "I am his tree" (61).

The awakening of Florens's passion marks but the beginning of her path to selfhood. Perhaps the most significant part of Florens's journey to wholeness occurs when, sometime after the blacksmith has departed the patroonship, she must locate him because smallpox has (again) visited the Vaark patroonship. Rebekka's life depends upon the ill-prepared but willing Florens, who is sent out into the wilderness to find the blacksmith (whose whereabouts are only vaguely known) since he had successfully cured Sorrow the previous year. Shod with Sir's boots, which are lined with hay and cornhusks for comfort because they "fit a man not a girl" (4), we are reminded of Florens's continued bondage; it has simply been transferred from the D'Ortega plantation to the Vaark patroonship. Though she is able to read signs in nature and recognize the smell of animals to discern their level of fright or danger, Florens still believes she needs the protection of someone else's footwear to give her solid grounding.

The question of Florens's identity—and it is a question—is first signified by the letter she carries, written by Rebekka and meant to justify not just Florens's right to passage but whatever she might need to continue her travels. Significantly, the letter does not identify Florens by name. It refers to her only as "the female person into whose hands [the letter] has been placed" (112). Her very personhood is in question upon her arrival at Widow Ealing's, where she is mistaken for a witch. When the widow is visited in the morning by members of the community about her own Daughter Jane's suspicious wandering eye, one of the widow's visitors points his walking stick at Florens, asking who she is, determining finally that she "is Afric. Afric and much more, says another. . . . The Black Man is among us. This is his minion." Florens is confused by these comments since she believes that the letter she is carrying from Rebekka proves she "is nobody's minion but my Mistress" (111). Despite the letter, Florens is made to strip and is inspected like an animal: "No hate is there or scare or disgust but they are looking at my body across distances *without recognition*" (113, emphasis added). The inspection reinforces her sense of a missing self: to Jacob, Rebekka, and D'Ortega, she is simply fungible property; to these village people, she is "the black man's minion"; and to the blacksmith, she later learns, she is a slave (141).

After Widow Ealing's Daughter Jane helps her to escape what promises to become a mortal thrashing, Florens feels that something about her is changing, at which point a strong sense of *threat* to self begins to emerge clearly. She reflects on who she believes she is and has become, both ontologically and epistemologically. The passage is worth quoting at length:

> I walk alone except for the eyes that join me on my journey. Eyes that do not recognize me, eyes that examine me for a tail, an extra teat, a man's whip between my legs. . . . Inside I am shrinking. I climb the streambed under the watching trees and know I am not the same. I am losing something with every step I take. I can feel the drain. Something precious is leaving me. I am a thing apart. With the letter I belong and am lawful. Without it I am a weak calf abandon by the herd, a turtle without shell, a minion with no telltale signs but a darkness I am born with, outside, yes, but inside as well and the inside dark is small, feathered, and toothy. Is that what my mother knows? Why she chooses me to live without? (114–15)

Florens muses to herself that when she sees the blacksmith, she will be "live," which may be read both as corporeally alive and as existentially living. Here, Florens suggests moments of clarity heretofore unacknowledged, although her self-understanding remains inchoate. She has not reunited with the blacksmith, but at the same time, she realizes she does not belong anywhere specifically and that something "precious" (that heretofore unacknowledged Other self?) is draining from her. At Widow Ealing's home she believes herself not to be the black man's minion, though here she admits as much, as well as acknowledges being abandoned, defenseless, "a thing apart." Significantly, she begins to recognize and give more presence to the animal-like Other that comprises her alter-ego. Recall that in her opening narrative she hints at this by promising "never again to unfold [my] limbs to rise up and bare teeth" (3). At the same time, however, Florens acknowledges her wild side, a minha mãe declaring, for example, that she is "dangerous" and "wild" (4), and the blacksmith swearing at her, "you are nothing but wilderness" (141). It is this wilderness, this animalistic self that Florens ultimately reconciles into one knowing self, being in and of the world.

Though the blacksmith is a catalyst for Florens's coming to self-consciousness and epistemic awareness, he is neither the cause nor the agent of it. In what ends up being a penultimate moment of clarity, while Florens and Malaik are waiting for him to return from healing Rebekka, Florens dreams that she is near water and looking in, but she cannot see her reflection:

> I see my face is not there. Where my face should be is nothing. I put a finger in and watch the water circle. . . . I am not even a shadow there. Where is it hiding? Why is it? Soon Daughter Jane is kneeling next to me. She too looks in the water. Oh, Precious, don't fret, she is saying, you will find it. (138)

Florens wakes to "see" a minha mãe holding Malaik's hand, lips mouthing silent words that Florens cannot hear. At this moment, though Florens cannot see her reflection, she realizes this fact and is comforted by the ghost of Daughter Jane. What Florens does not yet know is that her self resides within her—and while not "recognized" by the blacksmith in the way I have been using the term, she is beginning to recognize the existence of her *self* and is about to unleash the wildness within her that may be the essence of what she needs in order to form a complete whole. The two related traumas of nonrecognition—at Widow Ealing's and at the pond where she cannot see her reflection—as well as a third trauma at the blacksmith's home ignite a force that drives Florens's complete transformation.

Upon arriving at the blacksmith's and finding Malaik, the foundling who she presumes to be a competitor for the blacksmith's affection, Florens reacts by promising to herself that "this expel can never happen again" (137). The beginning of the end—or rather, the end of the beginning—of Florens's narrative occurs when she cannot find Sir's boots—Malaik has hidden them (139)—and she must walk barefoot in and around the blacksmith's cabin, where "bits of metal score and bite" her feet (139). Eventually, this scoring will produce the scarring and calluses needed to toughen her skin and allow her to walk safely and confidently in a world in which she once was "too tender for life" and "useless" (4). Moreover, when she realizes through her violent encounter with the blacksmith that she is "nothing but wilderness" and "a slave by choice," Florens initially believes she is lost. Fighting the animal instinct to annihilate that which she believes has rejected her—"I hold down the feathers lifting" (140)—she finally awakens, comes alive, "to the dying inside" (142). The self dependent upon external references for validation has died; now the phoenix within rises up, feathers unfurl, and claws "scratch and scratch until the hammer is in [her] hand" (141–2). Ironically, Florens does not want to annihilate the force that struck her down, the one whose hands once had caressed her; she cannot fatally harm the one who initially awakened her desire. Though her "claws scratch and scratch until the hammer is in [her] hand" (142), "it dies in weakness". She is finally able to recognize the parts of her self, the "animal" within and the person without, taking ownership of her wildness and assuring her interlocutor that he "should be" afraid after all (157). "See?" She reminds the blacksmith, "You are correct. A minha mãe too. I am become wilderness but I am also Florens. In full. . . . Slave. Free. I last" (161). By reconciling her two selves and by transcending the other/self dialectic, she has recognized and affirmed that self to the one who did not, initially, recognize her as well as to herself. Moreover, she comes to realize that she is always already wilderness, signified by the verb "am" and is simultaneously in a constant state of becoming wilderness. Florens has finally arrived at the self-consciousness that she needs in order to assume agency.

Her demand for recognition by the external other has transformed into the confident narrator of her life. Florens's heretofore self-imposed subordinate relationship to the blacksmith is now a "female-looking shape marching" down the road toward the patroonship, "bloody but proud" (148), signaling a newborn wild animal sure of itself and wholly intact. The hand that once wielded fireplace tongs in an attempt to mortally wound the smithy is the one that inscribes her story on the walls of Vaark's empty plantation home. The novel—Florens's narrative—comes full circle when she admits, finally, "my way is clear" (157). The moments of trauma and force that mark both her literal path and her figurative journey are complete. Both Florens and the reader now grasp the significance of this rebirth and can fill in the gaps that Florens's telling has left out at various points in the narrative. As Butler explains, "The notion of 'inner difference' of the unity of opposites which is so central to Hegel's mode of dialectical thinking is enhanced through the notion of Force" (26). The Hegelian concept of force is crucial to the transition of the consciousness into self-consciousness insofar as it presumes an externality to which it is related (26). Without a forceful externalizing action, such as the blacksmith's "rejection" of her (as well as those I have already noted above), Florens might never have come to a complete cognition of her selfhood.

The myriad but vague references to her feet needing to be shod with Senhora's "pointy toe" shoes or with Sir's boots, her "prettify ways," and her "useless" feet "too tender for life" (4) finally make sense to the reader. Florens did not believe she possessed the agency that would have allowed her to walk, literally, on her own two feet because she had never been in complete possession of her *self*.

Conclusion: Narratology as epistemology

The narrative has come full circle now: beginning with "Don't be afraid. My telling can't hurt you" (3), it ends with the dare to be afraid, indeed. Both the story and its teller have become one. It is literally "in [her] hands," an oblique yet clear reference to the story Morrison recounts in her 1993 *Nobel Lecture* in which the bird (a metaphor for language) is the responsibility of its holder. The tale has metamorphosed from one being merely inscribed onto the walls with a nail to one in which the words "must talk to themselves," released into the world. Although the blacksmith may not be able to read it, the story and Florens remain. She *is* the narrative, embodying it through the symbolic journey in which the soles of her feet "[become] hard as cypress" (161), rendering her able to walk in the world. She embodies it through the imagery of the phoenix described both at the novel's opening (4) and at the end, during her struggle with the blacksmith ("The feathers close. For now" [158]). Finally, through the vehicle of narrative Florens has transformed from a waif hiding behind the skirts of her mother's apron to a woman "untouchable" and "un-rape-able" (152), sure of herself and the story she has to tell. In the words of Butler:

> [T]he Hegelian subject expands in the course of its adventure through alterity; it internalizes the world that it desires, and expands

to encompass, to be, what it initially confronts as other to itself. The final satisfaction of desire is the discovery of substance as subject, the experience of the world as everywhere confirming that subject's sense of immanent metaphysical place. (8–9)

Florens is clearly "of" the world not only when the blacksmith recognizes her wildness but also and more importantly when she herself has internalized it: she has become "substance as subject." This is most evident when Scully notices Florens returning from the blacksmith's:

> It was easy to spot that combination of defenselessness, eagerness to please and, most of all, a willingness to blame herself for the meanness of others. Clearly, from the look of her now, that was no longer true. The instant he saw her *marching* down the road—whether ghost or soldier—he knew that she had become untouchable. . . . [H]er change from "have me always" to "don't touch me ever" seemed to him as predictable as it was marked. (152, emphasis added)

In the words of Butler, "The subject journeys with compulsive metaphysical honesty toward its ultimate dialectical harmony with the world" (22).

In considering that narrative epistemology is constructed intersubjectively, we may view Florens's storytelling as a process of sense- and self-making. The desire that Florens exhibits throughout the narrative is not, as I have argued, for sexual gratification per se; that is a secondary aim. Her real desire, subconscious at first, is for self-knowledge and self-consciousness, which could only occur through recognition, and that could only come through the telling of the story. With the cooperation of the chorus of voices in the community—Lina, Jacob and Rebekka Vaark, Scully and Bond, Sorrow, and a minha mãe—who help to tell this story, as well as the reader, whose ability to fill in the gaps left by the others participate in making it meaningful, we have ensured that it is a story to "pass on" (*Beloved* 324). Though "pass on" may be interpreted in a number of ways, here the phrase should be understood as literally handed down: orally passed on to the next generation and, in the case of this narrative, also written down to be read. This is all the more important because the community in the novel has all but disintegrated. All that remains is the narrative. Inscribed on the walls, uttered aloud, imprinted on the pages of the book itself, the words themselves signify the novel as a collective work of art authored by and about what Morrison calls "the village" and "the community" ("Rootedness" 64). Florens's return to the patroonship, barefoot and wild, signals as much. Morrison explained to Neary that in creating the characters in *A Mercy*:

> I wanted this group to be sort of the earliest version of American individuality, American self-sufficiency, and I think I wanted to show the dangers of that. You really do need a community. You do need a structure. Whether it's a church, or religion, as Rebekka thinks. . . . There is no outside thing that holds them together.

Elsewhere, Morrison has discussed this same issue. Regarding the importance of the reciprocal relationship between the reader and the chorus, Morrison adds that the "presence of an ancestor . . . determined the success or happiness of the character. It was the absence of an ancestor that was frightening, that was threatening, and it caused huge destruction and disarray in the work itself" ("Rootedness" 62). Clearly this is the case not only for Florens but also for some of the other characters in the novel, such as Rebekka, Sorrow, Scully, and Bond, who are widowed, abandoned, and indentured, respectively, as well. At the same time, however, Florens has produced—and we along with her—an originary narrative that will sustain future generations.

Florens herself never explicitly learns the true reasons for her mother's decision to urge Vaark to settle on the daughter wearing the "way-too-big woman's shoes" (26). As readers and intimate participants in and cocreators of the narrative, however, we become privy to it via the epilogue in which a minha mãe is finally able to share her story of the Middle Passage, her destiny as the property of Senhor and his wife (166), and finally, her reasons for needing a mercy. It is indeed "a mercy" that Florens and not her mother or younger brother is traded to Jacob Vaark to settle D'Ortega's debt. What is more, Florens is enjoined to listen to *a tua mãe* now, "each night and every day until you understand what I know" (167), and because she herself has completed the journey to selfhood, she may be able to hear that which she could not hear before: it is "a wicked thing" to give dominion of yourself to another" (161). In the end, these words, too, are part of the story.

9

"What Lay Beneath the Names": The Language and Landscapes of *A Mercy*

Marc C. Conner

Naming the land: Mastery versus mapping

At the opening of her 1992 study of race and the American novel, *Playing in the Dark*, Toni Morrison announces the following ambition: "I want to draw a map, so to speak, of a critical geography and use that map to open as much space for discovery, intellectual adventure, and close exploration as did the original charting of the New World—without the mandate for conquest" (3). This idea of a "critical geography," I believe, forms a pervading concern of Morrison's novels, nowhere more so than in her ninth novel, *A Mercy*. On the first page of *A Mercy*, the narrator (who we later learn is Florens, a young woman of African descent whose quest has ended in frustration, if not failure) poses two short questions that will pervade the entire book: "One question is who is responsible? Another is can you read?" (3).

These twin questions, one addressing the issues of ethics and autonomy, the other the areas of knowledge and interpretation, form the heart of Morrison's investigations in this book. For this is a novel obsessed with the ethics of knowledge, a fascination that marks all of Morrison's recent work—witness her use of the Gnostic *Nag Hammadi* writings as the epigraphs to *Jazz* (1992) and *Paradise* (1998), which heighten our attention to questions of gnosis and the ways in which human knowledge can connect us to the divine. Morrison's narrative strategies at least since *Beloved* (1987) provoke the question of how we know what we know, the limits of our knowing, the dangerous uses to which our knowledge may be put, and the ways in which knowing can set us free, can even lead us to a metaphysical freedom. This explains her attraction to Gnostic writings, in which, as Hans Jonas explains, "the emphasis on *knowledge* as the means for the attainment of salvation, or even as the form of salvation itself," is essential (32). *A Mercy* introduces an additional concern to these abiding themes: the need to explore the connections between knowledge and landscape—the ways in which the human urge to know is related to the earth and our responses to the land. Morrison's need to understand *how knowledge and geography speak to each other within narrative* forms a defining concern of this novel.

Unlike many of Morrison's previous novels, *A Mercy* has no epigraphs to announce its fundamental elements; yet it too begins, before it begins, with—not language—but landscape: the title page reproduces a seventeenth-century map, "courtesy of the American Antiquarian Society." This map shows the mid-Atlantic east coast region of what will become the United States, with all the place-names emerging from the Native American civilizations that predate white presence in the land. The novel thus opens by depicting a land that is to some in the novel a brave new world and to others a very ancient, familiar landscape. Morrison's novels since 1977 have opened with sacred texts—either biblical quotations or quotations from the noncanonical Gnostic writings that are roughly contemporary with the New Testament. *A Mercy* suggests that the map itself and its place-names are sacred text, a secret code the interpretation of which can lead one to visionary insight, even union with divinity.

At the heart of Morrison's effort to understand the relations between language and landscape is the concept of dominion. Jacob Vaark, the patriarchal Adamic figure of the novel, seeks to claim, dominate, and define the land. His own house and demesne he calls "Jacob's Land" (91), asserting ownership and dominion. But his attitude meets its opposite in Florens: she is of (at least part) African descent, born a slave, without the concept of even self-ownership, and when she traverses the land she refuses to name or to enter into a relationship of conquest. Each character expresses a different relationship to the land, and hence to the idea of mapping. The result is to force the novel's readers to revise their own understanding of that "New England" territory presented on the title page. It is as if the map is brought into a different relief elevating what had been submerged and leveling out the definitions that had stood in the history books for generations. This is cartography as liberation, an opening up of vision, or, to invoke one of Morrison's favorite metaphors, a clearing away of cataracts.

Morrison attests that the novel began with her own interest in the land that was there before any European arrived to begin mapping, dividing, claiming, and replanting. She has said that the first book she consulted to prepare her for this novel was "called 'Changes in the Land' [by William Cronon[1]] [which was] about what grasses and seeds were here before Europeans came" (Brophy-Warren). This book, published in 1983, describes itself as "an ecological history of colonial New England . . . a history which extends its boundaries beyond human institutions—economies, class and gender systems, political organizations, cultural rituals—to the natural ecosystems which provide the context for those institutions" (Cronon vii). Cronon's argument in this book is consonant with Morrison's in *A Mercy*: "To the cultural consequences of the European invasion— what historians sometimes call 'the frontier process'—we must add the ecological ones as well. All were connected by complex relationships which require the tools of an ecologist as well as those of a historian to be properly understood" (vii). Cronon reflects on Thoreau's lament over the change in the land from the 1630s to the mid-nineteenth century, in a passage that could well describe the timbre of Morrison's novel in its mournful evocation of a landscape that, from our own perspective in the early twenty-first century, has always been already lost:

> There is a certain plaintiveness in this catalog of Thoreau's, a romantic's lament for the pristine world of an earlier and now lost time. The myth of a fallen humanity in a fallen world is never far beneath the surface in Thoreau's writing, and nowhere is this more visible than in his descriptions of past landscapes. (4)

Morrison's inspiration from Cronon's work reflects her fascination in *A Mercy* with the human interaction with the land—her desire to investigate, quite literally, leaves of grass, to borrow the famous phrase of another great American remapper, Walt Whitman.

The most important and transformative act of cartography in the novel is the naming of places, most evident in Jacob's naming the Vaark farm "Jacob's land." But of course, as the opening map suggests, this is a renaming, displacing the land's authentic name by the dominant assertion of his own proper name. Jacob violates the series of organic interactions that results in genuine human mapping, which is precisely the site where the human imagination and the physical land come into contact. As the cultural cartographer Tim Robinson has argued, "Placenames are the interlock of landscape and language," for in place-names we "hear the language as if it were spoken by the landscape" (155, 153). Jacob's act of dominant renaming violates this spiritual interplay between the created world and human utterance constituting a crime against the human function of language.

This is not new terrain for Morrison. For decades, her language project has constituted a remapping of physical, literary, and cognitive terrain. She locates American placelore in divergent, multiple existences and cultures. The most powerful example of this occurs in *Song of Solomon*, as Milkman, having heard the Sugarman rhyme and begun his own reconnection with his ancestors, begins to understand the defining interaction between land and the human imagination:

> He read the road signs with interest now, wondering what lay beneath the names. The Algonquins had named the territory he lived in Great Water, *michi gami*. How many dead lives and fading memories were buried in and beneath the names of the places in this country. Under the recorded names were other names, just as "Macon Dead," recorded for all time in some dusty file, hid from view the real names of people, places, and things. Names that had meaning. No wonder Pilate put hers in her ear. When you know your name, you should hang on to it, for unless it is noted down and remembered, it will die when you do. (329)

Milkman undergoes a change of consciousness through this new understanding of place-name; this realization of the sacred quality of the name and the space it signifies constitutes Morrison's definition of wisdom. Just as in religious texts, in which a sacred place and the naming of that place is inextricably linked, so too for Morrison the earth can take on a luminous relationship to language when that language rightly names and reveals the sacred quality of the land. This concept is identical to what Mircea Eliade describes as "the manifestation of the sacred," the "primary religious experience . . . that allows the world to be constituted, because it reveals the fixed point, the central axis for all future orientation" (23). This is precisely what Morrison's characters seek in so many of her writings—to name and abide in the land whose beauty and magic is so tantalizingly apparent to them, as when Paul D in *Beloved* recalls being "astonished at the beauty of this land that was not his" (268). Morrison's concept of the interlock of language and landscape parallels Tim Robinson's argument that "a landscape [is] not just the terrain but also the human perspectives on it, the land plus its overburden of meanings." It is in properly naming a place that this eruption of meaning occurs: "The act of naming, or of learning its name, strikes a place like lightning, magnetizing it, attracting observations and the accumulation of placelore" (163). Morrison suggests that the names of mastery, such as "Jacob's land," violate this analogy of language and landscape and that we must rethink our way back to the previous names, which held a sacred connection to the place named.

Jacob's journey: Creation, dominion, damnation

The novel's fascination with place-names, mapping, and the relation of words to landscape is indicated by its multiple journeys and explorations, when characters chart their way through previously unknown terrain. One such journey occurs in the second chapter, which is really the beginning of the novel's central story. This second chapter, though still narrated in third person, is limited to the consciousness of Jacob, the patriarch and controlling male figure of the novel. We first encounter Jacob, not in relation to the extended family of women that surrounds him, but rather as an archetypal male who journeys outward from his farm, into the landscape, to the decadent plantation of D'Ortega to collect a debt. D'Ortega's plantation, with its curious blend of Old World aristocratic fashion and the harsh brutalities of a Southern slave system, immerses Jacob in worldliness, the trappings of ineluctable human markings that determine his fate. But Jacob's initial approach to this land is less determined, filled with possibilities of choice, of vision, and of promise:

> The man moved through the surf, stepping carefully over pebbles and sand to shore. Fog, Atlantic and reeking of plant life, blanketed the bay and slowed him. He could see his boots sloshing but not his satchel nor his hands. When the surf was behind him and his soles sank in mud, he turned to wave to the sloopmen, but because the mast had disappeared in the fog he could not tell whether they remained anchored or risked sailing on—hugging the shore and approximating the location of wharves and docks. Unlike the English fogs he had known since he could walk, or those way north where he lived now, this one was sun fired, turning the world into thick, hot gold. Penetrating it was like struggling through a dream. As mud became swamp grass, he turned left, stepping gingerly until he stumbled against wooden planks leading up beach toward the village. Other than his own breath and tread, the world was soundless. It was only after he reached the live oak trees that the fog wavered and split. He moved faster then, more in control but missing, too, the blinding gold he had come through. (9–10)

This remarkable tableau of how humanity relates to the landscape begins with that mythical act of creation of the "new world," as the representative man steps through water onto shore; but the blinding fog suggests that he neither knows what this land will look like, nor, once he arrives, can he see the world from which he came. The immense promise of this land is suggested by the repetition of "gold," the "dream" of which will pull Jacob down into the maelstrom of the slave trade and cause him to miss the pristine beauty of this scarcely created, "soundless," still forming world.

Jacob is a version of the American Adam, but he brings his corruption with him. Immediately he leaves this pristine new world behind and returns to the world of trade and commerce, where he can obtain a horse to carry him across this strange land without "a deposit if the man signed a note: Jacob Vaark" (10). Morrison gives the name a portentous significance, for it is a name that carries an immense burden of meaning: the biblical Jacob, like Morrison's Jacob, is a figure of countless parts, described by Genesis commentator William Kass as "a man of many turns and many ways, the biblical counterpart of Odysseus" (405). His biblical roles fit Morrison's character with resonant precision: Jacob as the man of self-reliance and long endurance, but who also runs the risk of the sin of pride, of thinking himself sufficient unto himself: "Precisely because of his enormous talents and self-reliance," Kass writes, "he must avoid the all-too-human propensity to ignore or forget about God, to regard himself as his own self-sufficing source," for "like the builders of Babel, he—quite literally—dreams of reaching heaven" (406). This emphasizes Jacob's other defining characteristic, as the seer of visions and dreams, in which God promises "gifts of land, progeny, and a blessed name" (414). And the Jacob of *A Mercy* is simultaneously a worker or maker: the enigmatic name "Vaark" may derive, at least in part, from the Old English noun for "work," that is *weorc* with the additional implications of something that is done, what a person does; as well as the sense of moral works, the works done to attain salvation, as opposed to faith or grace ("Work"). In other words, Jacob is connected with the anti-Puritanical emphasis on attaining grace through works, a tendency that, as Weber long ago showed, feeds into the Protestant work ethic that so fueled America from its early colonial days to the present. In sum, Morrison has created a representative man who embodies both the blessings and the curses of the American Adam.

These concepts define Jacob Vaark, as he moves through landscape that, for him, only takes meaningful form in relation to himself:

> Despite the long sail in three vessels down three different bodies of water, and now the hard ride over the Lenape trail, he took delight in the journey. Breathing the air of a world so new, almost alarming in rawness and temptation, never failed to invigorate him. Once beyond the warm gold of the bay, he saw forests untouched since Noah, shorelines beautiful enough to bring tears, wild food for the taking. . . . Now here he was, a ratty orphan become landowner, making a place out of no place, a temperate living from raw life. (12)

Vaark is part F. Scott Fitzgerald's Jay Gatsby, marveling at the splendor of "the old island here that flowered once for Dutch sailor's eyes—a fresh green breast of the New World. . . . face to face for the last time in history with something commensurate to his capacity for wonder" (189)—and part Thomas Sutpen (*Absalom, Absalom!* 1936)—having risen from orphanhood to be a ruthless landowner, powerful enough to claim the land and transform it from "raw life" into his own "place" (*A Mercy* 12). Jacob Vaark's desire is similar to Sutpen's when Sutpen is turned away from the splendid Virginia mansion and determines that "to combat them you have got to have what they have that made them do what he did. You got to have land and niggers and a fine house to combat them with" (Faulkner 192). Both Jacob and Sutpen fall victims to the obsession of owning things, of taking the created world and turning it into one's own possession—a condition that Morrison has also adumbrated in Macon Dead, who imparts this wisdom to his son: "Let me tell you right now the one important thing you'll ever need to know: Own things. And let the things you own own other things. Then you'll own yourself and other people too" (*Song of Solomon* 55). And just as Sutpen seeks that fortune—and the dominion it would give him—in the West Indies, so too Jacob's fall will embroil him in the sugar plantations of that land so devastated by enslavement.

Yet like Sutpen and Gatsby, Vaark's doom has already been sown—he has entered into the economies of commerce and trade, and so when D'Ortega can only pay his debt in human flesh, Jacob agrees.

D'Ortega is not the serpent in the garden that tempts Jacob to his fall; Jacob already seeks his own doom. For when he leaves D'Ortega's plantation, he reveals the envy that he feels toward the wealthy landowner: "On his way to the narrow track, he turned Regina around, waved at the couple and, once again, in spite of himself, envied the house, the gate, the fence. . . . And realized, not for the first time, that only things, not bloodlines or character, separated them. So mighten it be nice to have such a fence to enclose the headstones in his own meadow? And one day, not too far away, to build a house that size on his own property?" (27).

At the chapter's end, Jacob's "dreams were of a grand house of many rooms rising on a hill above the fog" (35). The chapter concludes with Jacob mingling his earthly hands with the landscape itself: "He gazed at the occasional dapple of starlight on the water, then bent down and placed his hands in it"—as he imagines that landscape translated into the heavenly bliss he craves: "Right, he thought, looking at a sky vulgar with stars. Clear and right. The silver that glittered there was not at all unreachable. And that wide swath of cream pouring through the stars was his for the tasting" (35). Jacobs's vision here is a version of the "'incomparable milk of wonder" (Fitzgerald 117) at the heart of Fitzgerald's *Gatsby*. And, like Jay Gatsby, Jacob expresses a sense of prideful ownership of the stars themselves, mingled with a marvel at the beauty of this creation.

Morrison's theology:
The creator and the creation

A Mercy's great irony is that it begins with Jacobs's ethos of conquest and domination of the landscape, and readers might anticipate the Sutpen or Gatsby sort of story that American literature knows only too well, but at this point Morrison abandons Jacobs's dreams of dominion, and the rest of the book consists largely of the female voices of nondomination that seek harmony with the land. We see this in Florens's journey, which literally maps the remainder of the book and contrasts markedly with Jacob's journey. Whereas Jacob asserts a male language of dominion onto the land, Florens moves into and through a landscape in which dominion does not exist, and the only language available to her is a female language that does not wish to dominate, but only to find the way. Seeking the blacksmith, Florens begins her journey on a wagon that conveys two other women, who are "certain their years of debt are over but the master says no" (39–40), and also "[a] boy with a yellow pigtail . . . his hands tied to his ankles" (39). Florens travels through a series of sites of the have-nots, among the historical ciphers by and upon whom America was built: indentured servants, people who are the property of others, the poor and dispossessed and never-possessed—in short, those who have no place in this world, who make no mark upon its map. This litany of the preterite results in a new mapping of what will become America, revealing a thicker concept of slavery than Morrison has ever presented. She has said that her interest in this novel was in "a period before racism was inextricably related to slavery. The only place was this period before a race hierarchy was established legally and later culturally. . . . My book is pre-racial in that it happens before it became institutionalized" (Brophy-Warren). The resulting portrait of America shows that it is, among other things, precisely the product of a range of human enslavements.

This means, however, that Florens, like the reader, has no map to follow through this world. As an enslaved person who can claim dominion over nothing, not even herself, her only clues for place and direction are remembered words from her mistress Rebekka and the language spoken to her by the land itself. Rebekka has made Florens "memorize the way." Florens journeys first with the wagon, then takes "the Abenaki trail which I will know by the sapling bent into the earth with one sprout growing skyward" (39–40). This sapling signifies Florens's own situation: grounded into the earth, but stretching into the sky, seeking the freedom that can come only through successfully completing her journey. When the other travelers all make their escape, Florens knows she must also flee: "I go west into the trees. Everything I want is west." But Florens becomes confused, for she is not yet able to read the land, "Hard as I try I lose the road"; she then laments the signals the land sends her, "I don't know how to read that" (41). She lacks the guiding words that another woman could provide: "I need Lina to say how to shelter in wilderness" (42). Through Florens's initial journey, Morrison suggests the difficulty of navigating the wilderness without dominating it. Just as Florens seeks the language that will guide her to the blacksmith, so too Morrison herself is trying to write an alternative language that seeks not to master, but to harmoniously inhabit and traverse the landscape itself.

In seeking this alternative language, Morrison departs midway from the story of Florens's journey, and the narrative shifts to explore the crucial story of Lina, the Native American girl whose village was wiped out by smallpox, who was subsequently sheltered and named by "the Presbyterians," and then abandoned by them and acquired by Jacob. Native American characters and culture are consistently valorized in Morrison's work (we think of Sixo in *Beloved*, Consuela and the Algonquian girls in *Paradise*); Lina speaks for the values Morrison associates with native culture, and she also serves to express Morrison's contempt for the culture of domination asserted by "the Europes" who:

would forever fence land, ship whole trees to faraway countries, take any woman for quick pleasure, ruin soil, befoul sacred places and worship a dull, unimaginative god. They let their hogs browse the ocean shore turning it into dunes of sand where nothing green can ever grow again. Cut loose from the earth's soul, they insisted on purchase of its soil, and like all orphans they were insatiable. It was their destiny to chew up the world and spit out a horribleness that would destroy all primary peoples. (54)

Lina tells Florens a story that serves as a paradigm of the plight of the various motherless women in this novel. A mother eagle is defeated by a man who speaks the language of dominion: "The traveler laughs at the beauty saying, 'This is perfect. This is mine.' And the word swells, booming like thunder into valleys, over acres of primrose and mallow. Creatures come out of caves wondering what it means. Mine. Mine. Mine." He then strikes the eagle down with his stick. The mother, Lina narrates, is still falling, but the eggs hatch and live, just as she and Florens and Sorrow and the other motherless daughters do in this novel (62–3). The story is didactic, even obvious, but this is an important aspect of Morrison's writing—in many ways she is equally allegorist and novelist, having as much in common with John Bunyan as she does with Charles Dickens.

The trauma of being a motherless daughter expresses the heart of Morrison's social argument in this book. This condition makes Lina, Florens, and Sorrow *unpropertied*, subject to no one's dominion—which means they are subject to anyone's dominion. In a crucial passage, Lina prays that Rebekka will not die, not out of desire or love but out of the terror of being unclaimed in a predatory world:

Female and illegal, they would be interlopers, squatters, if they stayed on after Mistress died, subject to purchase, hire, assault, abduction, exile. . . . Sir and Mistress believed they could have honest free-thinking lives, yet without heirs, all their work meant less than a swallow's nest. . . . Pride, she thought. Pride alone made them think that they needed only themselves, could shape life that way, like Adam and Eve, like gods from nowhere beholden to nothing except their own creations. She should have warned them, but her devotion cautioned against impertinence.

As long as Sir was alive it was easy to veil the truth: that they were not a family—not even a like-minded group. They were orphans, each and all. (58–9)

Morrison's invocation of Adam and Eve conveys the fundamental sin that haunts so much of her writing: the sin of self-sufficiency, the prideful assertion that one is self-created, dependent on nothing. Her characters, one after another, realize their dependency on larger communities, whether these be ancestors (Son in *Tar Baby*, Milkman in *Song of Solomon*); neighbors (Sethe and Denver in *Beloved*); partners (Joe and Violet in *Jazz*); a larger concept of God than they had heretofore admitted (Deacon in *Paradise*); or a sense of commitment that goes beyond one's own desires and pleasures (Romen in *Love*). In this, Morrison pushes against the strong American motif of self-reliance. By making Jacob Vaark the center of this sin in *A Mercy*, she further participates in (and revises) the vision of Fitzgerald and Faulkner, whose Gatsby and Sutpen commit the same fundamental sin. Here Morrison's theology is resolutely orthodox: she perceives that at the heart of all sins is the rejection of the Creator. *A Mercy* is passionate about these religious ideas, particularly the figure of the maker; its theological position is expressed in the question of Isaiah: "shall the work say of him that made it, He made me not? Or shall the thing framed say of him that framed it, He had no understanding?" (Isaiah 29.16).

This theology is consonant with Morrison's other works, but *A Mercy* goes further in showing that the rejection of the Creator is also a rejection of the Creation, a sin against the earth itself. When Adam and Eve reject their created status, their subsequent punishment is not merely exile from Paradise, but a cursed relationship to the earth itself:

And unto Adam he said . . . cursed is the ground for thy sake; in sorrow shalt thou eat of it all the days of thy life; Thorns also and thistles shall it bring forth to thee; and thou shalt eat the herb of the field; In the sweat of thy face shalt thou eat bread, till thou return unto the ground; for out of it wast thou taken: for dust thou art, and unto dust shalt thou return. (Genesis 3.17–19)

Humanity's alienation from the land occurs in its first turning-away from the land's creator. Morrison makes clear that Jacob's grand vision of a magnificent home and lasting estate is precisely a crime against the earth. Lina laments that the "third and presumably final house that Sir insisted on building distorted sunlight and required the death of fifty trees. And now having died in it he will haunt its rooms forever" (43). The building of this house is a prideful crime against the earth that brings a wicked delight to Jacob: "when he decided to kill the trees and replace them with a profane monument to himself, he was cheerful every waking moment." But such a crime will bring judgment and justice, Lina knows that "[k]illing trees in that number, without asking their permission, of course his efforts would stir up malfortune. Sure enough, when the house was close to completion he fell sick with nothing else on his mind" (44). Jacob's final wish, to be carried into that unfinished house in his very death-throes, confirms that the house is his tomb, a monument to death, for in its construction Jacob has turned his face against the principle of life: "He went quickly. Screaming at Mistress. Then whispering, begging to be taken to his third house. The big one, useless now that there were no children or children's children to live in it . . . Lina felt as though she were entering the world of the damned" (50–1). This is precisely the wisdom contained in the "cursed is the ground" passage from Genesis, cursing man to "malfortune" indeed for his sin, as Kass explains:

> Man now knows that he is hardly a ruler; on the contrary, his choice for independence makes him like a slave who must work and serve the earth, in order to eke out a living for himself and his family. Woman periodically will suffer painful labor, but man will labor painfully all the days of his life. His portion is sorrow, sweat, toil, and death: the dusty earth opposes his needs, resists his plow, and finally devours him whole. (116)

In *A Mercy* Morrison offers a strong reading of Genesis 3, particularly its understanding that through his assertion of mastery man becomes "like a slave."

The female quest and a
new language for the land

The crucial chapter told from Rebekka's perspective follows Lina's
section. In Morrison's most extended foray into the consciousness
of a white woman, we see a remarkable expression of the different
relation women can attain to the landscape: not domination but
timelessness and harmony. The central part of Rebekka's narrative
is her journey by ship from England to America, in which she
traveled, "packed like cod between decks" in the "dark space below
next to the animal stalls" (73, 81) with a band of cast-off women,
aboard a ship called the *Angelus*. (Alluding to the centuries-old
Catholic devotion to Mary and the Incarnation, the ship's name
suggests complex ideals of motherhood.) Functioning like other
Morrisonian female communities (such as the Convent Women
in *Paradise*), "these exiled, thrown-away women"—prostitutes,
thieves, women "sent away in disgrace" (82)—give Rebekka the
courage to complete the arduous journey. Their voyage is a version
of the Middle Passage, certainly not as horrific nor as brutal, but
meant to evoke a certain parallel, to show that European women
and African slaves bear a certain sympathy in their fates, that each
is sent into a kind of slavery, and that slavery in America is more
multivalent than history has supposed it to be.

In a novel that is so obsessed with land, it is crucial that Rebekka
communes with the sea, which becomes another of her female
companions, offering her comfort, wisdom, and erotic pleasure:
"Then she talked to the sea. 'Stay still, don't hurtle me. No. Move,
move, excite me. Trust me, I will keep your secrets: that the smell
of you is like fresh monthly blood; that you own the globe and
land is afterthought to entertain you; that the world beneath you is
both graveyard and heaven'" (73). The women create a communion
moment, sharing wine (watery tea mixed with rum) and wafer (stale
biscuits) during their crossing, and in this moment they are, however
temporarily, free from the twin dominators of men and land, and
safe in the arms of the sea which is neither male nor land:

> Wretched as was the space they crouched in, it was nevertheless
> blank where a past did not haunt nor a future beckon. Women
> of and for men, in those few moments they were neither. And

when finally the lamp died, swaddling them in black, for a long time, oblivious to the footsteps above them, or the lowing behind them, they did not stir. For them, unable to see the sky, time became simply the running sea, unmarked, eternal and of no matter. (85)

This changed sense of time, indeed the absence of time in the human sense—time as the marked and linear progression through the hours, the time against which men like Jacob Vaark, Jay Gatsby, and Thomas Sutpen wage a hopeless battle—constitutes the novel's opposite condition to the ethos of domination and ownership. Here the women experience the evanescence of time, as they exist in pure eternity, almost in a womb-like fluidity in which time and death do not have purchase.

These two long chapters focused on Lina's and Rebekka's quests prepare us for Florens's longest chapter, which forms the novel's shaping narrative element—her journey through the landscape. Her journey has all the elements of a classic American quest narrative, as Florens works her way through brush and brambles, always heading north and west, encountering Natives who aid her on her travel with water and food, and a community of Puritans who associate her with devilry and "the Black Man" (109) and try to impede her quest. Florens's figure of aid, like Sethe's Amy Denver, is another young girl similarly suspected of witchcraft, Daughter Jane. In a complex blend of sororal sympathy, rebellious adolescence, and self-preservation, Jane guides Florens away from the oppressive, points out her way along the path, passes along the gift of eggs (always a complex symbol in Morrison's work), and inverts the demonic from a curse to an act of rebellion:

Daughter Jane hands me the cloth of eggs. She explains how I am to go, where the trail will be that takes me to the post road that takes me to the hamlet where I hope you are. I say thank you and lift her hand to kiss it. She says no, I thank you. They look at you and forget about me. . . . Are you a demon I ask her. Her wayward eye is steady. She smiles. Yes, she says. Oh, yes. Go now. (114)

The Puritans have taken Florens's letter from Rebekka, the letter that shows her property status and gives her identity, and Florens fears that now she is in greater danger. But her emotion—"I am a thing apart. With the letter I belong and am lawful" (115)—actually expresses her new freedom. No longer defined by the written word, no longer claimed by (and hence in the dominion of) another, she now is free to claim both the darkness and her desire for the blacksmith: "The sun's going leaves darkness behind and the dark is me. Is we. Is my home" (115). As her quest appears to be nearing a successful achievement, her remapping of the landscape seems complete, no longer defined for her by the language nor the geography of domination.

Although Florens is successful in her journey to reach the blacksmith, her true quest, to establish love between them—a love that would replace the lost love she experienced when her mother gave her to Jacob—ends in anguish and failure. She quickly realizes that the blacksmith's primary relation is with his adopted son, a relation that recalls for Florens the experience of her mother sending her away, "it is me peering around my mother's dress hoping for her hand that is only for her little boy. . . . This cannot happen. I feel the clutch inside. This expel can never happen again" (136–7). That original trauma of being forsaken by her mother has left Florens with a desperate need to be loved—she cannot yet possess herself, for she can only feel her worth if she is possessed by another. "I can never not have you have me" (137) she thinks to herself (and perhaps states to the blacksmith). This is a dangerous evacuation of the self, and one of the principal arguments of this novel is that such dependence is precisely another form of slavery. As the voice of Florens's mother will say on the novel's final page, "to give dominion of yourself to another is a wicked thing" (167). The blacksmith offers the same condemnation of Florens, "Own yourself, woman, ... You are nothing but wilderness. No constraint. No mind. . . . a slave by choice" (141). When Florens injures the boy, the blacksmith rejects her because of her dependence: "I want you to go," he tells her, "Because you are a slave" (141).

The blacksmith cries to her, "where is your ruth?" (140)—a fascinating word, already archaic by the late seventeenth century, it connotes sorrow for another, the quality of being compassionate, and even in its early usages it means "mercy" . . . precisely the philosophical concept that is the opposite of the worldview of slavery ("Ruth"). To enslave another requires complete disidentification with the enslaved, an alienation from her existence so thorough that no common cause can be found. There must be, in short, an absence of *ruth*. The term's most famous usage occurs in 1638 when Milton exclaims in the great elegy "Lycidas," "look homeward, angel now, and melt with ruth." Throughout *A Mercy*, Morrison shows a powerful fascination with Milton, which I have described elsewhere as Morrison's long "mediation" on ("Modernity and the Homeless"), and what Tessa Roynon designates as "the extensive dialogue between *A Mercy* and *Paradise Lost*" (45). This is particularly evident in the elegy's concluding words over the loss of a beloved friend, which certainly inform Florens's devastation at the blacksmith's "expel" of her: "But O the heavy change now thou art gone, / Now thou art gone and never must return!" (Milton, ll.163.37–8, 192–3). If Florens (and by extension America) is to be free, she must escape domination and attain ruth.

Joining language and landscape: The sacred sense of place

Yet this rejection of Florens is, ultimately, liberating, for through the blacksmith's rejection of her she is able to emerge as a storyteller, as a voice that can express itself—as, it turns out, the book's writer (or its writing). For now she is able to wed language and landscape, words and world, in a relationship that is harmonious and poetic, rather than dominating and enslaving. When the blacksmith rejects her, Florens strikes back with power and violence, generating fear in him ("Is that a tremble on your mouth, in your eye? Are you afraid? You should be" [157]) and, crucially, striking at him with his masculine tools, the hammer and the tongs. Her movement away from him is figured as an "escape," as she moves back into the landscape of ice and river with "no kicking heart no home no tomorrow" (158). Freed from her need to be dominated by the blacksmith, she now sees a natural world that she could not behold before: "It is three months since I run from you and I never before see leaves make this much blood and brass. Color so loud it hurts the eye and for relief I must stare at the heavens high above the tree line"(158). Florens then reveals that she has been sneaking into Jacob's ruined house at night and, on the floorboards, with a nail, she has been inscribing "the telling"—writing the story that we ourselves are reading, much like on the final page of *Jazz* when we realize that the narrator is speaking to us directly from the book we are holding in our hands. This remarkable moment is exactly what Tim Robinson describes as the event when language and land come together, when "the language and the place, the landscape, spoke with one tongue, and spoke of something that is in danger of being forgotten by the busier languages and places of the world" (151).

Florens suggests that she is writing the words in the hope that the blacksmith will someday come and read them, but she may also be imploring her mother to come one day and enter this house, "part the snakes in the gate you made, enter this big awing house, climb the stairs and come inside this talking room in daylight. If you never read this, no one will. These careful words, closed up and wide open, will talk to themselves" (161). The writing is Florens's effort to heal the rift in herself caused by the two "expels," twin rejections by mother and lover; yet through the writing, she is able to express her story and, ultimately, return it to the landscape—the mother earth—that she has never before seen with such glory and such power. Only when the words enter the world, when language and landscape blend, can each realize its original, creative glory:

> Perhaps these words need the air that is out in the world. Need to fly up then fall, fall like ash over acres of primrose and mallow. Over a turquoise lake, beyond the eternal hemlocks, through clouds cut by rainbow and flavor the soil of the earth. (161)

This passage echoes the process in which "little myths . . . tempt you to hear the language as if it were spoken by the landscape." Florens is learning what Morrison herself is seeking to achieve: "the idea of a deep connection between a landscape and its language" (Robinson 153).

Conclusion

The contemporary of Morrison's who best understands this interlock of world and word is her fellow Nobel Laureate, Irish poet Seamus Heaney, whose argument is remarkably consonant with Morrison's ideas of the sacred landscape evoked in language:

"our sense, or—better still—our *sensing* of place . . . was once more or less sacred. The landscape was sacramental, instinct with signs, implying a system of reality beyond the visible realities" ("Sense of Place" 132). This idea of landscape pervades Morrison's writing, a sacramental landscape, literally mapping the intersection of humanity and divinity. Her places are not merely human; nor are they entirely spiritual. They mark the intersection of the two domains and call us to remember, to think back to the time when places were called by their authentic names, as when Adam first named the creation. As Robinson notes, this is "true place, with all its dimensions of subjectivity, of memory and the forgotten." Robinson has coined a new term to express this vision shared by writers ancient and modern, "'geophany.' A theophany is the showing forth, the manifestation, of God, or of a god; geophany therefore must be the showing forth of the Earth" (163–4).

Thus Morrison engages in what the ancient Irish poets termed "Dinnsheanchas," defined by the Irish language poet Nuala ni Dhomhnaill as writing that "involved itself with the numinosity of place and the values of blood and soil which are fundamental tenets of cultural nationalism, indicating to us how or why a place comes to be 'notable'" (25). And just as Morrison seeks throughout her novels to give voice to the unspoken stories of African Americans at crucial junctures of their history, so too this numinous writing of place seeks "to encompass . . . the genealogies of powerful families, tribal lore, stories of conquest or migration, traditional laws and customs of the tribe" (ni Dhomhnaill 25). This is a poetry that yokes place to the most important elements within a people, to their sacred stories, their most luminous names. In this poetic effort in *A Mercy*, we see Morrison returning to her most cherished studies, the Middle Passage experience, the terror of being a hunted woman in the wild, the passion of men and women who give themselves wholly to each other. The concluding conceit, of Florens inscribing her tale on the floor of her dead master's unfinished house, is a brilliant analogue to Morrison's own project: to rewrite the defining American narratives of conquest and domination, and offer a powerful revision of the maps of mastery.

10

Visions and Revisions of American Masculinity in *A Mercy*

Susan Neal Mayberry

Morphing European thralldom into American-style slavery

A Mercy not only locates the metamorphosis of Old World serfdom in the New World, but it also highlights the origins of American masculinity. Appearing serendipitously in November 2008, at an historic moment just after the election of the first black president of the United States, Toni Morrison's ninth novel focuses on nation-building as she confronts America's foundational myths, including its creation of equal manhood. Morrison maintains that she wanted to tell the other story about the development of racism in the United States, not just "the Puritan, Plymouth Rock stuff" (Nance 48). She claims to have been looking for a period "before racism was inextricably related to slavery . . . before a race hierarchy was established legally and later culturally in the states" (Brophy-Warren 5).

Upon his arrival in North America, *A Mercy*'s European male shakes his head in puzzlement at a Virginia territory in which his friend is conflated with foe. Mulling over the brutal colonial uprising that has come to be known as Bacon's Rebellion, Jacob Vaark remembers the militia that pitted "blacks, natives, whites, mulattoes—freedmen, slaves and indentured" against the local gentry and the ruling class. The colonial elites responded by passing laws that hardened the racial caste as a way of controlling the colony's marginalized people:

> By eliminating manumission, gatherings, travel and bearing arms for black people only; by granting license to any white to kill any black for any reason; by compensating owners for a slave's maiming or death, they separated and protected all whites from all others forever. Any social ease between gentry and laborers, forged before and during that rebellion, crumbled beneath a hammer wielded in the interests of the gentry's profits. (11–12)

If increasing the enslaved black population enabled planters to reduce an armed white labor force and resolve volatile white class tensions, a by-product was the creation of a biracial society. Unsuccessful at eliminating Native Americans from Virginia, the laws helped to convert multiracial European thralldom into black American slavery.

Building a new national manhood

The injustice inspired by Virginia racial cast[e]ing helped to hinder the development of progressive notions of gender and sexuality as well. My analysis of Morrison's oeuvre tracks her ideas about American masculinity from the winding down of the Middle Passage to the 1990s—over 160 years. Viewed collectively, Morrison's male characters suggest that issues of race, class, gender, sexuality (and religion) cannot be segregated and that conflicts between African American men and women result not from sexual disease but from cultural dis-ease, the cure for which includes radical structural surgery. To single out Morrison's men is not to negate the preeminence of her women. It is, rather, to recognize the interconnectedness of the masculine and the feminine, affirming the balance between them. It also welcomes the androgyny endorsed by "black male feminism," a flexible black masculinity that eschews homophobia and encourages gender equality. Singling out men confronts the limitations while it simultaneously celebrates the power of authentic, multifaceted, African American masculinity— Morrison's "free black male" or Neal's "New Black Man."[1] As *A Mercy* traces the rise of slavery in the New World, it delineates the beginnings of (white) American masculinity, connecting it to burgeoning American capitalism. In the process, Morrison develops notions of homosexual masculinity more than she has done thus far, associating its fluidity with sensitivity to women and children, and defines the free black man via his disruptive presence and the complex nature of freedom.

Creating a man's castle out of "out there"

Most of the white heterosexual males in *A Mercy* are orphans trying to get a piece of the (New World) rock, and Jacob Vaark takes delight in any dangerous journey. So when he inherits 120 acres of a dormant patroonship in virgin North America from the Dutch uncle who deserted him, he seeks to conquer terra incognita and, named after the Old Testament Jacob yet looking a lot like a new English Adam, finds himself treading "the edge of an immense Eden" (Updike 112). [Un]fortunately, like that first Man, Jacob Vaark turns into a fallen man for all seasons. He despises Maryland's relentless heat, Catholic leanings, and flesh market, but covets the landed estates so strongly associated with masculine power among Europeans.

Morrison initially presents the image of Jacob as "ratty orphan become landowner, making a place out of no place, a temperate living from raw life" (13). In *Playing in the Dark: Whiteness and the Literary Imagination* (1992), she argues that "cultural identities are formed and informed by a nation's literature" and theorizes how "the image of reined-in, bound, suppressed, and repressed darkness became objectified in American literature as an Africanist persona." She outlines what has been on the "mind" of US literature since Emerson's *The American Scholar*: the "self-conscious but highly problematic construction of the American as a new white man" (*Playing in the Dark* 38–9). Collective hardship forces disparate but displaced Europeans to establish solidarity in spite of difference.

These new North American arrivals manage to constitute an American Africanism as darkness and savagery, a characterization that not only shapes and makes possible white desires for autonomy, authority, and absolute power, but also embodies major themes in American literature. A rebellious but serviceable black slave population, more accessible than the nonwhite indigenous population, handily enables otherwise disconnected white men to create bonds of privilege based on differences. In other words, the need for New World manhood and the color of skin transform European immigrants like Jacob Vaark into a new American male. Whatever his social status in London or Amsterdam, the white male immigrant becomes more of a "gentleman" in the New World. Shared guilt about being invigorated by rawness as he struggles to survive in a hostile environment, that is, "collective needs to allay internal fears and to rationalize external exploitation," persuades him that dark savagery is "out there" (44–5) and that his house makes him *the* Man.

Laying the brickwork for Jacob's jubilation

A Mercy individualizes the socialization of this new white man in the story of Jacob's money-brokering expedition to Maryland's Jublio Plantation on an October Sunday. Despite the lines he had to memorize in the children's quarter of a London poorhouse, which mandated contempt toward the vain, voluptuous "cunning of the Papists," enterprise forces the American moneylender to set aside his Protestant primer and his disdain for that "arrant whore of Rome" (15). Guilty pleasure ensues. Before he arrives there, Jacob has not been prepared for D'Ortega's iron-gated, honey-colored house, more like a palace or House of Parliament than a dwelling. Jacob begins climbing his American ladder with three brick steps. He has to stand back and retrace his steps again before he finds the focus of his mixed feelings in the form of a pungent-smelling cook and "a small, contradictory man" who answers the door before Jacob can knock, "aged and ageless, deferential and mocking, white hair black face" (17). Ushered into Portugal's rendition of a New World paradise by the courteously disturbing Angolan butler, Jacob becomes immediately ashamed of his appearance and almost overcome by the heat. He marvels at the dryness of D'Ortega's skin despite his heavy coat, silk stockings, and fanciful wig. They drink sassafras beer behind windows shut to the boiling air, and Jacob has his considerable hunger shrunk by food that is too heavily spiced and overcooked for his English taste. Directed from a small table dominated by graven images into a vast dining room space where the company just gets more inhibiting, he is made acutely aware of his rough clothes, perspiration-limp hair, body odor, and dirty hands stained with the blood of a young raccoon whose hind leg he freed that morning.

As a black woman smelling of cloves serves their meal, Jacob Vaark is compelled to listen to his host's financial complaints. D'Ortega's disaster amounts to the destruction of a third of his human goods while his ship lay anchored for a month one nautical mile from shore waiting to be filled to capacity. While the additional freight was delayed indefinitely, D'Ortega refused to cut his losses, the ship sank, and he forfeited not only the initial third but "all, except the crew who were unchained, of course, and four unsalable Angolans red-eyed with anger" (19). D'Ortega now wants from Vaark more credit and additional time to pay his original debt. The reference to chains and unsalable Angolans alone identify the "cargo." Morrison confronts the horror hiding behind the slaveholder's words by juxtaposing his financial loss, so personally painful to him, against his cavalier dismissal of human beings. While describing people in the crass monetary language usually reserved for expendable things, D'Ortega whines about having been fined "five thousand pounds of tobacco by the Lord Proprietarys' magistrate for throwing their bodies too close to the bay" and the associated expenditures of pikes, nets, and drays required to find the corpses and cart them away (18–19).

In telling this story, Morrison highlights the dullness of D'Ortega's sensibilities as she augments the blunting of Jacob Vaark's. Vaark has already heard the shocking outcome, yet he listens politely and with some sympathy to D'Ortega's details and, more repelled by the latter's inept commercial practices than his mistreatment of people, merely wants to avoid any awkwardness. Multiple feelings fight one another to a draw within Jacob's psyche: the temptation of Maryland's free trade versus his contempt for its Catholic government; admiration for D'Ortega's house versus abhorrence of the slave system that built it; the necessity to listen courteously to D'Ortega's tale versus disgust with D'Ortega's business tactics. Throughout, the presence of Jublio's provocative black butler and cook stand as steadfast reminders of the moral implications of free agency and the consequences of D'Ortega's business dealings.

Doing business with that arrant whore

Jacob Vaark also remains conflicted over his own Protestant plainness and childhood deprivation in the face of the Catholic planter's indulgence. He tries to tamp his envy of the D'Ortega's ostentatious display of wealth while entertaining himself with condescending thoughts about the couple's wasteful ways and fancied flaws in their marriage. Observing the silence of the two sons old enough to sit at table in silly periwigs like their father's, Jacob discovers his own speech stifled. He becomes uncomfortably aware of the widening gulf between communication and feeling: "Perhaps it was their pronunciation; their narrow grasp of the English language, but it seemed to Jacob that nothing transpired in the conversation that had footing in the real world" (20).

Their Portuguese accent, however, is not the problem. Instead, it is the "the face behind the face . . . the words hiding behind talk" (*Love* 28). The D'Ortegas' mask of social elegance and gracious propriety disguises their excess and abuse. Their conversation returns again and again to Portugal's Angolan slave pool: how the progression from herding cattle to trading humankind offers a swift and immensely rewarding profit; how difficulties encountered in this untamed world provide practically endless opportunities to display dedication to God; how caring for supposedly ill, definitely recalcitrant, always unpredictable labor virtually warrants canonization. Jacob suspects a staged performance calculated to make him sweat, and his humiliation sours into resentment. D'Ortega's sons also remind him of D'Ortega's newly acquired patrimony, even as the "third son of a cattleman, in line for nothing" (21), and of his own bitterness at having no offspring to benefit from the sweat of his brow. All three of Jacob's sons have succumbed to infant mortality; his 5-year-old daughter, tellingly named Patrician, died when a pull horse brought in to build his palatial house kicked her in the head.

Once more, it is a black presence, this time the clove-smelling cook, who distracts Jacob from his disruptive thoughts. During their inspection of his estate, D'Ortega pressures Jacob to take a slave in

lieu of cash; Jacob selects the cook "on a whim," and the cook offers
him Florens (27). A minha mãe's insight, sharpened from her own
unspeakable past, persuades her that the tall man sees Florens "as
a human child, not pieces of eight. She knelt before him. Hoping
for a miracle. He said yes" (195). Surrounded by slaves whose loud
silence reverberates like an afterboom and sickened by the idea of
a human trade, Jacob at first begs off. His acceptance of the child
as payment for D'Ortega's debt represents the final capitulation to
his overwhelmingly conflicted feelings. Helpless to collect the cash,
beleaguered by the prospect of a lawsuit unwinnable because of
his lower social rank, royally annoyed by D'Ortega's strut and the
suggestion in him of something soft, the skilled usurer feels "the
shame of his weakened position like a soiling of the blood" (27). So,
when he spots the piquantly smelling woman holding one child on
her hip, another hiding behind her skirts, he capriciously chooses the
woman. If a minha mãe giving away her daughter is the mercy that
haunts *A Mercy*, then Jacob's assent represents the new white father's
unscrupulous—even unwitting—surrender of his moral values to
his business interests. In *A Mercy* and elsewhere, Morrison suggests
that obsession with ownership kills American males, morally and
physically. If Adam's love for Eve causes him to eat the forbidden
apple, Jacob's compassion for the slave, induced by self-pity for his
bereft childhood, tempts him to take the girl. Naïve or not, Jacob
endorses slavery. Florens becomes one of the group of young women
he keeps as dependents, unpaid servants, and slaves.

It is not until the end of the novel that we fully understand
the actions of Florens's mother (a minha mãe), who has seen
the eyes of the "old married couple" and their lips ready for the
pleasure of young Florens's breasts. A minha mãe comprehends
that, with Florens's breasts rapidly rising and her compulsion for
fine shoes, there will be no safety (190–1). The mother cannot
know the self-centered motivation behind Jacob's sympathy for
orphans and strays, but she senses the creditor's compassion for
children. Like most of Morrison's white knights, including *Tar
Baby*'s sugar daddy Valerian Street; *Beloved*'s "bleached nigger"
Scots Quaker Edwin Bodwin; and, most similarly, its Sweet
Home, Kentucky's Mr. Garner, who "call[s] his own niggers men,"
Jacob is ignorant rather than good (260, 11). With his good-
natured but facile willingness to examine his motives, to consider
reasonably but superficially what appear to be his weaknesses, the

willful innocence of this New Eden's Adam makes him at least as dangerous as other Morrison patriarchs because the outwardly good man cannot control the savagery of the reckless boy within.

Transforming the frontier chronicle of conquest into the City upon a Hill

Morrison's design of Jacob's subsequent career reflects Michael K. Johnson's assertions about the influence of the frontier on American masculinity. Johnson finds the frontier narrative's chronicle of conquest a story of male identity formation, which rests upon the belief that an encounter with otherness transforms the subjectivity of the hero. The hero in effect becomes a new man and the representative of a new manhood. His masculinity outranks both the putative savagery of the American Indian and the ultracivilized maleness of the European because American manhood combines the best elements of both.

Thus, Jacob Vaark's encounter with D'Ortega, the effete upper-class, supercilious yet superfluous son, proves to the new white male that neither bloodlines nor character makes the Man. When he identifies the only things in the New World separating the worthiness of the Portuguese third son from that of the Anglo-Dutch orphan to be the degree of their things and the death of his sons, Jacob Vaark locates the source of white American masculinity. Morrison describes the epiphany which fuses sophisticated negotiator with the savage boy:

> Jacob raised his eyes to D'Ortega's, noticing the cowardice of unarmed gentry confronted with a commoner. Out here in wilderness dependent on paid guards nowhere in sight this Sunday. He felt like laughing. Where else but in this disorganized world would such an encounter be possible? Where else could rank tremble before courage? It was a curious moment. Along with his contempt, he felt a wave of exhilaration. Potent. Steady. An inside shift from careful negotiator to the raw boy that once prowled the lanes of town and country. (29)

Having sounded the wellspring of his potency and demonstrated his superiority by scornfully turning his exposed back during his final negotiations with D'Ortega, Jacob turns his energies into constructing his rendition of the Pilgrims' City upon a Hill. His Virginia estate would be purer, nobler than the decadent ones farther south, eschewing pagan excess and uncompromised by "wealth dependent on a captured workforce that required more force to maintain. Thin as they were, the dregs of his kind of Protestantism recoiled at whips, chains and armed overseers. He was determined to prove that his own industry could amass the fortune, the station, D'Ortega claimed without trading his conscience for coin" (32). So Jacob Vaark "secured a wife and someone to help her, planted, built, fathered. . . ." (ful)filling his Virginia version of Noah's ark (39). His limitations at husbandry, however, reinforce his ties to slavery. He ultimately makes rum-running, so closely intertwined with the slave trade, his primary enterprise.

Thenceforth, the language and behavior of the (ad)venture capitalist whose forename means "supplanter" increasingly indulge his willful innocence. Maintaining women to be more innately reliable than men, he permits himself to forego a dowry in exchange for sturdy female labor. Wary of dodgy males who might rape, pillage, or run, especially with a frequently absent master, he is reluctant to buy—or hire—men. Instead, he trades his neighbor grazing rights for free toil, making good use of indentured servants Willard and Scully, who pose no threat to women at all. He views the acquisition of Sorrow and Florens as rescue and partial replacement for Patrician: and if 7-year-old Florens's swimming in loose shoes gets kicked in the head by a mare, the loss "would not rock Rebekka so" (31). Only Lina (a.k.a. Messalina) had been "purchased outright and deliberately, but she was a woman, not a child. And there was a profound difference between the intimacy of slave bodies at Jublio and a remote labor force in Barbados. Right? Right, he thought, looking at a sky vulgar with stars. Clear and right" (40–1).

Good men endowing mothers and children with their rights too!

Morrison ultimately distinguishes the ethical [up]rightness of her ideal masculine by the respective quality of her male characters' connections with women and children: the less their wealth and rank, the more *A Mercy's* male orphans empathize with them. Vulgarly gentrified D'Ortega empowers the mother of his children to engage in pedophilia; while Vaark's rough youth enables him to understand that a street waif must depend on the kindness of strangers. Thus troubled by the exposed vulnerability of orphans and strays, Vaark saves from unlivable situations Messalina, Sorrow, Florens, and Rebekka, who comes to define him as the "true meaning of mate" because, like the others, she has been more abused by other competitive males (117). Rescue, however, eventually becomes another word for patronage and, finally, patronizing control. Few things reveal better the measure of a man than the way he treats others. A significant measure of Jacob's craving for absolute power can be discerned from his decision to establish a household of powerless outcasts—a cadre of subjugated women.

Messalina

Messalina's is a story of Native Americans "domesticated" by new white men to become financial, religious, and/or sexual commodities. Jacob purchases the Indian girl to help cultivate his farm while he awaits the European mail-order bride who will complete his estate. Even a 14-year-old with little knowledge of farming can see that his impatient desire for order makes Vaark a poor husbandman: he dislikes the look of unruly squash among tall corn despite the unmistakable value of vines smothering weeds. Displaced Messalina reinvents herself by teaching him how to survive in the wild, even as she struggles with the memory of her smallpox-soaked village infected and then set on fire by "Europes" in blue uniforms, who first shot the wolves sated on contaminated bodies. She appeases the guilt of having survived the destruction of her families with a vow never to betray or abandon anyone she cherishes.

The soldiers later turn Lina over to "kindly Presbyterians," who rename her "Messalina" for aging Emperor Claudius's promiscuously unpredictable adolescent wife "just in case, but shortened it to Lina to signal a sliver of hope" (55). The worthies, in turn, abandon her for promiscuity: "The Presbyterians stare at her face and the blood wipes on her clothes but say nothing. They visit the printer and offer her up for sale" (123). Having been randomly brutalized by her European lover, Lina is blamed for her own victimization by the same sort of "bloody, silly" white people (*Beloved* 198–9) who take her in and tolerate systematic wife beating.

Such uneven treatment teaches Lina to cobble together from all her experiences, indigenous and colonized, a way to exist in the world, eliminate everything else, and evaluate individuals one by one. Forced to become an exile in her own land and of necessity an expert in hermit skills, Messalina has learned to think for herself. "Europes" have taught her that their New Eden is a dangerous place for native women and children. Thus she, Florens, and Sorrow, "three unmastered women," and Sorrow's infant "out here, alone, belonging to no one, became wild game for anyone" (68). Messalina ultimately expresses her philosophy in her warning to Florens: "Men have two hungers. The beak that grooms also bites" (124).

Rebekka

Rebekka's story buries a different dimension of masculine dominance within the Enlightenment version of the trophy wife. Only two years older than her servant Lina, Rebekka has been bartered long-distance by her father to be Jacob's bride. Given the spectacle of public hangings and disembowelings she endured as a 2-year-old in religion-torn London, Rebekka manifests no fear of the savage wilderness her fanatically religious mother warned her about, and she commits to a pact of exclusive comradeship with her new husband "seal and deal": "He would offer her no pampering. She would not accept it if he did. A perfect equation for the work that lay ahead" (101). Yet this same solitary traveler who for six weeks "shat among strangers" packed like cod in the bowels of a ship flees from a majestically uninterested moose into her husband's arms, and she will increasingly confide her miseries to Lina alone. When Florens asks Lina why Rebekka is unwilling to accept her freedom to choose but rather runs frantically into Sir's embrace, Rebekka's sole female friend replies: "Because [now] she can" (83).

However committed to her role, the sturdy new wife does risk refusing Jacob's increasingly less practical gifts and offers an alternative view of what a good man might be. Rebekka tells her husband as she shaves him that good common people do not need such fripperies in a place where reputation is all. Asserting that "[w]hat a man leaves behind is what a man is" as he wipes his own chin and succumbs to the fever of building, Jacob informs his arranged wife: "Understand me: I will have it" (104). With dark-skinned Lina as witness and relief, Rebekka assuages her uneasiness by rationalizing that Jacob is home and happy—until they have to haul his deadweight into his uncompleted grand manor. Now Rebekka must fight smallpox without her "perfect mate" and choose between visitations from her outlaw soul mates or visits from the repressed Anabaptists in the nearby village.

In her pain Rebekka has her own epiphany about others: "What excited and challenged her shipmates horrified the churched women and each set believed the other deeply, dangerously flawed. Although they shared no common views, they had everything in common with one thing: the promise and threat of men. Here, they agreed, was where security and risk [i.e. freedom] lay" (115). If all the women must in one way or another navigate the nature of the man in charge, Rebekka believes she has found a mutually sufficient bargain: man and wife "leaned on each other root and crown" (102). When the root is gone, however, the crown has no clue that sustained risk is prerequisite for real freedom and that dependence on a single person is perilous. The newly recovered widow reverts to the life-denying religion of her parents and neighbors for the sake of safety, whispers to the Puritan Father to tell her what to think, and becomes more and more like a child.

Sorrow

Caught between the white devil and the deep blue sea, Sorrow presents a figure of life-affirming femininity among the male-dominated females of the Vaark household. Believing her to be a "lad," two sawyers' sons trawled her in out of the North River after she shimmied onto shore from the foundered ship where she had been braving icy weather alone with her imaginary Twin. The biracial daughter of a ship captain who prevented her from living on land and used her to sew sailcloth, she reacted with recurring boils and frequent wandering. Eleven years old and named for her abandonment, Sorrow is both wild and obedient and, as soon as she has her first period, pregnant—initially in silent submission to the sawyer brothers who take turns with her behind a woodpile and a second time from the hurried affair in a church pew with the deacon—or Sir—or the smithy. Since the look in her thick-lashed, smoke-gray eyes inflames Lina, Sorrow is prevented the company of Patrician or Florens. The child endures her sea-bound and then land-locked solitude by creating an imaginary friend she calls Twin, "who was her safety, her entertainment, her guide," especially after her first baby dies, from premature delivery, says Lina; from "breathing water under Lina's palm," speculates Sorrow (141, 145). Her second child, a daughter, survives—with the help of two flexible male castoffs and castaways, Willard and Scully.

Redefining homosexual masculinity

Social disdain and the master's death having taught them that there is no safety, indentured servants Willard Bond and Scully learn to think beyond patriarchal absolutes and, so are able to sympathetically address the plight of the various uprooted women and children in their adopted household. Putting their heads together, they see that beneath her calm Lina is simmering; Rebekka will marry the deacon soon upon serving out her mourning; "[v]ixen-eyed Sorrow with black teeth and a head of never groomed wooly hair the color of a setting sun" has suffered a sea change that, among all those altered after Jacob's death, looks like her salvation (59); and defenseless Florens has returned from the blacksmith having turned feral.

Morrison devotes more attention to homosexual masculinity in *A Mercy* than in any of her previous novels. Middle-aging Willard has yet to work off a passage lengthened from 7 years to 20 something for carousing, rabble rousing, and running away. At 14 he finds himself farming tobacco for a Virginia planter. Despite the brutal work, he enjoys the company of 23 racially divided laborers united in hatred of their overseer, and "[n]o women anywhere" (174–5). His physical load may have been lifted when the planter sells him north, but his days stretch out with no people anywhere. Like *Beloved's* Sweet Home men who show restraint when they run "smack into their nature" by "fucking cows, dreaming of rape" (140, 11), Willard endures hard days "watching cattle munch and mate" (174). Dreading what moves in animated darkness, suffering visions of living and dead from his solitary hammock, he welcomes the addition of a boy. Scully, "young, fine-boned, with light scars tracing his back," must complete his unrepentant but dead mother's punishment for lewdness and dereliction and then reimburse expenses claimed by the "father" who leases him to the Anglican Synod only to settle his balance and lease him again. Convinced his enslavement will expire before he does but unable to read the document he thinks will insure his freedom fee, he does not object to "lying with Willard when sleep was not the point" (67–8). Although he is smarter, soberer, and far more refined than Willard, 22-year-old Scully has also known no women.

Morrison presents Scully's sexual preference for men as a by-product of church politics. Complementing Willard, who concentrates on action, Scully considers himself an astute judge of character since he has seen more human folly than most people his age: "By the time he was twelve he had been schooled, loved and betrayed by an Anglican curate" (180). But Scully does not blame his ensuing flogging on the curate, who faced execution as well as defrocking had he not converted their affair into Scully's lasciviousness. Sully had simply planned to run away after the Synod sent him to work with a lone herdsman. A violent ice storm, however, destroyed most of those animals not huddled within the herd, while the herdsmen's bodies clung together in the warmth of the barn. Changing his plans and choosing to bide his time, Scully continues to display no carnal interest in females, though he quietly enjoys a "voyeur's obsession with Lina's body" as he watches her bathe in the river, "[l]ong ago the world of men and only men had stamped him" (179).

Morrison intimates that survival sometimes plays a crucial role in sexuality, and sexual choice often evolves out of early sexual experiences. Scully's past experiences, which incorporate mother, father, and church into one powerful trinity of influence, cause him to covet what he could not see elsewhere, a female letting down hair "aggressive, seductive, black as witchcraft" (170). Scully, nevertheless, perceives her nakedness as purity, her loyalty not as submission but as evidence of her own self-respect. Accompanying Willard in mocking Sorrow, he nonetheless prefers her complex mystery to the personalities of the other women. He judges her decisions as sound, her privacy as protection, and her "easy coupling a present to herself" (178). If Scully were interested in seduction, he would choose lying-in-wait Sorrow; if he were interested in rape,

he would select needy, self-blaming Florens. Sensing Rebekka's
transformation into a cold, disaffected penitent, Scully joins his
partner in attempting to placate her for the sake of old times and
ensuing practicality, but had he an option, he would prefer not to
interact with born-again Widow Vaark at all.

The social lives of both men improve with Vaark's building
project and the arrival of the blacksmith. Willard is especially
happy working with skilled labor again until he notices,
sullenly resents, and passively resists the *black*smith being paid.
The free black man merely chuckles at the bound white man's
need for masculine dignity and tickles his fancy by calling him
"Mr. Bond." Willard "knew his rank, but did not know the lift
that small courtesy allowed him" (177). Abused but appeased, the
indentured servant can now more fully appreciate the other man:
his craft, his charm, his open grin, his sexual allure to women.
While colonial law might not allow the white servants to be as
free as or as well compensated as the blacksmith, the free black
man helps them discover that a future might be possible. Their
rejuvenated imagination helps envision a different future. It is
Scully and Willard who deliver Sorrow's daughter and assume
godfather status afterwards. "Right fine midwife, I'd say," one
congratulates the other for cutting her cord. "No question," the
other man answers (157). These unmasterful white men help to
bring more than one new life into being. Recognizing "the gray
glisten of a winter sea while a ship sailed by-the-lee" mirrored
in her thriving newborn's eyes, Sorrow stops her wandering and
commits herself to the needs of her child (158). Mother and
daughter become integrated in the way that describes the free
black man—Complete.

In her tribute to her male couple's masculinity, Morrison suggests
that definitions then and now frequently belong to the definers, not
the defined. In 1690 it is primarily bloodlines, property, religion,
skill, courage and sexual preference—not race, sense or sensibility—
that constitute early American manhood. Unwitting definer Jacob
Vaark takes advantage of the girls' fears of other male predators
and their preference for purchased wife or servant instead of
prostitute to "save" them and make him look manly (133). He also
trades on a white indentured male partnership in his quest for new
world control. He considers the unencumbered African craftsman,
however, not yet a threat but a building brother.

Spotting the dangerously free black male

When Jacob dies of smallpox, all the orphans in his constructed family turn naturally to the free black man: a feverish Rebekka sends an eager Florens on a risky mission to fetch him. Although Morrison allows the male named for his craft few speaking scenes, he is omnipresent in *A Mercy*. Like Bill Cosey's complicated effect on people in *Love*, the blacksmith's intricate ironwork could be considered art or "a frivolous waste of a grown man's time" (59). But his laughing presence is serious. Unlike Cosey, however, this male rests easy in his skin, unaware of his disturbing effect, which cannot be narrowly defined: "Was he the danger Lina saw in him or was her fear mere jealousy? Was he Sir's perfect building partner or a curse on Florens, altering her behavior from open to furtive?" (147–8). As distracting savior, the blacksmith looks directly at but doffs his hat to Rebekka; as soothing devil, he creates a spectacular Edenic gate on which gilded serpents conclude in flowers instead of fangs. He cures Sorrow of smallpox. He awakens Florens to womanhood after which he leaves her without saying good-bye. He recognizes his heterosexual virility but respects the homosexual man.

Unlike the high-strung, single-note Guitar who claims black women as "mine" (*Song of Solomon*), the shape-shifting artist/healer seeks to realize certain inalienable rights for himself and his son. Welcoming Florens into his home with glee and open arms, he just as easily [r]ejects her for hurting his foundling child Malaik, and she responds violently to taking second place a second time to a boy. Her encounter with Malaik arousing her fears of displacement, Florens accidentally injures him and, in her childlike feelings of dependence, expects the blacksmith to protect her. Unlike Jacob, who survives by supplanting others, the free black male chooses his child, slaps Florens and calls her pleas of devotion empty-headed slavery. When he tells the groveling girl that she has opted to be a slave because she lacks constraint, growling, "Own yourself, woman, and leave us be," she rises up to attack her lover with his hammer (166). The blacksmith's assertion of self triggers the rage that Florens ultimately needs to break into a new appreciation of herself.

Accounting the African "too shiny, way too tall, both arrogant and skilled," Lina alone predicts "the breakdown stealing toward

[Florens's safe haven]. The only one who foresaw the disruption, the shattering a [dangerously] free black man would cause" (71). What his contradictory presence ultimately posits is freedom, as both a positive and a negative force. His dismissal of Florens allows her to connect the dots that determine her chart of freedom and put her story next to his: "You say you see slaves freer than free men. One is a lion in the skin of an ass. The other is an ass in the skin of a lion. That it is the withering inside that enslaves and opens the door for what is wild" (160).

Florens believes her withering was born in Widow Ealing's closet en route to her he-lion's lair. The smith's blow forces her to recall the humiliation of being stripped naked by Puritans believing her to be the Black Man's minion because of her skin. She recollects no emotion in their eyes, only an examination of her body "across distances without recognition." Being taken for the wild Other separates Florens from her lover, but it saves the life of the Widow's daughter Jane. The neighbors "look at you, and forget about me," Jane tells her, as she leads Florens to the stream that leads to freedom (133–5). Jane's decision to free a slave illuminates for Florens what freedom means. If Jane's strange wayward eye terrifies free Separatists, it awakens the slave girl to the accountability that comes with agency. Writing her female version of the story in the talking room of Vaark's abandoned Big House, she distinguishes between a simple display of power and the complex assumption of responsibility that separates free from slave, as she reminds the blacksmith about the Other thing: the "lion who thinks his mane is all. A she-lion who does not. I learn this from Daughter Jane. Her bloody legs do not stop her. She risks. Risks all to save the slave you throw out" (188).

Recouping the she-lion's mane-man

Like most of Morrison's novels, A Mercy ends inconclusively. We do not know whether or not Florens has killed the illiterate blacksmith or whether he ever sees what she has written. We can, however, compare the potential of the partnership between an artist/healer and a flourishing Florens with the Vaarks' "seal and deal." We remember Lina's erratic beatings by her learned lover,

Rebekka's shipmate Abigail becoming Captain's pick, Sorrow's rape by the sawyer brothers and the bribes brought her by the deacon, Scully's Synod-directed flogging—all caught by and in what Morrison names the master narrative or white male gaze, all victims of the new white man's uniquely American compulsion to control. We recollect the drayman's hand on Florens's behind in contrast to the Indian rider who offers her food and water even as he mocks her innocence.

Unsurprised to find betrayal the romantic order of the day, on the one hand, Scully finds the ravages of Vaark's death sad, "the consequences of women in thrall to men or pointedly without them." On the other hand, he draws hope from the curate's description of the mess existing before Creation, the "dark matter out there, thick, unknowable, aching to be made into a world" (182–3). Florens's willingness to put herself at risk and the blacksmith's free black maleness allow Florens to allow herself a mercy. Morrison claims a special affection for the girl who "learns the hard way that even love is no substitute for independent thinking." And as Kevin Nance observes, Florens "turns into something fairly feral, a tough-minded person, who's willing to stand up for herself. . . . Too bad about the guy, but at least she's meaner, and she might survive" (54).

As Morrison presages in her 1993 Nobel Prize lecture, Florens cannot fully understand how to be a woman until she knows what it means to be a man. She must accept the paradox that, though he cannot own any life, a man has to be free to possess a fully lived life as he simultaneously takes responsibility for all lives, especially the children's. She must also learn that a woman has "got to be a daughter first" (*Tar Baby* 281). Unforgiven and unforgiving Florens must comprehend that her withering actually began at her mother's side long before she entered the Widow's closet. Florens must decipher in full the ways of a new white man, a free black man, and a minha mãe's unspeakable words unspoken. Her mother's terrible gift to her is not a miracle bestowed by God but a mercy offered by a human: to be given dominion over another is a hard thing; to wrest dominion over another is a wrong thing; to give dominion of your [best] self to another is a wicked thing" (196).

The sole/soul mercy Morrison claims in *A Mercy* maintains that the New World Big House that Jacob built will be haunted by Florens until the women decide to burn it down. Since black male feminism allows both women and men to occupy a fluid space of contradiction somewhere out there and in between patriarchally imposed absolutes about religion, race, class, gender and sexuality, real freedom and respect[ful]able manhood remain enticingly possible for America's New Black Man. Because the new white man's construction of American masculinity has been compromised by African slavery, its hope now depends on the mercies offered (and accepted) by all those occupying the land of the free—and the home of Others.

NOTES ON CHAPTERS

1. Introduction: The Grace and Gravity of Toni Morrison

The following editions of Morrison's works are used in this chapter: *The Bluest Eye* (New York: Plume, 2005); *Love* (New York: Vintage International, 2005); *A Mercy* (New York: Vintage International, 2009); *Paradise* (New York: Plume, 1999); Sula (New York: Vintage International, 2004).

1 It is interesting to note that Morrison expressed similar sentiments about her own losses—the stars: "They [stars] used to be up there in Lorain. . . . As kids we saw the Milky Way. Seeing them was something you could count on. Life is different if you can look up and see the stars." See Adam Langer, "Star Power," Denard, *Toni Morrison: Conversations*, 213.

2. Separate Spheres?: The Appropriation of Female Space in *Paradise*

This chapter refers to the following edition of *Paradise* (New York: Plume, 1999).

3. The Working Through of the Disconsolate: Transformative Spirituality in *Paradise*

The following editions of Morrison's novels are used in this chapter: *A Mercy* (New York: Knopf, 2008); *Paradise* (New York: Plume, 1999).

4. Reclaiming the Presence of the Marginalized: Silence, Violence, and Nature in *Paradise*

The following editions of Morrison's novels are used in this chapter: *A Mercy* (New York: Knopf, 2008); *Paradise* (New York: Knopf, 1998).

5. "Some to Hold, Some to Tell": Secrets and the Trope of Silence in *Love*

This chapter refers to the following editions of Morrison's novels: *Beloved* (New York: Knopf, 1987); *The Bluest Eye* (New York: Rinehart and Winston, 1970); *Love* (New York: Knopf, 2003); *Paradise* (New York: Knopf, 1998); *Song of Solomon* (New York: Knopf, 1977); *Sula* (New York: Knopf, 1973); *Tar Baby* (New York: Knopf, 1981).

1 Pig Latin is an English word game where words are twisted to obscure and create confusion. Pig Latin had its origins in English language as early as the sixteenth century when people outside of the aristocracy made up their own versions of Latin. In its earliest uses, Pig Latin was a kind of "argot of the underworld, sometimes used in conversation to confuse outsiders." It has survived in the United States as a children's word game where children move the first consonants of a word to the end of the word and add the "ay" sound on to the consonant at the end, as inigpay atinlay" for "Pig Latin." See "What Is the Origin of Pig Latin?" *The Straight Dope* <www.straightdope.com/columns/read/2163/whats-the-origin-of-pig-latin> [June 1, 2010].

6. Power and Betrayal: Social Hierarchies and the Trauma of Loss in *Love*

This chapter refers to the following edition of *Love* (New York: Vintage International, 2005).

7. The Power in "Yes": Pleasure, Dominion, and Conceptual Doubling in *Love*

This chapter refers to the following editions of Morrison's novels: *Beloved* (New York: Knopf, 1987); *The Bluest Eye* (New York: Plume, 1994); *Jazz* (New York: Plume, 1993); *Love* (New York: Plume, 2005); *Paradise* (New York: Plume, 1999); *Song of Solomon* (New York: Plume, 1994); *Sula* (New York: Plume, 1982).

8. Narrative Epistemology: Storytelling as Agency in *A Mercy*

This chapter uses the following editions of Morrison's novels: *Beloved* (New York: Vintage International, 2004); *A Mercy* (New York: Knopf, 2008).

9. "What lay beneath the names": The Language and Landscapes of *A Mercy*

This chapter refers to the following editions of Morrison's novels: *Beloved* (New York: Knopf, 1987); *Jazz* (New York: Plume, 1993); *A Mercy* (New York: Knopf, 2008); Paradise (New York: Plume, 1999); *Song of Solomon* (New York: Plume, 1997).

1 This chapter refers to William Cronon's *Changes in the Land* (New York: Farrar, Straus and Giroux, 1983).

10. Visions and Revisions of American Masculinity in *A Mercy*

This chapter refers to the following editions of Morrison's novels: *Beloved* (New York: Knopf, 1987); *Love* (New York: Knopf, 2003); *A Mercy* (New York: Vintage International, 2009); *Song of Solomon* (New York: Plume, 1987); *Tar Baby* (New York: Knopf, 1981).

1 Riffing on Emerson's 1837 description of the "new white man," Mark Anthony Neal's study of the *New Black Man* embraces what several scholars have called black male feminism.

WORKS CITED

Primary sources

Morrison, Toni. *Beloved*. New York: Alfred A. Knopf, 1987.
—. *Beloved*. New York: Plume, 1988.
—. *Beloved*. New York: Vintage International, 2004.
—. *The Bluest Eye*. New York: Rinehart and Winston, 1970.
—. *The Bluest Eye*. New York: Plume, 1994.
—. *The Bluest Eye*. New York: Plume, 2005.
—. *The Dancing Mind*. New York: Alfred A. Knopf, 1997.
—. *Five Poems* (illustrated by Kara E. Walker). Las Vegas, NV: Rainmaker Editions, 2002.
—. "Foreword." *Love*. New York: Vintage International, 2005.
—. "Home." *The House That Race Built: Original Essays by Toni Morrison, Angela Y. Davis, Cornel West, and Others on Black Americans and Politics in America Today*. Ed. Wahneema Lubiano. New York: Vintage Books, 1998, pp. 3–12.
—. *Jazz*. New York: Alfred A. Knopf, 1992.
—. *Jazz*. New York: Plume, 1993.
—. *Lecture and Speech of Acceptance, Upon the Award of the Nobel Prize for Literature*. New York: Alfred A. Knopf, 1994.
—. *Love*. New York: Alfred A. Knopf, 2003.
—. *Love*. New York: Vintage International, 2005.
—. *A Mercy*. New York: Alfred A. Knopf, 2008.
—. *A Mercy*. New York: Vintage International, 2009.
—. *Nobel Lecture*. Nobel Prize. org. 1993. <http://nobelprize.org/> [Web. March 1, 2011].
—. *The Nobel Lecture in Literature*. New York: Alfred A. Knopf, 2002.
—. *Paradise*. New York: Alfred A. Knopf, 1997.
—. *Paradise*. New York: Plume, 1999.
—. *Playing in the Dark: Whiteness and the Literary Imagination*. Cambridge, MA: Harvard University Press, 1992.
—. "Rootedness: The Ancestor as Foundation." *What Moves at the Margin*. Ed. Carolyn Denard. Jackson: University Press of Mississippi, 2008, pp. 56–64.
—. *Selected Nonfiction*. Ed. Carolyn C. Denard. Jackson: University Press of Mississippi, 2008, pp. 198–207.

—. *Song of Solomon*. New York: Alfred A. Knopf, 1977.

—. *Song of Solomon*. New York: Plume, 1987.

—. *Song of Solomon*. New York: Plume, 1994.

—. *Sula*. New York: Alfred A. Knopf, 1973.

—. *Sula*. New York: Plume, 1982.

—. *Sula*. New York: Vintage International, 2004.

—. *Tar Baby*. New York: Alfred A. Knopf, 1981.

—. *Toni Morrison: What Moves at the Margins: Selected Nonfiction*. Ed. Carolyn Denard. Jackson: University Press of Mississippi, 2008.

—. "Unspeakable Things Unspoken: The Afro-American Presence in American Literature." *Michigan Quarterly Review* 28 (1989): 1–34.

Interviews

—. "Bench by the Road." Interview in *The World: The Magazine of the Unitarian Universalist Association*. January/February 1989, pp. 4–5; 37–41.

—. *Profile of A Writer: Toni Morrison*. VHS recording, London Weekend Television, 1987.

—. *Toni Morrison: Conversations*. Ed. Carolyn Denard. Jackson: University Press of Mississippi, 2008.

—. "Toni Morrison Discusses *A Mercy*." Interview by Lynn Neary. *Book Tour. National Public Radio*. October 27, 2008. <www.npr.org/templates/story/story.php?storyId=95961382> [Web. June 1, 2011].

—. "Toni Morrison: More Than Words Can Say." *Rolling Out* 3.43 (April 29, 2004): 16–17.

Morrison, Toni and Christine Smallwood. "Back Talk: Toni Morrison." *Nation* December 8, 2008. <www.thenation.com/article/back-talk-toni-morrison> [Web. August 10, 2010].

Secondary sources

Adamson, Joni and Scott Slovic, eds. "Guest Editors' Introduction: The Shoulders We Stand On: An Introduction to Ethnicity and Ecocriticism." *MELUS* 34.2 (2009): 5–24.

Allen, Walter R. "The Dilemma Persists: Race, Class and Inequality in American Life." *"Race," Ethnicity and Nation: International Perspectives on Social Conflict*. Ed. Peter Ratcliffe. London: UCL, 1994, pp. 48–67.

Als, Hilton. "Ghosts in the House: How Toni Morrison Fostered a Generation of Black Writers." *New Yorker* (October 27, 2003): 64–75.

Arthur, Rose Horman. *The Wisdom Goddess: Feminine Motifs in Eight Nag Hammadi Documents*. Lanham, MD: University Press of America, 1984.

Barchfield, Jenny. "Toni Morrison Inducted into France's Legion of Honor." <www.huffingtonpost.com/2010/11/03/toni-morrison-legion-of-honor_n_778315.html> [Web. June 6, 2011].

Baxter, Charles. *The Art of the Subtext: Beyond Plot*. Minneapolis, MN: Graywolf Press, 2007.

"The Bench by the Road: In Memory of Louis Delgrès, 1766–1802." Toni Morrison Society Biennial Conference Program (November 2010): 10–11.

Benston, Kimberly. "I Yam What I Yam: Naming and Unnaming in Afro-American Literature." *Black American Literature Forum* 16 (Spring 1992): 3–11.

Bent, Geoffrey. "Less Than Divine: Toni Morrison's *Paradise*." *Southern Review* 35 (Winter 1999): 145–9.

Bergoffen, Debra. "Queering the Phallus." *Disseminating Lacan*. Ed. David Pettigrew and François Raffoul. Albany: State University of New York Press, 1996, pp. 273–91.

The Bible. Introduction and notes by Robert Carroll and Stephen Pickett. Oxford: Oxford University Press, 1998. Oxford World's Classics. Authorized King James Version.

Boles, Janet K. and others. *Historical Dictionary of Feminism*. 2nd edn. Lanham, MD: Scarecrow, 2004.

Booth, Wayne. "Why Ethical Criticism Can Never Be Simple." *Ethics, Literature, and Theory: An Introductory Reader*. Ed. Stephen K. George. Lanham, MD: Rowman and Littlefield, 2005, pp. 23–35.

Bouson, J. Brooks. *Quiet As It's Kept: Shame, Trauma, and Race in the Novels of Toni Morrison*. Albany: State University of New York Press, 2000.

Brenner, Charles. *An Elementary Textbook of Psychoanalysis*. New York: Doubleday, 1957.

Brophy-Warren, Jamin. "A Writer's Vote." *Wall Street Journal* (November 7, 2008): W5.

Brown, Elaine. *A Taste of Power: A Black Woman's Story*. New York: Pantheon, 1992.

Butler, Judith. *Subjects of Desire: Hegelian Reflections in Twentieth-Century France*. New York: Columbia University Press, 1987.

Carson, Clayborne. *In Struggle: SNCC and the Black Awakening of the 1960s*. Cambridge, MA: Harvard University Press, 1981; 1995.

Chandra, Giti. *Narrating Violence, Constructing Collective Identities: To Witness These Wrongs Unspeakable*. New York: Palgrave Macmillan, 2009.

Cheung, King-Kok. *Articulate Silences: Hisaye Yamamoto, Maxine Hong Kingston, Joy Kogawa*. Ithaca, NY: Cornell University Press, 1993.

Chou, Shiuh-huah Serena. "Pruning the Past, Shaping the Future: David Mas Masumoto and Organic Nothingness." *MELUS* 34.2 (2009): 157–74.

Christopher, Lindsay M. "The Geographical Imagination in Toni Morrison's *Paradise*." *Rocky Mountain Review* 63 (Spring 2009): 89–95.

Claiborne, Corrie. "Leaving Abjection: Where 'Black' Meets Theory." *Modern Language Studies* 26.4 (Autumn 1996): 27–36.

Clarke, Simon. *Social Theory, Psychoanalysis, and Racism*. New York: Palgrave, 2003.

Clifton, Lucille. "I Am Accused of Tending to the Past." *Quilting: Poems 1987–1990*. Brockport, NY: BOA Editions, 1991.

Clinton, Catherine. "'With a Whip in His Hand': Rape, Memory, and African-American Women." *History and Memory in African-American Culture*. Ed. Genevieve Fabre and Robert O'Meally. Oxford: Oxford University Press, 1994.

Coffey, Jesse. "Toni Morrison Honored in Paris." *Lexington Literature Examiner*. November 4, 2010. <www.examiner.com/literature-in-lexington/toni-morrison-honored-paris> [Web. June 6, 2011].

Cohodas, Nadine. *Princess Noire: The Tumultuous Reign of Nina Simone*. New York: Pantheon Books, 2010.

Conner, Marc. "Modernity and the Homeless: Toni Morrison and the Fictions of Modernism." Address Delivered at Toni Morrison Society Biennial Conference. Charleston, SC, July 2008.

Cortina, Mauricio and Giovanni Liotti. "Building on Attachment Theory: Toward a Multimotivational and Intersubjective Model of Human Nature." Annual meeting of the Rapaport-Klein Study Group. June 11, 2005.

Cronon, William. *Changes in the Land: Indians, Colonists, and the Ecology of New England*. New York: Farrar, Straus and Giroux, 1983.

—. *Changes in the Land: Indians, Colonists, and the Ecology of New England*. New York: Hill & Wang, 2003.

Crouch, Stanley. "Aunt Medea." *Notes of a Hanging Judge: Essays and Reviews, 1979–1989*. New York: Oxford University Press, 1990, pp. 202–9.

David, Ron. *Toni Morrison Explained: A Reader's Road Map to the Novels*. New York: Random House, 2000.

Dreifus, Claudia. "Chloe Wofford Talks About Toni Morrison." *Toni Morrison: Conversations*. Ed. Carolyn C. Denard. Jackson: University Press of Mississippi, 2008, pp. 98–106.

Du Bois, W. E. B. *The Souls of Black Folk*. New York: Library of America, 1989.

Duncan, Patti. *Tell This Silence: Asian American Women Writers and the Politics of Speech.* Iowa City: University of Iowa Press, 2004.

Durrant, Sam. *Postcolonial Narrative and the Work of Mourning: J. M. Coetzee, Wilson Harris, and Toni Morrison.* Albany: State University of New York Press, 2004.

Duvall, John N. *The Identifying Fictions of Toni Morrison: Modernist Authenticity and Postmodern Blackness.* New York: Palgrave, 2000.

Ehrenreich, Barbara and Dierdre English. *Witches, Midwives, and Nurses: A History of Women Healers.* New York: Feminist Press at CUNY, 1993.

Eliade, Mircea. *The Sacred and the Profane: The Nature of Religion.* Trans. Willard R. Trask. New York: Harcourt, 1957.

Erickson, Kai. "Notes of Trauma and Community." *Trauma: Explorations in Memory.* Ed. Cathy Caruth. Baltimore: Johns Hopkins University Press, 1980, pp. 183–99.

Evans, Mari. "I Am a Black Woman." In *The Norton Anthology of African American Literature.* Ed. Henry Louis Gates, Jr. and Nellie McKay. New York: Norton, 1997, p. 1808.

Fanon, Frantz. *Black Skin, White Masks.* Trans. Charles Lam Markmann. London: MacGibbon & Kee, 1968.

Faulkner, William. *Absalom, Absalom!* New York: Vintage Books, 1990.

Fitzgerald, F. Scott. *The Great Gatsby.* New York: Macmillan, 1992.

Foucault, Michel. *Power/Knowledge: Selected Interviews & Other Writings, 1972–1977.* Ed. Colin Gordon. New York: Pantheon Books, 1980.

Franklin, Jimmie Lewis. *Journey Toward Hope: A History of Blacks in Oklahoma.* Norman: University of Oklahoma Press, 1982.

Freud, Sigmund. *Beyond the Pleasure Principle.* New York: W.W. Norton, 1920, rpt. 1961.

Getty, Adele. *Goddess: Mother of Living Nature.* London: Thames and Hudson, 1990.

Gilroy, Paul. "Living Memory: A Meeting with Toni Morrison." *Small Acts: Thoughts on the Politics of Black Culture.* London: Serpent's Tail, 1993, pp. 175–82.

Glotfelty, Cheryll and Harold Fromm. *The Ecocriticism Reader.* Athens: University of Georgia Press, 1996.

Gray, Paul. "Paradise Found." *Time* (January 19, 1998): 62–6.

Hamilton, Kenneth Marvin. *Black Towns and Profit: Promotion and Development in the Trans-Appalachian West, 1877–1915.* Urbana: University of Illinois Press, 1991.

Hartman, Saidiya V. *Scenes of Subjection: Terror, Slavery, and Self-Making in Nineteenth-Century America.* New York: Oxford University Press, 1997.

Hawthorn, Jeremy. *A Glossary of Contemporary Literary Theory.* 4th edn. New York: Oxford University Press, 2000.

Hayes, Elizabeth T. "The Named and the Nameless: Morrison's 124 and Naylor's 'The Other Place' as Semiotic Chorae." *African American Review* 38 (Winter 2004): 669–81.

Heaney, Seamus. "The Sense of Place." *Preoccupations: Selected Prose, 1968–1978*. New York: Farrar, Straus and Giroux, 1980.

Heinert, Jennifer Lee Jordan. *Narrative Conventions and Race in the Novels of Toni Morrison*. New York: Routledge, 2009.

Ho, Wing-ching. "Editor's Preface." *EurAmerica: A Journal of European and American Studies* 36 (December 2006): 515–20.

Hoofard, Jennifer. "An Interview with Toni Morrison: 'Thinking about a Story.'" *Writing the Edge* 17.2 (Spring 2007): 86–99. <http://woe.ucdavis.edu> [Web. March 30, 2011].

"Isis." *The Facts on File Encyclopedia of World Mythology and Legend*. New York: Facts On File, 1988.

"Isis Suckling a Young Horus." *Encyclopedia Mythica Online*. <www.pantheon.org/areas/gallery/mythology/africa/egyptian/isis-horus.html> [Web. October 17, 2011].

Jameson, Anna Brownell. *Legends of the Madonna*. Detroit: Gale Research Company, 1972.

Jaxon-Bear, Eli. *The Enneagram of Liberation: From Fixation to Freedom*. Bolinas, CA: Leela Foundation, 2001.

Jenkins, Candice M. "Pure Black: Class, Color, and Intraracial Politics in Toni Morrison's *Paradise*." *Modern Fiction Studies* 52.2 (Summer 2006): 270–96.

Jennings, La Vinia Delois. *Toni Morrison and the Idea of Africa*. Cambridge, UK: Cambridge University Press, 2008.

Johnson, Charles. "The Philosopher and the American Novel." *Passing Three Gates: Interviews with Charles Johnson*. Ed. Jim McWilliams. Seattle: University of Washington Press, 2004, pp. 53–67.

Johnson, Hannibal B. *Acres of Aspiration: The All-Black Towns in Oklahoma*. Austin, TX: Eakin Press, 2002.

Johnson, Michael K. *Black Masculinity and the Frontier Myth in American Literature*. Norman: University of Oklahoma Press, 2002.

Jonas, Hans. *The Gnostic Religion: The Message of the Alien God and the Beginnings of Christianity*. 3rd edn. Boston: Beacon Press, 2001.

Jones, Carolyn M. "*Sula* and *Beloved*: Images of Cain in the Novels of Toni Morrison." *African American Review* 27.4 (1993): 615–26.

Kakutani, Michiko. Book review of *Love*. *The International Herald Tribune*. Rpt. from the *New York Times* (November 6, 2003): 20.

Kass, Leon R. *The Beginning of Wisdom: Reading Genesis*. New York: Simon and Schuster, 2003.

Katz, Naomi. "For Love of a Sea Goddess." *Américas* 38.4 (1986): 40–5.

Kella, Elizabeth. *Beloved Communities: Solidarity and Difference in Fiction by Michael Ondaatje, Toni Morrison, and Joy Kogawa.* Uppsala, Sweden: Uppsala University Press, 2000.

Killingsworth, M. Jimmie. "Rhetorical Appeals: A Revision." *Rhetoric Review* 24.3 (2005): 249–63.

Kojève, Alexandre. *Introduction to the Reading of Hegel.* Ed. Allan Bloom. Trans. James H. Nichols, Jr. Ithaca, NY: Cornell University Press, 1969.

Lacan, Jacques. *Four Fundamental Concepts of Psycho-Analysis.* Ed. Jacques-Alain Miller. Trans. Alan Sheridan. New York: Norton, 1981.

—. The Seminar of Jacques Lacan: Book II, *The Ego in Freud's Theory and in the Technique of Psychoanalysis, 1954–1955.* Ed. Jacques-Alain Miller. Trans. Sylvana Tomaselli. New York: Norton, 1991.

LaCapra, Dominick. *Writing History, Writing Trauma.* Baltimore: Johns Hopkins University Press, 2000.

Langer, Adam. "Star Power." *Toni Morrison: Conversations.* Ed. Carolyn C. Denard. Jackson: University Press of Mississippi, 2008, pp. 206–13.

Ling, Peter J. and Sharon Monteith, eds. *Gender and the Civil Rights Movement.* New Brunswick, NJ: Rutgers University Press, 2004.

Little, Jonathan. "An Interview with Charles Johnson (1993)." *Passing Three Gates: Interviews with Charles Johnson.* Ed. Jim McWilliams. Seattle: University of Washington Press, 2004, pp. 97–122.

"The Louvre Invites Toni Morrison." *Louvre* (November 6–29): 1–14. <www.louvre.fr/media/repository/ressources/sources/pdf/DPToniMorrisonlightENGLISH_v2_m56577569831144595.pdf> [Web. September 19, 2011].

Mackey, Nathaniel. *Discrepant Engagement: Dissonance, Cross-Culturality, and Experimental Writing.* Cambridge, UK: Cambridge University Press, 1993.

"Magdalene, Mary." *Historical Dictionary of Feminism.* Ed. Janet K. Boles and Diane Long Hoeveler. Lanham, MD: Scarecrow, 1996.

Masumoto, David M. *Epitaph for a Peach: Four Seasons on My Family Farm.* New York: HarperCollins, 1995.

Mayberry, Susan Neal. *Can't I Love What I Criticize?: The Masculine and Morrison.* Athens: University of Georgia Press, 2007.

McDougall, Joyce. "Parent Loss." *The Reconstruction of Trauma: Its Significance in Clinical Work.* Ed. Arnold Rothstein. Madison, CT: International Universities Press, 1986, pp. 135–51.

Michael, Magall Cornier. "Re-Imaging Agency: Toni Morrison's *Paradise.*" *African American Review* 36 (2002): 643–61.

Michelangelo di Lodovico Buonarroti Simoni. "The Pietà." St. Peter's Basilica <www.saintpetersbasilica.org> [Web. May 18, 2011].

—. "The Pieta." Duomo in Florence. ALIMDI.NET/Raimund Kutter. <www.saintpetersbasilica.org> [Web. May 18, 2011].

Milton, John. *The Complete Poetry and Essential Prose.* Ed. William Kerrigan, John Rumrich, and Stephen M. Fallon. New York: Modern Library, 2007.

Minh-ha, Trinh T. *Woman, Native, Other: Writing Postcoloniality and Feminism.* Bloomington: Indiana University Press, 1989.

Morrisette, Noelle. "Both the Law and Its Transgression: Toni Morrison's *Paradise* and 'Post'-Black Feminism." *Cultural Sites of Critical Insight* (2007): 139–57.

Moss, Leonard W. and Stephen C. Cappannari. "In Quest of the Black Virgin: She Is Black Because She Is Black." *Mother Worship: Theme and Variations.* Chapel Hill: University of North Carolina Press, 1982, pp. 53–74.

Moyers, Bill. "Bill Moyers Interviews John Leonard." *Now,* November 28, 2003. <www.pbs.org/now/transcript/transcript_leonard.html> [Web. August 10, 2011]

Nance, Kevin. "The Spirit and the Strength." *Poets and Writers Magazine* 36.6 (November/December 2008): 47–54.

Neal, Mark Anthony. *New Black Man.* New York: Routledge, 2005.

Neumann, Erich. *Depth Psychology and a New Ethic.* Trans. Eugene Rolfe. Boston: Shambhala, 1990.

Newton, Adam Zachary. *Narrative Ethics.* Cambridge, MA: Harvard University Press, 1995.

Ni Dhomhnaill, Nuala. "Dinnsheanchas: The Naming of High or Holy Places." *Selected Essays.* Ed. Oona Frawley. Dublin: New Island, 2005.

Nussbaum, Martha. "Perceptive Equilibrium." *Love's Knowledge: Essays on Philosophy and Literature.* New York: Oxford University Press, 1990, pp. 168–94.

Olson, Lynne. *Freedom's Daughters: The Unsung Heroines of the Civil Rights Movement from 1930 to 1970.* New York: Scribner, 2001.

Pagels, Elaine. *Gnostic Gospels.* New York: Random House, 1979.

Parrott, Douglas M. *Nag Hammadi Codices V. 2–5 and VI.* Leiden: E. J. Brill, 1979.

Patterson, Laura Sloan. *Stirring the Pot: The Kitchen and Domesticity in the Fiction of Southern Women.* Jefferson, NC: McFarland, 2008.

Phelan, James. "Sethe's Choice: *Beloved* and the Ethics of Reading." *Ethics, Literature, and Theory: An Introductory Reader.* Ed. Stephen K. George. Lanham, MD: Rowman and Littlefield, 2005, pp. 299–314.

Prose, Francine. *Reading Like a Writer: A Guide for People Who Love Books and for Those Who Want to Write Them.* New York: HarperCollins, 2006.

Robinson, James M., ed. *The Nag Hammadi Library.* New York: Harpers, 1990.

Robinson, Tim. "Listening to the Landscape." *Setting Foot on the Shores of Connemara and Other Writings.* Dublin: Lilliput Press, 1996.

Rodriguez, Junius P., ed. *Encyclopedia of Slave Resistance and Rebellion, Volume 1*. Westport, CT: Greenwood Press, 2007.

Romero, Channette. "Creating the Beloved Community. Religion, Race, and Nation in Toni Morrison's *Paradise*." *African American Review* 39 (2005): 415–30.

Roynon, Tessa. "Miltonic Journeys in *A Mercy*." *A Mercy: Critical Approaches*. Ed. Shirley A. Stave and Justine Tally. Cambridge, UK: Cambridge Scholars Publishing, 2011, pp. 45–61.

"Ruth." *The Middle English Dictionary, 1100–1500*, online version. <http://quod.lib.umich.edu/m/med>. "Ruth" found at: <http://quod.lib.umich.edu/cgi/m/mec/med-idx?type=id&id=MED37312&egs=all&egdisplay=open> [Web. May 15, 2011].

Schroder, Nicole. *Spaces and Places in Motion: Spatial Concepts in Contemporary American Literature*. Tubingen: Gunter Narr Verlag, 2006.

Sempruch, Justyna. "The Sacred Mothers, the Evil Witches, and the Politics of Household in Toni Morrison's *Paradise*." *Journal of the Association for Research on Mothering* 7 (Spring/Summer 2005): 98–109.

Shields, Carol. "Heaven on Earth." *Washington Post, Book World* (January 26, 1998): 33.

Smith, Denitia. "Toni Morrison's Mix of Tragedy, Domesticity and Folklore." *New York Times* (January 8, 1998): E1 and E3.

Stave, Shirley A. "The Master's Tools: Toni Morrison's *Paradise* and the Problem of Christianity." In *Toni Morrison and the Bible: Contested Intertextualities*. Ed. Shirley A. Stave. New York: Peter Lang, 2006, pp. 215–31.

Tally, Justine, ed. *The Cambridge Companion to Toni Morrison*. Cambridge, UK: Cambridge University Press, 2007.

Tobin, Jacqueline L. and Raymond G. Dobard. *Hidden in Plain View*. New York: Anchor, 2000.

Toni Morrison Society. <www.tonimorrisonsociety.org/> [Web. March 15, 2011].

Tsai, Chia. "Historiography, Communal Identity and Feminine Jouissance—on Toni Morrison's *Paradise*." *Ou Mei yanjui* 38 (2008): 161–209.

Updike, John. "Dreamy Wilderness." *New Yorker* (November 3, 2008): 112–13.

Van den Broek, R. *The Myth of the Phoenix, According to Classical and Christian Traditions*. Leiden, Netherlands: E. J. Brill, 1972.

Van der Kolk, Bessel A. "Trauma, Neuroscience, and the Etiology of Hysteria: An Exploration of the Relevance of Breuer and Freud's 1893 Article in Light of Modern Science." *Journal of the American Academy of Psychoanalysis* 28 (2000): 237–62.

Van Deusen, John G. "The Exodus of 1879." *The Journal of Negro History* 21.2 (1936): 11–129.

Verdelle, A. J. "Loose Magic: A. J. Verdelle Interviews Toni Morrison." *Toni Morrison Conversations*. Ed. Carolyn C. Denard. Jackson: University Press of Mississippi, 2008, pp. 159–70.

Volkan, Vamik. *Blind Trust: Large Groups and Their Leaders in Times of Crisis and Terror*. Charlottesville, VA: Pitchstone, 2004.

Waegner, Cathy Covell. "Ruthless Epic Footsteps: Shoes, Migrants, and the Settlement of the Americas in Toni Morrison's *A Mercy*." *Post-National Enquiries: Essays on Ethnic and Racial Border Crossings*. Ed. Jopi Nyman. Newcastle upon Tyne, UK: Cambridge Scholars Publishing, 2009, pp. 91–112.

Wallace, Kathleen R. and Karla Armbruster. *Beyond Nature Writing*. Charlottesville: University Press of Virginia, 2001.

"Witch." *The Oxford English Dictionary*. 2nd edn. CD-ROM. Oxford: Oxford University Press, 1999.

Woodward, Joan. "Introduction to Attachment Theory." *Attachment and Human Survival*. Ed. Marci Green and Marc Scholes. London: Karnac, 2004, pp. 7–20.

"Work." *Oxford English Dictionary*.<www.oed.com.ezproxy.rice.edu/view/Entry/230216?rskey=2fzjB4&result=1&isAdvanced=false#eid> [Web. May 23, 2012].

Wyatt, Jean. "*Love*'s Time and the Reader: Ethical Effects of Nachtraglichkeit in Toni Morrison's *Love*." *Narrative* 16.2 (May 2008): 193–221.

Yoon, Seongho. "Home for the Outdoored: Geographies of Exclusion, Gendered Space, and Postethnicity in Toni Morrison's *Paradise*." *CEA Critic* 67 (Spring–Summer, 2005): 65–80.

Young, Allan. "Bodily Memory and Traumatic Memory." *Tense Past: Cultural Essays in Trauma and Memory*. Ed. Paul Antze and Michael Lambek. New York: Routledge, 1996.

Zauditu-Selassie, K. *African Spiritual Traditions in the Novels of Toni Morrison*. Gainesville: University Press of Florida, 2009.

FURTHER READING

Toni Morrison's fiction, rooted in African American history and culture, presumes a certain degree of knowledge about American history on the part of her readers. Many of the works below are intended for readers seeking a broader understanding of American/African American history and culture and a deeper insight into *Paradise*, *Love*, and *A Mercy*. The list also includes companions and guides for readers seeking ready references to characters, places, and events, critical studies on the novels in this volume and Morrison's other works. Two sources are especially noteworthy: a recent publication, *Toni Morrison*, by Pelagia Goulimari, which brings together the most current scholarship on Toni Morrison's writing and the Toni Morrison Society website [www.tonimorrisonsociety. org/bibliography3.html].

Beaulieu, Elizabeth Ann, ed. *The Toni Morrison Encyclopedia*. Westport, CT: Greenwood Press, 2003.

Carson, Clayborne. *In Struggle: SNCC and the Black Awakening of the 1960s*. Cambridge, MA: Harvard University Press, 1981; 1995.

Fultz, Lucille P. *Toni Morrison: Playing with Difference*. Urbana: University of Illinois Press, 2003.

Gillespie, Carmen. *A Critical Companion to Toni Morrison: A Literary Reference to Her Life and Work*. New York: Facts on File, 2008.

Goulimari, Pelagia. *Toni Morrison*. New York: Routledge, 2011.

Gray, Edward G. *Colonial America: A History in Documents*. New York: Oxford University Press, 2003.

Jordan, Don and Michael Walsh. *White Cargo: The Forgotten History of Britain's White Slaves in America*. Edinburgh, Scotland: Mainstream Publishers, 2007.

Katz-Hyman, Martha B. and Kym S. Rice, eds. *World of a Slave: Encyclopedia of the Material Life of Slaves in the United States* (2 vols). Westport, CT: Greenwood Press, 2011.

Kockelmann, Holger. *Praising the Goddess: A Comparative and Annotated Re-Edition of Six Demotic Hymns and Praises to Isis*. Berlin, Germany: Walter de Gruyter, 2008.

Lewis, Charlene M. Boyer. *Ladies and Gentlemen on Display: Planter Society at the Virginia Springs 1790–1860*. Charlottesville: University Press of Virginia, 2001.

Lowery, Charles D. and John F. Marszalek, eds. *The Greenwood Encyclopedia of African American Civil Rights: From Emancipation to the Twenty-First Century* (2 vols). Westport, CT: Greenwood Press, 2003.

Martin, Sean. *The Gnostics: The First Christian Heretics*. Harpenden, UK: Pocket Essentials, 2006.

O'Rourke, David K. *How America's First Settlers Invented Chattel Slavery: dehumanizing Native Americans and Africans with Language, Laws, Guns, and Religion*. New York: Peter Lang, 2005.

Rawick, George P. *The American Slave: A Composite Autobiography* (Vol. 16). Westport, CT: Greenwood Press, 1972.

Reames, Kelly. *Toni Morrison's Paradise: A Reader's Guide*. New York: Continuum, 2001.

Roberson, Gloria Grant. *The World of Toni Morrison: A Guide to Characters and Places in Her Novels*. Westport, CT: Greenwood Press, 2003.

Sitkoff, Harvard. *The Struggle for Black Equality, 1954–1980*. New York: Hill and Wang, 1981.

Summa, K. *The Novels of Toni Morrison: A Study in Race, Gender, and Class*. New Delhi, India: Prestige Books, 1998.

Wilkerson, Isabel. *The Warmth of Other Suns: The Epic Story of America's Great Migration*. New York: Random House, 2010.

Wright, Donald R. *African Americans in the Colonial Era: From African Origins through the American Revolution*. Wheeling, IL: Harlan Davidson, Inc., 1990, 2000.

NOTES ON CONTRIBUTORS

Volume editor

Lucille P. Fultz is Associate Professor Emerita in English at Rice University. She is the author of *Toni Morrison: Playing with Difference* (University of Illinois Press, 2003), winner of the Toni Morrison Society Book Award in 2005; cocontributing editor of *Double Stitch: Black Women Write About Mothers and Daughters* (Beacon Press, 1991); former associate editor of *SAGE: A Scholarly Journal on Black Women*. She has published articles and reviews on Toni Morrison's fiction and served as peer reviewer for several literary journals. Excerpts from her work have been published in Harold Bloom's *Guides*. Fultz's essay, "*Love*: An Elegy for the African American Community," appears in a festschrift presented to Toni Morrison on the occasion of her eightieth birthday.

Contributors

Herman Beavers is Associate Professor of English at the University of Pennsylvania, where he teaches courses in Twentieth-Century African American literature. He is the author of *Wrestling Angels into Song: The Fictions of Ernest J. Gaines and James A. McPherson* and the poetry chapbook, *A Neighborhood of Feeling*. After spending the 2009–10 academic year as Visiting Fellow at Princeton's Center for African American Studies, he is completing two projects: a scholarly monograph on jazz and the politics of social conduct and another that utilizes chaos and system theory to read canonical texts in African American literature.

Jami Carlacio is the editor of the collection titled *The Fiction of Toni Morrison: Reading and Writing on Race, Culture, and Identity*. After having taught writing and literature since the early 1990s, she has shifted her focus to education policy. She still produces scholarship in her former areas of interest, including the fiction of Toni Morrison, digital media and composition, and the literacy practices of secondary and postsecondary students. She has most recently published (with Lance Heidig) "Teaching Digital Literacy Digitally: A Collaborative Approach" (in *Dancing with Digital Natives: Staying in Step with the Generation That's Transforming the Way Business Is Done*. Ed. Heidi Gautschi and Michelle Manafy, Medford, NJ: Cyberage Books, 2011).

Marc C. Conner is Professor of English and Director of African-American Studies at Washington and Lee University in Virginia. His books include *The Aesthetics of Toni Morrison: Speaking the Unspeakable*, and *Charles Johnson: The Novelist as Philosopher* (with William Nash), both published by the University Press of Mississippi, and *The Poetry of James Joyce Reconsidered*, from the University Press of Florida. In addition, Conner has published dozens of essays and reviews on American and Irish Modernism.

Carolyn Denard is Founder and Board Chair of the Toni Morrison Society. She currently serves as Assistant Vice Provost for Academic Affairs at Emory University. Her research focuses on African American myths, ethics, and cultural tropes in Toni Morrison's fiction. She has contributed to critical anthologies and essay collections on Morrison's work. She is editor of *What Moves at the Margin: Selected Non-Fiction* by Toni Morrison and *Toni Morrison: Conversations*, a collection of interviews. Denard is currently completing a book-length study on history and community in selected Morrison novels.

Gurleen Grewal is Associate Professor of English at the University of South Florida, where she has taught and published in women's studies, global postcolonial literature, and ethnic literatures of the United States. Her book *Circles of Sorrow/Lines of Struggle: The Novels of Toni Morrison* was awarded the Toni Morrison Society Book Prize in 2000. Grewal is the recipient of two university-wide teaching awards and the ACLS Contemplative Practice Fellowship in 2007. Since 2009 she has served as the founding Director of the Center for India Studies at USF Tampa. She is currently working on her book *Nature Consciousness: Contemplative Environmental Writings* (working title).

Susan Neal Mayberry is Professor of English at Alfred University. She writes on Early Modern literature, literature of the American South, African American literature, and Toni Morrison. She explores the masculine and Morrison in *Can't I Love What I Criticize?* (University of Georgia Press, 2007). Mayberry is presently working on a multidisciplinary project—*Thoroughly Modern, Theatrically Classical Dames*—that considers how contemporary British classical actresses who are regarded worldwide far more seriously than American movie stars but are paid far less even though they (British actresses) have influenced and been affected by changes in the modern roles of women on both sides of the Atlantic. Mayberry is a participant in the Shakespeare Association of America and a life member of the Toni Morrison Society.

Aoi Mori is Professor of English at Hiroshima Jogakuin University, Japan. She was the recipient of a Fulbright Fellowship affiliated with State University of New York, Buffalo, where she received her Ph.D. in English. In 2004, she spent a sabbatical year in African American Studies at Princeton University. She is the author of the following books: *Toni Morrison and Womanist Discourse* (Peter Lang, 1999) and *Toni Morrison Paradaisu wo Yomu* (*African-American History and Creativity in Toni Morrison's Paradise*) (Sairyu-sha, 2009). Mori is coeditor of *Gendai Sakka Gaido 4 Toni Morison* (*Guide to Contemporary Authors 4: Toni Morrison*) (Sairyu-sha, 2000).

Evelyn Jaffe Schreiber is Associate Professor of English at the George Washington University in Washington, DC. Her first book, *Subversive Voices: Eroticizing the Other in William Faulkner and Toni Morrison*, examines identity and race via the theory of Jacques Lacan and cultural studies. The book was awarded the Toni Morrison Society Book Prize in 2003. Her second book, *Race, Trauma, and Home in the Novels of Toni Morrison* (Louisiana State University Press, 2010) is an interdisciplinary study of trauma in Morrison's fiction. Schreiber's articles appear in *Mississippi Quarterly*; *The Faulkner Journal*; *Literature & Psychology*; *Style*; and *Journal of* *the Fantastic in the Arts.* She has contributed chapters to *Blackwell's Companion to Faulkner*; *Teaching Faulkner: Approaches and Methods*; *A Gathering of Evidence: Essays on William Faulkner's Intruder in the Dust*; and *Memory and Meaning: Essays in Honor of Toni Morrison.*

Shirley A. (Holly) Stave is Professor at the Louisiana Scholars' College at Northwestern State University. She is a specialist in the novel and the author of *The Decline of the Goddess: Women, Nature, and Culture in Thomas Hardy's Wessex* (Greenwood, 1995). She is the editor of a collection of essays on Gloria Naylor (University of Delaware Press, 2000), the coauthor of a book on contemporary Wicca (Praeger, 1994), and editor of *Contested Intertextualities: Toni Morrison and the Bible* (Peter Lang, 2006)—a collection of essays. She is a contributor to *The Cambridge Companion to Toni Morrison* and a festschrift presented to Toni Morrison on the occasion of her eightieth birthday. Most recently, she is coeditor of *Toni Morrison's A Mercy: Critical Approaches* (Cambridge Scholars Publishing, 2011).

INDEX